SEA

Haran

ASSYRIA

Assur

Nuzu

Mari

Euphrates

Tigris

ACCAD

Babylon

ELAM

BABYLONIA

MER

Ur

SEA

PERSIAN GULF

NEAR EAST

100   200   300

MILES

GOR BTDL99

BEFORE THE BIBLE

Babylonian seal found at Platanos: Goddess and hero

Gold bowl from Ugarit, showing bulls and gazelles hunted from a chariot;
the theme and treatment combine Aegean and Levantine characteristics

BEFORE THE BIBLE

The Common Background
of Greek and Hebrew
Civilisations

by

CYRUS H. GORDON

PROFESSOR OF NEAR EASTERN STUDIES
BRANDEIS UNIVERSITY
WALTHAM
MASSACHUSETTS

HARPER & ROW, PUBLISHERS

*New York, Evanston
and London*

Dedicated
to my father
Benjamin Lee Gordon
physician and Hebraist
who taught me to cherish ancient tradition
as well as modern enlightenment

CONTENTS

ILLUSTRATIONS

Illustrations

I

Introduction

Archaeological discoveries at sites like Ugarit prevent us from regarding Greece as the hermetically sealed Olympian miracle, or Israel as the vacuum-packed miracle from Sinai. The thesis of this book is simply that *Greek and Hebrew civilisations are parallel structures built upon the same East Mediterranean foundation.* This statement, like any brief formulation of a complex subject, is meaningful only in the light of the evidence. It will soon be plain to the reader that there is no dearth of evidence. To the contrary, the evidence is so abundant that our problem is one of selection and arrangement.[1]

Lest the reader suppose that our thesis may detract from the Greek or Hebrew achievement, let us state here and now that the

[1] A topical arrangement would tend to convey the false impression that Greeks, Hebrews, Egyptians, Babylonians, etc., were the same, whereas they were very different (albeit intercommunicating) groups. I therefore present the material according to the sources, with a special chapter on each literature to bring out its individuality. Comparisons made in the early chapters necessarily anticipate the later chapters, and comparisons in the later chapters sometimes refer back to material covered in the earlier chapters. Every effort has been made to reduce repetitions to a minimum. Because the comparisons in the early chapters cover so much Greek and Hebrew material, the final chapters on Homer and on the Bible are not complete or well-rounded discussions. Instead they serve only to bring out some highlights and to add some details not covered in the previous chapters. Accordingly this book should be read and understood as a whole, and not as a series of more or less independent essays.

9

greatness of Homer and Bible emerges, as never before, when we see how they towered above their predecessors and contemporaries.

For centuries scholars have been forced to grapple with the problem of accounting for the parallels between Greek literature and the Bible. Did Greece borrow from Israel? Or did Israel borrow from Greece? Can the parallels be accidental? And even if they are accidental, do they not obliterate the uniqueness of both Israel and Greece? These and other questions have been asked.

Pagan critics of early Christianity confronted the Church Fathers with some embarrassing parallels, but the Fathers were equal to the challenge and provided answers in keeping with the spirit of their times. There were Fathers who honestly recognised the reality of the parallels but explained them as the mischief of demons who had planted them in Greek literature to harass the Church. For better or worse, demonology has given way to other schools of thought in academic circles, and accordingly the problem has in modern times been handled in other (but not always better) ways. V. Bérard attributed the links mainly to the role of the Phoenicians. P. Jensen explained matters through the diffusion of the Gilgamesh Epic. Much can still be said in favour of these and other proposed solutions but their one-sidedness and exaggeration brought them, and indeed the problem itself, into disrepute among critical scholars.

The history of the problem has been ably documented by W. Baumgartner[1] and there is no need to duplicate his work.

---

[1] W. Baumgartner, "Israelitisch-griechische Sagebeziehungen," *Schweizerische Archiv für Volkskunde* 41, 1944, pp. 1-29; now reproduced in a collection of Baumgartner's studies called *Zum Alten Testament und seiner Umwelt*, Brill, Leiden, 1959. Already in pre-Christian Alexandria, pagan critics had begun to invoke Greek myths to discredit the Bible of their Jewish neighbours (H. A. Wolfson, "The Philonic God of Revelation and his Latter-Day Deniers," *Harvard Theological Review* 53, 1960, pp. 101-124; see p. 110).

Introduction

Suffice it to say that the prevailing attitude[1] (which is gradually losing its grip) may be described as the tacit assumption that ancient Israel and Greece are two water-tight compartments, totally different from each other. One is said to be sacred; the other, profane; one, Semitic; the other, Indo-European. One, Asiatic and Oriental; the other, European and Occidental. But the fact is that both flourished during the same centuries, in the same East Mediterranean corner of the globe, with both ethnic groups in contact with each other from the start.

As a university student, I studied Hebrew and Greek simultaneously. Interestingly enough, the professors of Hebrew were quite conversant with Greek, and the professors of Greek at least knew the contents of the Bible in translation. But each set of teachers taught their subject as though it were totally unrelated to the other.[2] In retrospect it seems strange that so many generations of Old Testament scholars, trained in Greek as well as Hebrew literature, have managed to keep their Greek and Hebrew studies rigidly compartmentalised. Nothing could bring out more clearly the fact that we absorb attitudes as well as subject matter in the learning process. Moreover the attitudes

[1] This refers to the numerical majority, which is by no means a monopoly, in academic circles. More than a quarter of a century ago, Franz Dornseiff called attention to the ancient Near East stratum underlying Greek and Hebrew literatures, and to the fact that the two literatures (specifically from 1000 to 200 B.C.) were never really isolated from each other. More recently the Greek side, without reference to the Hebrew, has received considerable attention. For example, Spyridon N. Marinatos has shown that the Mycenaean Greeks were part of the international East Mediterranean synthesis, and should not be equated with the later classical Greeks (" *Diogeneîs Basilées* " in *Studies Presented to David Moore Robinson*, pp. 126-134). For a recent well-documented discussion, see Denys L. Page, *History and the Homeric Iliad*, Univ. of Cal. Press, Berkeley and Los Angeles, 1959.

[2] The reader will bear in mind that this book does not deal with the Hellenistic Age, when the union of Greece with the rest of the Near East is universally recognised. We are instead primarily concerned with the " Heroic Age " of Greece and Israel (*ca.* 15th to 10th centuries B.C.).

tend to determine what we see, and what we fail to see, in the subject matter. This is why attitude is just as important as content in the educational process.

The Greco-Hebrew parallels have repeatedly come to the fore to disturb our compartmentalised approach, because they pose a real problem. Due to insufficient connecting links, the attempts to answer the problem have been unconvincing, and, one after the other, have been discredited or forgotten. But the age of archaeological discovery in which we live has changed the picture. Egyptian and cuneiform texts have come to light from all over the Near East, providing many a missing link. Since 1929, Ugarit has yielded an especially important corpus of literary tablets bridging the gap between the oldest Greek and Hebrew compositions. As we shall note later, Ugaritic literature often parallels the subsequent Greek and Hebrew texts simultaneously, showing that Israel and Hellas drew on a common East Mediterranean heritage of the second millennium B.C. In short, this book is evoked not by any urge to tell a twice-told tale; nor by any hope or desire to win success with the same tools wherewith others have met with failure. It is rather because newly discovered material enables us to cope with the problem on a far more factual and well-rounded basis, that more satisfying results can now be achieved.

If we want to understand the roots of our culture around the East Mediterranean in the second millennium B.C., we shall have to exercise our capacity to detect real sameness in apparent difference, and real difference in apparent sameness. Otherwise, a comparative study such as the one before us will lie beyond our grasp.

We may begin our investigation by considering a few assorted parallels of limited scope. Exodus 17: 8-13 records the tradition of a victory secured through the agency of a divine implement: "Amalek came and fought against Israel in

Rephidim. And Moses said to Joshua: ' Choose for us men, and go out to fight against Amalek. Tomorrow I'll be standing on the summit of the hill, with the Staff of God in my hand.' Joshua did as Moses had commanded him to fight against Amalek. And Moses, Aaron and Hur went up to the summit of the hill. And it happened that when Moses raised his hand, Israel prevailed; but when he dropped his hand, Amalek prevailed. Because the hands of Moses were heavy, they took a stone and placed it under him and he sat upon it; and Aaron and Hur supported his hands, one on this side, and one on that, so that his hands were steadfast until the sun set. And Joshua vanquished Amalek and its people by the sword." Divinely fashioned staffs that serve as weapons to secure victory are common in East Mediterranean myth and saga, but Homeric epic confronts us with a divine implement closely paralleling the Staff of God in Exodus 17. Iliad 15: 318-322 tells that Phoebus Apollo determined the tide of battle by the way he held the aegis. Similarly, Odyssey 22: 297-309 relates that " Athene held up the aegis that consumes mortals," thus securing victory for Odysseus over the wooers who were forthwith routed and slain. In these passages the Greek aegis is functionally the equivalent of the Hebrew Staff of God. The parallel need not be attributed to either Greeks or Hebrews borrowing from the other. More likely both fell heir to an international heritage that included this feature.

Iliad 1: 312-317 tells of a ritual whereby men made themselves ceremonially pure by casting their defilement into the sea: " Then they, embarking, sailed the watery paths; and the Son of Atreus ordered the people to purify themselves. So they purified themselves and threw the defilement into the sea, and sacrificed to Apollo perfect hecatombs of bulls and goats by the shore of the unharvested sea. And the savour reached heaven, curling amid the smoke." By washing away uncleanliness into the sea, people sought to get rid of their guilt and be set aright. " Cast into the depths of the sea all their sins " refers to the same ritual in Micah (7: 18-20): " What god is like Thee, forgiving sin and excusing transgression for the remnant of His inheritance. He will not stay angry forever, for He desires loving kindness. He will relent and pity us; He will conquer our sins. And Thou wilt cast into the depths of the sea all their sins. Thou wilt ascribe truth to Jacob and loving kindness to Abraham, as Thou hast sworn to our fathers since days of old." Traditional Judaism still preserves, in connection with this passage, the custom of purifying oneself for the New Year, by throwing into a body of water crumbs that are fancied as laden with one's transgressions. The Homeric passage is interesting also for its reference to the sea as " watery paths." The Greeks viewed the Mediterranean not as a barrier but as a network of routes connecting the people who dwelt along its shores. This is familiar to any student of Greece. But what is not so well known is that the Hebrews express themselves similarly in passages like Psalm 8: 9 (" crossing the paths of the seas "). Sea-lanes connected the East Mediterranean peoples including Hebrews and Greeks, thus accounting for much of the cultural interchange.[1] But there is another more specific aspect of the parallel under consideration in this paragraph. It is the religious aspect, for, as we shall note later, the priestly guilds were highly mobile, with the result that cultic practices crossed ethnic lines over wide areas.

Some of the parallels are due to common East Mediterranean

---

[1] In 1960, Martin Noth (*The History of Israel*, 2nd English ed., A. & C. Black, London), the distinguished Old Testament scholar, still maintains " The fact that the land was shut off from the neighbouring sea explains why seafaring and sea-trading played no part at all in Israel . . . and where the sea is mentioned in the Old Testament it hardly ever appears as a means of communication between different countries but rather as a menace on the edge of the inhabited earth . . ." (p. 13). This estimate of the situation is astounding in the light of Israel's well-known Mediterranean contacts covered by Noth himself on pp. 23, 31, 37, 150, 178, etc.

social institutions underlying Hebrew as well as Greek society. Manslaughter was requited through blood revenge. Accordingly the offender, to escape the avenger, would be forced to flee, cut off from his land and people, at the mercy of strangers far from home. Particularly pathetic was the man who, after slaying a kinsman, had to flee from an avenger of his own family. The situation is described from the mother's viewpoint in 2 Samuel (14: 5-7): "I am a widow for my husband has died. I had two sons who fought with each other in the field, with no rescuer between them, and one smote the other and killed him. And now the whole clan has risen against me and said: 'Hand over the fratricide that we may kill him for the life of his brother whom he has slain; and we shall destroy also the heir.' Thus they would extinguish my ember that survives, without leaving my husband any name or survival on the face of the earth." This tragic situation lends itself to sympathetic treatment. Iliad 16: 571-574 tells of "goodly Epeigeus, who had formerly been king in well-peopled Budeum; but when he had killed a worthy kinsman, he came as a suppliant to Peleus and to silver-footed Thetis." Note that another such slayer is also treated sympathetically in the Odyssey (15: 271-278): "Then godlike Theoclymenus answered him: 'Thus am I too away from my fatherland, for I slew a kinsman. Many are the brethren and kinsmen in horse-pasturing Argos, who wield great power over the Achaeans. I am in flight to avoid death and black fate from them, for now it is my lot to be a wanderer among men. But set me on the ship, for I, a fugitive, come to you as a suppliant lest they slay me. For I think they are in pursuit'." Just as Peleus and Thetis had compassion upon Epeigeus, Telemachus also shelters Theoclymenus. It is against this background that we are to understand the plight of Cain, who had slain his brother Abel. When Cain says: "I shall be a vagabond and wanderer in the land, and any who finds me shall slay me" (Genesis 4: 14), the ancient

Hebrew would be moved to compassion for Cain, rather than dwell on the enormity of the crime he had committed. Indeed Cain is represented as the recipient of God's sympathetic protection: " Yahweh said to him: ' Therefore anyone who kills Cain will be punished sevenfold.' And He put a mark on Cain so that none who met him would slay him" (Genesis 4: 15). This parallel illustrates how we must be ready to revise our approach to familiar texts. Though his crime was heinous, Cain is represented not as a villain but as a tragic character. We are accustomed to think of him with revulsion; but the text of Genesis aims rather at evoking our sympathy for a man who atoned for his crime with homelessness and fear: a fate worse than death.

We may now turn to a type of parallel of a still more specific nature. Homeric tradition often represents military organisation as contingents of troops under a triad of officers for each contingent, as in passages like Iliad 2: 563-7 and Odyssey 14: 470-471. Iliad 12: 85-107 tells of five triads of officers in command of the five companies in the Trojan alliance (cf. Iliad 2: 819-823). " Some went with Hector and flawless Polydamas; these were the most numerous and best, and pressed on most eagerly to break through the wall, to fight by the hollow ships; and with them Cebriones followed as the third; for by the chariot Hector had left another inferior to Cebriones. Paris, Alcathous and Agenor led the second company. Leading the third company were Helenus and godlike Deiphobus, two sons of Priam; the third was the hero Asius: Asius son of Hyrtacus, whom great tawny horses had fetched from Arisbe, from the river Selleis. Aeneas, the goodly son of Anchises, led the fourth company; with him were the two sons of Antenor: Archelochus and Acamas, well skilled in all kinds of combat. And Sarpedon led glorious warriors; and he selected (as colleagues) Glaucus and warlike Asteropaeus, for they seemed to him to be decidedly the

best of all after himself, but he was distinguished above all"
(Iliad 12: 88-104). This passage is to be compared with the list of
David's officers in 2 Samuel 23 and 1 Chronicles 11. Triads of
officers appear in 2 Samuel 23: 9, 16, 17, 18, 19, 22, and 23 to
mention only the clear examples. Triads in this catalogue of
David's officers are also reflected in problematic forms of the
numeral " 3," which may have been distorted in the course of
textual transmission because the Davidic system was not fully
understood by later generations. The Homeric terminology ties
in with the Biblical in some detail. Just as Cebriones and Asius
(Iliad 12: 91, 95) in the passage translated above, are called
trítos " third," officers are frequently called *šālíš* (from the same
root as *šālôš* " 3 ") in Hebrew. It is furthermore not unusual in
both traditions to designate one officer in each triad as the chief.
Much as Sarpedon is called superior to his two associates (Iliad 12:
101-104), Abishai is honoured in 2 Samuel 23: 18 as " chief of the
triad " and as having won special " fame among the three."
1 Chronicles 11: 21 states that of the three " he was more
honoured than the other two and became their general."

The agreement we have just observed between early Greek
and early Hebrew usage is due to forces that can be pinned down
in time and place. Regardless of the later stages of the fixing of
the Greek and Hebrew texts, they reflect authentic traditions of
what we may call the heroic age of the East Mediterranean
during the last half of the second millennium B.C. The text of
Homer about the Mycenaean Age with its memories of the
Trojan War, and the Hebrew text covering from the Conquest
through David's reign, cover ground with much in common
geographically, chronologically and ethnically. Just as Mycenaean civilisation is a development of the Minoan, so too the
Philistines who came to Palestine from Caphtor were an offshoot
of the same general Aegean civilisation. Moreover, until David's
victories around 1000 B.C., the Philistines dominated the Hebrews

so that, militarily at least, the Davidic monarchy was the Hebrew response to the Philistine stimulus. Indeed, David served Achish, the Philistine King of Gath, as a vassal; and David learned much about the art of war from his Philistine associations. David and his successors for several generations made use of Philistine mercenary troops. Thus the Achaeans, Trojans, Philistines and Hebrews during the closing centuries of the second millennium belonged to the same international complex of peoples, sharing many conventions and institutions, specifically in military matters. When we read that the men of Jabesh-Gilead retrieved the corpses of Saul and his sons, who had been slain by the Philistines, and that they burned them (I Samuel 31: 12) prior to burial, we are dealing with an institution familiar from the Iliad. Hector's body was retrieved from Achilles by Priam and finally the Trojans " shedding tears, carried out brave Hector and set the corpse on the highest pyre and cast fire thereon " (Iliad 24: 786-787). " Later his brethren and companions gathered the white bones, weeping, and a great tear flowed down their cheeks. They gathered and put the bones into a golden vase, covering it with soft purple robes, and swiftly placed it in a hollow grave " (Iliad 24: 792-797). Also Patroclus was burned before burial. The Hittites practised somewhat similar rites. Mount Gilboa, where Saul met his death at the hands of the Philistines, and Troy, where Hector was slain by Achilles, were parts of the same East Mediterranean milieu during the closing centuries of the second millennium. The customs of both Greeks and Hebrews in that heroic age were often alien to their respective descendants in the classical periods. We shall have to bear in mind that the gulf separating classical Israel (of the great Prophets) from classical Greece (of the scientists and philosophers) must not be read back into the heroic age when both peoples formed part of the same international complex.

The Greco-Hebrew parallels need not conceal the evident and

profound Greco-Hebrew differences. No two nations forming part of a large cultural sphere are identical. Hungary and Norway, despite their unrelated languages and other major differences, are nonetheless component parts of what we recognise as European civilisation. Comparing Hungary and Norway alone might bring out their differences; but if the comparison be extended to include also Bantu and American Indian tribes, the genuine cultural relationship between Norway and Hungary would become evident. Similarly, a study limited to the Greek and Hebrew cultures has the effect of bringing out the many differences between the two. But the similarities between them come to the fore if we contrast them with cultures alien to the East Mediterranean.

The early Hebrews are no more different from the early Greeks than they are from the Egyptians or Mesopotamians where the interrelations (side by side with the drastic differences) are universally recognised.

It would be foolhardy to swell the pages of this book with an exhaustive list of Greco-Hebrew differences. Everyone knows that Homer is very different from the Bible. What is not sufficiently known is the fact that the two share a common East Mediterranean heritage. This common denominator is of prime importance in the history of our culture. This is why the parallels are worth discussing at length, and why the more numerous differences are not spelled out in detail.

The parallels that form the core of this book fit into a historical framework in the wake of the Amarna Age during the closing centuries of the second millennium. Prior to the Amarna Age (i.e., before 1400 B.C.) Egyptian, Canaanite, Mesopotamian, Anatolian, Aegean and other influences met around the East Mediterranean to form an international order, by which each was in turn affected. Out of the Amarna Age synthesis emerged the earliest traditions of Israel and Greece. Such is the background that accounts for many of the parallels. The distribution of these parallel elements can be accounted for in time, in place and via specific human channels.

We shall be reckoning with whole compositions as well as with their component parts. That both the Gilgamesh Epic and the Odyssey deal with the episodic wanderings of a hero, would not be sufficiently specific to establish a genuine relation between them. But when both epics begin with the declaration that the hero gained experience from his wide wanderings, and end with his homecoming, a relationship dimly appears. Finally, when we note that whole episodes are in essential agreement, we are on firmer ground. For instance, both Gilgamesh and Odysseus reject a goddess's proposal of marriage; and each of the heroes interviews his dead companion in Hades.

The preceding paragraphs have indicated the problem and its historic framework. The methodology, which is inherent in our presentations of the actual parallels, must remain flexible in conformity with the varying material that confronts us. The source material must not be forced to fit a prearranged scheme or methodology. Historical, sociological, literary, linguistic, archaeological and other techniques must be brought to bear when they are applicable to the material at hand. Methods, as well as conclusions, stem from the evidence. Our attention will be focused squarely on the primary,[1] rather than secondary,[2] sources. I have gone—and in the future shall continue to go—wherever they lead me.

[1] Where I have omitted to document well-known Near East sources, the reader can nearly always find the standard bibliography in the prefatory notes to each composition in J. B. Pritchard, *Ancient Near Eastern Texts*, 2nd Ed., Princeton, 1955. Old Testament references are always according to the Hebrew chapter and verse numbering. Greek authors are cited sometimes from the Loeb, and sometimes from the Oxford editions.

[2] It is impractical to give a large secondary bibliography. I have cited quite a few modern authorities in my earlier writings on this subject. Among the

Introduction

It is a pleasant duty to acknowledge my indebtedness to those who have helped me prepare this book. Miss Gloria Adelson typed the manuscript. My able and erudite colleague, Dr. D. W. Young, and my promising student, Mr. Gerald Swaim, have read the typescript and, in addition to eliminating some of my more jarring repetitions and solecisms, have made constructive contributions to the substance of this book. I am grateful to Brandeis University not only for enabling me to engage in teaching, research and writing, but also for the opportunity to visit the Aegean in 1957 and in 1961. Above all I want to express my thanks to my students, for they have been my chief source of inspiration over the years.

---

many excellent books to which I am indebted, I wish to single out Gilbert Murray, *The Rise of the Greek Epic*, 4th ed., Oxford U. Press, 1934; and G. Germain, *Genèse de l'Odyssée*, Paris, 1954.

II

Channels of Transmission

Culture cannot be transmitted through abstract processes without human agency. Only people can carry culture; and cultural fusion results from the mingling of different groups of people. Because there is no one formula for the transmission of civilisation, we shall consider a variety of the more important channels attested around the ancient East Mediterranean.

Since remote antiquity, tribal units have been driven to seek grass and water for their flocks in far-off places when their native haunts have been hit hard by famine or drought. When, for this or any other reason, ethnic groups are on the move, some people are bound to be dispossessed so that a chain reaction of migration may be touched off.

Sometimes the migrants keep up contacts with their homeland. This is regularly the case when the travel is in the foreign service of the homeland. Diplomacy is not the only form of peaceful foreign service. Productive civilisations often require raw materials from abroad. While Babylonia is devoid of mineral resources, the Sumerian civilisation there required metals and stones for processing. Accordingly, through trade and foreign colonies, Sumer secured the raw materials indispensable for Sumerian life. Without stone seals and statuettes, or without metal knives, it is hard to imagine any culture that could be termed "Sumerian".[1] This raises the question as to whether

[1] For an introduction to Sumerian culture, see S. N. Kramer, *History Begins at Sumer*, Doubleday (Anchor), Garden City, N.Y., 1959.

Sumerian civilisation got started in Sumer or elsewhere. It is incredible that in a land devoid of stone or metal, the Sumerians could have risen from barbarism to a remarkably developed culture excelling in the arts of the lapidary and smith. There is every reason to believe that the Sumerians came to " Sumer " with a considerable degree of civilisation, and with connections already established in areas producing the needed raw materials. Some of the mines may have actually been worked by Sumerians; but in any case Sumerians must have been stationed there in administrative capacity. In late Sumerian times, as we shall note, Ur of Sumer had trading colonies far to the north.

Pottery found at early Greek sites such as Lerna, Dimini and Sesklo often has unmistakable affinities with Mesopotamian pottery from as far back as the Tell Halaf Period, around 3500 B.C.[1] We shall presently explain the character of the human agents that account for the transmission of ceramic production, but meanwhile we may observe that ceramic affinities between Mesopotamia and the Aegean are proof of contact between the two areas long before the dawn of writing; over two thousand years before the Amarna synthesis out of which the early Greek and Hebrew traditions sprang. At no historic time were the Near East and the Aegean out of touch with each other, though in some periods, such as the Amarna and Hellenistic Ages, the contacts were especially strong. Classical scholars know about the orientalising periods in Greek art; and Near Eastern specialists are familiar with Minoan, Mycenaean, Hellenistic and still later Greek influence in Western Asia and Egypt. The interconnections antedate not only the earliest Hebrew and Greek writings, but also the earliest texts of Sumer and Egypt.

The most familiar and swiftest form of ethnic impact is military invasion and conquest. The first Semitic empire,

[1] Cf. F. Schachermeyr, *Die ältesten Kulturen Griechenlands*, Kohlhammer, Stuttgart, 1955.

23

namely the Akkad Dynasty in Mesopotamia (*ca.* 2350–2150 B.C.), could boast of conquests up to, and even beyond, the shores of the Mediterranean. Seal cylinders of the Akkad Dynasty have been found on the island of Cyprus, making it quite likely that Sargon, who founded the Dynasty, reached Cyprus and brought it under his sway. Other Mesopotamian monarchs whose operations reached the Mediterranean in early times, include Naram-Sin of the Akkad Dynasty, Sargon the First of Assyria, and Naram-Sin of Eshnunna.[1] Quite often, great movements connected with these and other sovereigns are documented all too vaguely; but the testimony of written records and archaeological objects leaves no doubt as to their historicity. Often enough the texts in question are not contemporary with the events. For example, Sargon of Akkad's conquest of Asia Minor has given rise to an epic called " King of Battle ". In the Amarna Age, this epic was so popular that it was studied and copied by cuneiform scribes as far off as Egypt. The popularity of this composition in the outposts of Babylonian influence during the Amarna Age may be due to the fact that the scribes, and more especially the Babylonian traders for whom they worked, sometimes needed the protection of the Babylonian king. Accordingly, the tradition that Sargon, in response to the appeal of his merchants in Asia Minor, victoriously reasserted his power there, was long cherished by Mesopotamia's sons, trading far away for their country.

The King of Battle epic tells of Sargon planning to march over the difficult road to Buršaḫanda, in Asia Minor. Inasmuch as we do not possess all of the text, and what we have is incomplete (with the opening signs of each line lost), it is hard to give a full translation. But " the chief of the merchants " (obverse, l. 13) mentions the campaigns of Sargon, his suzerainty over the

---

[1] For a useful attempt to bring the historical data of the cuneiform world up to date, see H. Schmökel, *Geschichte des Alten Vorderasien* (*Handbuch der Orientalistik* II, 3), Brill, Leiden, 1957.

four quarters of the earth, and control over " the throne-rooms from the rising of the sun to the setting of the sun "(ll. 14-15). The strong feelings of the merchants (l. 16) are instrumental in getting Sargon to undertake the hazardous expedition. The merchants declare: " We have appealed to Sargon, King of the Universe. Let him come down to us so that we shall get strength. We are not heroes." They go on to say that they will foot the bill with gold (ll. 18-20). The reverse side of the tablet portrays Sargon's opponent, King Nur-Dagan, and the latter's troops uttering taunts and comforting each other with the recollection that in the past no king had invaded their territory. But meanwhile Sargon was proceeding, and he finally captured his foes. Nur-Dagan, now vanquished, must take back the taunts he had uttered before his defeat, and in Sargon's presence he exclaims: " What lands can rival Akkad! What king can rival you! " (rev., ll. 20-21).[1]

The popularity of this composition in the Amarna Age reflects the status of the merchant abroad. There came times when, far from home, he required the diplomatic or even military aid of his king. It is quite likely that although the merchants in the King of Battle epic disclaim any prowess as warriors, merchants often had to fend for themselves to cope with threats to their security on short notice. We shall soon note that Genesis 14 portrays Abraham as a fighting merchant prince.

The influx of Indo-European immigrants into the Near East during the second millennium B.C. revolutionised the art of war. The newcomers introduced the horse-drawn war-chariot, which gave a swift striking power hitherto unknown in the Near East.

---

[1] The most convenient publication of this poem is S. A. B. Mercer, *The Tell el-Amarna Tablets*, Macmillan, Toronto, 1939, vol. II, pp. 808-815. (In general, however, the most reliable edition of the Amarna tablets remains J. A. Knudtzon, *Die El-Amarna-Tafeln*, *Vorderasiatische Bibliothek*, Leipzig, 1907-15. See further my " The New Amarna Tablets," *Orientalia* 16, 1947, pp. 1-21, pls. I-II.)

The *élite* charioteer officers, who bear the Indo-European name of *maryannu*, soon became a new aristocracy throughout the entire area, including Egypt. With them appears also a new type of royal epic, which we may call the Indo-European War Epic. Embedded in it is a motif that has become commonplace in world literature: the Helen of Troy theme, whereby a hero loses his destined bride and must wage a war to win her back. Greek and Indic epic illustrate this theme, and it is from the Iliad that it has become popular in the modern West. However, it is completely absent from the romantic literatures of early Mesopotamia and Egypt, and it appears in the Semitic World only in the wake of the Indo-Europeans with their *maryannu* aristocracy. The Helen of Troy theme first appears at Ugarit of the Amarna Age, in a community where the Indo-European elements are present, including a firmly entrenched organisation of *maryannu*. As we shall note later, the theme permeates the early traditions of Israel, particularly the saga of Abraham.

One of the major channels of cultural transmission was the colony or enclave.[1] Whole communities were often transplanted to look after their nation's interests in far-off places. Sometimes these colonies were of a military character to secure the borders of a large empire. For example, the Egyptian Empire (which reached its maximum limits during the reign of Thothmes III), and later the Hebrew Empire of David and Solomon, seem to have planted colonies on their northern frontier, just east of Cilicia. In any case, the northern districts called Muṣur (" Egypt") and "Judah "[2] (" Ya'udi " in the native inscriptions) may well have been named after the homelands of the colonising powers. Indeed, we have to be on the look-out in the texts we read, to

[1] Cf. my " Colonies and Enclaves," *Studi Orientalistici in onore di Giorgio Levi Della Vida*, Rome, 1956, vol. I, pp. 409-419.

[2] See my *World of the Old Testament*, Doubleday, Garden City, N.Y., 1958, pp. 197, 215, 219.

know whether Muṣur and "Judah" designate the homeland or the colony. In addition to military duties, such colonies often had commercial functions as well.

Some colonies were primarily commercial, others military. For example, it is quite likely that the Third Dynasty of Ur, in Sumer, established around 2000 B.C. a number of colonies called Ur in tablets from Nuzu, Alalakh and Hattusa. The Ur of the Chaldees, where Abraham was born, seems to have been one of the northern Urs. After the collapse of the Ur Dynasty, the colony continued its commercial way of life under the new masters who took over. As we shall see, as late as the 13th century B.C., one of the northern Urs was an active community of merchants in the service of the Hittite kings. Then again in 525 B.C., when Cambyses conquered Egypt, he found an already established military colony of Aramaic Jews guarding the fortress island of Elephantine far up the Nile.[1] This military colony continued to function for a long time under the Achaemenian rulers of Egypt. It is normal for people to continue their way of life even though new masters control their land.

The best-documented colonies are the Old Assyrian commercial settlements in Asia Minor, particularly the one at Kültepe. The establishment of such centres usually implies that the founding nation was stronger than the nation on whose soil the community was planted. At least such was the case subsequently when the Arameans of Damascus took cities away from Omri of Israel and established commercial agents in Samaria; whereas, when Omri's son Ahab vanquished the Arameans, he recovered the lost territory and posted his commercial agents in Damascus (I Kings 20: 34). However, military supremacy did not always have to precede commercial expansion. The long Mesopotamian tradition of business, book-keeping and law was welcome

[1] See my "The Origin of the Jews in Elephantine," *Journal of Near Eastern Studies* 14, 1955, pp. 56-58; and *World of the Old Testament*, p. 272.

in areas that had no well-developed equivalent of their own. Thus the spread of Mesopotamian trade was due in part to conquest, and in part to the process of useful developments filling a vacuum.

The Old Assyrian *kârum* (as the community of such commercial settlements was called) kept up its commercial interchange with the mother country by caravan, and maintained its business records in the Old Assyrian language. There is no better documented illustration of transmission of Mesopotamian culture to Asia Minor than the *kârum* at Kültepe.

That Old Babylonian expansion paralleled the Old Assyrian, is suggested by the fact that the Akkadian language written in the Amarna Age throughout the Near East (from Anatolia, through Canaan, and into Egypt) is the Babylonian, rather than the Assyrian, dialect. Still more cogent is the evidence of the Babylonian tablets found at Mari, along the middle Euphrates, establishing connections with Canaan, Asia Minor and even Crete on the eve of Hammurapi's widest conquests. Hammurapi's Babylonian Empire reached out, perhaps in the form of Babylonian colonies and enclaves, into the Aegean, as well as into Egypt. These outposts of his Empire did not take the form of outright conquest, but rather of commercial expansionism. In the Amarna Age itself, when Kassite Babylonia was politically and militarily weak, we find Babylonian used widely in the spheres of diplomacy, business and law all over the Near East. This triumph of Babylonian cannot be the accomplishment of the shrinking Kassite kingdom; it is rather the legacy of the powerful Age of Hammurapi over three centuries earlier. It should come as no surprise if Babylonian tablets, spanning the period of Hammurapi[1] and the Amarna Age, will some day be found in Egypt.

---

[1] Whether Hammurapi began to reign early or late in the eighteenth century is a moot question. M. B. Rowton's dates for Hammurapi (1792-1750 B.C.) are more in keeping with the consensus of opinion than E. Weidner's dates (1704-1662 B.C.). See *World of the Old Testament*, pp. 74-75, n. 4.

(This would be quite in keeping with what is known of the Hyksos Empire which ruled territory in Asia as well as Egypt during the 17th and early 16th centuries B.C.) Discoveries are largely a matter of accident; the Amarna tablets themselves were discovered quite by accident; reputedly by a peasant woman in 1887 digging for fertiliser.

It is not unlikely that a sort of *kârum* was established in the Messara, near the south central coast of Crete. The plainest indication of Babylonian influence in the Messara are the finds discovered by Xanthoudides at Platanos in " Tholos B," including a typical Old Babylonian seal cylinder [1] showing the goddess with raised hands, and the " Amorite " hero. Workmanship, theme and material are all Old Babylonian without any provincial deviation. The port, where perhaps the remains of a *kârum*-type community may have flourished, may yet be found on the Messara coast, perhaps in one or more of the settlements at a site now called Komo. We shall examine, in Chapter VI, the evidence of the Hagia Triada tablets and Harvester Vase which point to Mesopotamian influence at Hagia Triada. These Hagia Triada materials, from about 1400 B.C., come in the wake of the Old Babylonian impact on the Messara, attested by the finds at Platanos.

The Hittites planted their enclaves abroad, too. In the 23rd chapter of Genesis, Abraham purchases real-estate from a Hittite, in the presence of the whole Hittite community near Hebron in southern Palestine. Until a few years ago, biblical scholars assumed that the Hittites of Genesis 23 (and of other biblical narratives pertaining to the Palestinian population) were not Hittites at all. However, it has been demonstrated[2] that the real-

[1] Cf. J. D. S. Pendlebury, *The Archaeology of Crete*, Methuen, London, 1939, p. 121.

[2] M. R. Lehmann, *Bulletin of the American Schools of Oriental Research* 129, 1953, pp. 15-18. See further J. C. L. Gibson, *Journal of Near Eastern Studies* 20, 1961, pp. 224-227.

estate transaction in Genesis 23 conforms with Hittite law, now known to us from Hittite tablets.

Ugarit provides us with the clearest picture of what was happening in the Near East during the Amarna Age. The community might be called Semitic, because the official local language (Ugaritic) is clearly Semitic. However, there was an influential Aegean enclave there, attested by Cypro-Minoan texts, Mycenaean art objects, and the presence of a Caphtorian god in the Ugaritic pantheon. Hittites, Hurrians, Alashiyans and other segments of the community are mentioned in the tablets. Assyrian and Egyptian enclaves are recorded side by side, though Ugarit certainly did not belong to either the Assyrian or Egyptian kings. While King Niqmad of Ugarit paid tribute to the Hittite sovereign (Suppiluliuma[1]), Ugarit was a member of the Hittite defensive alliance, rather than a conquered territory. The fact that Assyrian and Egyptian enclaves flourished at Ugarit shows that Ugarit enjoyed enough freedom to have peaceful relations with all nations, near and far. What we see at Ugarit is the interpenetration of commercial empires. At that important city, at the crossroads of east-west and north-south traffic, representatives of the Aegean, Hittite, Hurrian, Mesopotamian, Canaanite, Egyptian and other populations met to conduct their affairs in an international order.

The above sketch shows that the Levantine character of the Near East had got well under way by the third millennium, and was highly developed even before the Amarna Age. The Levantine pattern is the mingling of distinct communities side by side. If we contrast a Levantine city (such as Istanbul, Beirut or Alexandria) with an American city (such as New York or Boston), the difference between the Near East Levant and the American melting pot will become clear. The minorities in the Levant maintain their individuality for centuries, and even

[1] Ruled about 1380-1346 B.C.

millennia, whereas the norm in an American metropolis is assimilation. In America, immigrants speak their foreign languages, which their children can usually understand but not speak, but which their grandchildren cannot even understand. In a Levantine city, while the minority groups know the principal languages used in their area, they speak their own ancestral language at home. Thus Greeks, Armenians and other minority peoples of the Levant still preserve their own language in Church and home, even though they may live under the Turkish or U.A.R. flag. At the core of their individuality is the concept of separate peoplehood, whereas the children of immigrants in America want to be Americans, first and foremost. In America the high incidence of denominational intermarriage tends to break up the denominational continuity within the family. In the Levant, peoplehood goes hand in hand with religion. The Greek Orthodox are Greeks; the Armenian Orthodox are Armenians; the Coptic Orthodox are Egyptian Christians (who use a Coptic liturgy); etc. It is not a matter of theological persuasion; it is simply peoplehood that determines one's identity in the Levant. This is why a Levantine, when asked his nationality, will (in the case of the minority groups) tell what religion he adheres to. The institution of minority peoples forming a single state under one flag is different in the Levant from, let us say, Switzerland. In Switzerland, citizens call themselves Swiss regardless of whether their home language is German, French or Italian. In the Levant, a citizen calls himself a Greek, Jew or Armenian by way of signifying his primary identification. The traditional scheme in the Levant is called the Millet System, where the individual is related to the body politic, not directly or through the district in which he lives, but through his ethnic group (i.e., his *millet*, which is translated " nation " although it is rather *ethnos*). The Millet System is clearly documented for the Achaemenian Empire (6th-4th centuries B.C.), which probably inherited most of the structure from the preceding World Empires of the Assyrians and Neo-Babylonians. But the fact of a patch-quilt of ethnic groups under one government is already discernible in the Near East kingdoms of the Amarna Age.

Only two of the ethnic groups that emerged historically in the East Mediterranean of the second millennium have enjoyed a historically conscious continuity down to the present: the Greeks and the Hebrews. The recorded history of the Greeks can now be traced to the Amarna Age when, around 1400 B.C., the Mycenaean Greek tablets in the so-called Linear B script appear in Knossos and go on until the 12th century B.C. in the Peloponnesus.[1] Although Greek paganism eventually yielded to Christianity, the Greek language has thus survived as a written language on the same soil for at least 3350 years (and probably much longer as a spoken language). The Jews have preserved their religion and Hebrew Scriptures in an unbroken tradition; but the use of spoken Hebrew, and the establishment of Statehood in Israel, are the results of a restoration. Regardless of the differences between the continuity of the Greeks and Hebrews from the Amarna Age to the present day, the fact remains that they alone have preserved across the millennia an unbroken awareness of their past, and an attachment to their ancient land and language.

In the Achaemenian Empire, segments of Jewry lived widely separated from each other geographically and in way of life. The Jewish community in Iran, as depicted in the Book of Esther, is quite different from the Jewish colony in Elephantine.[2] Yet both claimed Jewish identification, and accepted the other Jews of the

[1] See M. Ventris and J. Chadwick, *Documents in Mycenaean Greek*, Cambridge U. Press, Cambridge, 1956.

[2] For background on this and other aspects of Old Testament times, I refer the reader to *World of the Old Testament*.

world as fellow Jews. When the State of Israel welcomes all Jews as citizens (from black Falashas of Abyssinia, to blue-eyed blondes from West Europe), it is clear that psychological ethnic identity is still the thing that counts.[1] Cyprus may never have belonged to Greece, although Greek colonies have been on the Island for over three thousand years. Nevertheless, Greece has in recent years claimed the Island because the majority of the people speak Greek and adhere to the Greek church. Makarios was the only real candidate for the presidency of the new Cypriote state, because as the religious chief of the majority group, he was *de facto* the Ethnarch of the Cypriote Greeks. The key to the Cyprus situation is the age-old concept of peoplehood. The Turks of Cyprus are just as much Cypriotes as the Greeks. But the criterion of peoplehood is more basic than citizenship in the West European or American sense. The barriers between the ethnic groups do not prevent the people from meeting in the market place and pooling their individual contributions into the fabric of Levantine culture. This process was already established in the ancient East Mediterranean prior to the emergence of the Greeks and Hebrews.

In addition to the trading colonies, there were mobile traders who went abroad on itinerant or short-term missions. Hammurapi's Code (#103) regulates relationships between the business entrepreneur (*tamkârum*) and his travelling agent (*šamallûm*). The *tamkârum* himself is represented as conducting business personally in foreign territory, where, in addition to looking after his own business, he had to attend to wider Babylonian interests as the occasion might demand. Thus he had to redeem Babylonians in exile so that they could be repatriated. Law #32 requires the *tamkârum* to advance the ransom for repatriating captive Babylonian soldiers. Laws ##280-281 regulate the

[1] Note that *ethnos* is a matter of social psychology rather than physical anthropology.

tamkârum's ransoming of runaway Babylonian slaves abroad, for repatriation.[1]

The Hittites followed the Assyro-Babylonian precedent of sending merchants abroad. The Hittite Code (I: 5) protects the merchant by imposing the exemplary fine of 100 minas of silver (plus other restitution) on anyone who kills him abroad in Luwiya or Pala, or in Hatti land.[2]

The Hittite kings sponsored merchants plying their trade in Canaan. Documents of Hattusili III (*ca.* 1282-1250 B.C.) have been found at Ugarit, regulating the activities of his merchants there. Complaints had been lodged against the merchants for their undue exploitation of Ugarit. Accordingly, Hattusili forbade his merchants to acquire Ugaritic real-estate, or to remain in Ugarit throughout the year. They were to function in Ugarit only during the summer season and return to their home base, the city of Ur(a), for the winter season. Thus the merchants of Ur(a) would be prevented from gaining a permanent foothold in Ugarit, by being kept on the move, and by being without land of their own in Ugarit. A number of tablets mention the Hittite-sponsored merchants of Ur(a), indicating that it was a commercial colony, whose citizens often embarked on foreign trading missions. This Ur(a) may possibly be Abraham's birthplace in the Haran/Urfa area. Hattusili protected the capital of his merchants by enforcing their right to enslave the debtors, together with their dependents, if loans were not repaid on time.[3]

These tablets of Hattusili have corroborated the repeated statement in the narrative of Genesis, that the Hebrew Patriarchs

[1] I have given an introduction to, analysis of, and bibliography for *Hammurapi's Code* in a pamphlet of that name published by Rinehart, New York, 1957.

[2] The latest ed. of the Hittite Code is J. Friedrich, *Die hetitischen Gesetze*, Brill, Leiden, 1959.

[3] See my "Abraham and the Merchants of Ura," *Journal of Near Eastern Studies* 17, 1958, pp. 28-31.

had mercantile interests.[1] One can say with confidence that Abraham is represented as a *tamkârum* from Ur of the Chaldees in the Hittite realm. Like many others from Ur, he embarked on a career in Canaan. But unlike the others, he succeeded in purchasing land and laying the foundation for his descendants' settlement there.

Genesis 14 portrays Abraham as the commander of his own company of troops, augmented by those of his Amorite allies. Moreover, he is successful in overtaking and defeating a coalition of invading kings. It is significant that in this chapter, Abraham is called a " Hebrew." This raises an interesting question, because many scholars are inclined to identify " Hebrew " with *Apiru* (written in Akkadian: *ḫa-pí-ru*). The phonetic difficulties in equating the words are considerable, but in the case of borrowings we cannot always establish the exact phonetic " laws " that are operative. The *Apiru* are widely distributed over the Near East throughout the second millennium. They are not an ethnic group, such as " Hebrew " came to designate early in Old Testament times. They are regularly outsiders, usually serving in some official capacity. Often they are warriors, though in Nuzu they are servile. Abraham is an outsider, serving in an official capacity, to judge from Genesis 23: 6, where the members of the Hittite enclave address him as " My Lord " and add " you are an exalted prince in our midst." In Genesis 14 he is a successful warrior, and it is precisely in that chapter that he is called the " Hebrew." Inasmuch as the *tamkârū* " merchants " were sponsored by their kings, and had to look after their national interests abroad, the *tamkârū* formed a guild with official duties and prerogatives. Since they were targets of attack (for it was always a temptation to rob them of their goods), they tended to develop a military capability for self-defence (and in some cases, perhaps, for offensive purposes such as eliminating rivals and

[1] Genesis 23: 16; 34: 10; 42: 34.

capturing new markets). Abraham the " Hebrew " has a combination of qualities that fit the *Apiru* well: outsider, trader, official, warrior.[1]

Homeric epic shows no concern for trade.[2] Homeric society gloried in an aristocracy of warriors who owned land and cattle as well as precious stuffs and gladly left commerce in the hands of Phoenicians and others with mercantile proclivities. Hebraic tradition, as epitomised in the saga of Abraham, combines Homeric with Phoenician values, and honours a fighting merchant prince as the founder of the People. Hesiod's ideal is different from Homer's. For Hesiod the best way of life is success in agriculture; but next comes success in trade.

The spread of the *tamkârū*, culminating in the Hammurapi Age, brought Babylonian business, law and writing to the ends of the Near East, including the Aegean in the northwest and Egypt in the south. For keeping accounts, making contracts, and correspondence the *tamkârū* introduced the Babylonian language wherever they went. Their scribes had first to be trained in the essentials of Babylonian literature so that a knowledge of the classics of Mesopotamia was exported wherever the *tamkârū* opened offices throughout the ancient world.

The *tamkârū* also spread business methods. The seeds of the capitalist system were produced in Mesopotamia and sown throughout the ancient world by the *tamkârū* and their successors. The most fundamental part of capitalistic economy is the encouragement of capital investment by the payment of interest. The Mesopotamians called such capital, or principal, *qaqqadum* (literally " head "). With the institution the name has been

[1] We cannot accurately describe Abraham's status with a single label. " Merchant prince " is as good a label as any suggested so far; but see Chapter VIII for further details.

[2] The Linear B tablets depict the economic and administrative sides of Mycenaean civilisation.

carried through Hebrew *rôš*,[1] Greek *kefálaion*,[2] and Latin *caput*,[3] whence English " capital " is derived. Conducting business by leaving security (pending payment) was also fostered by the *tamkârū* of the ancient Near East. In Canaan, the " security " was written *ᶜrbn* at Ugarit and pronounced *ᶜêrābôn* in Hebrew. The Greeks called it *arrabón*; the Romans, *arrabō* (gen. *arrabōnis*); and the French still call it *les arrhes*—the same word, although worn down through linguistic wear.

All societies are stratified and their component parts often have different modes of life, as well as different functions. Usually several different forces are at work, resulting in a variety of stratifications crisscrossing each other so that many individuals, as well as whole groups, are affected by a number of factors simultaneously. For example, the stratification into rich and poor does not always go in the expected way with the stratification into free and slave. Free men were often poor; and slaves were sometimes wealthy. Hammurapi's Code has a three-fold division of society into patrician, plebeian and slave. But other divisions are also operative in the Code: native vs. alien; priesthood vs. laity; military vs. civilian; government vs. subjects; herds-men vs. farmers; etc., etc. Amid all this complexity is the guild system whereby each craft has its own closed guild.[4] One normally had to be born into the guild and learn the craft from his father. However, a childless craftsman could adopt a child and teach him the craft, thus bringing him into the guild.

Guilds were an important channel of cultural transmission, for the reason given in the Odyssey 17: 382-386: " Who of himself really invites and summons a stranger from abroad? Unless they

[1] Means primarily " head "; and secondarily " capital " or " principal."
[2] " Capital, principal "; derived from *kefalé* " head."
[3] Means primarily " head "; and secondarily " capital " or " principal."
[4] See my " Stratification of Society in Hammurapi's Code," *The Joshua Starr Memorial Volume*, New York, 1953, pp. 17-28.

be *dēmioergoí*: a prophet, or a healer of ills, or a builder, or an inspired minstrel, who sings to a delighted audience. For these are called by mortals over the endless earth. But no one would call a beggar to impoverish himself." The implication of this passage is clear. Ordinary men such as dispossessed peasants and herdsmen were not welcome abroad. Only skilled specialists were desired and welcome the world over. The context tells us to translate *dēmioergoí* as "members of the guilds"; i.e., skilled craftsmen and professional men. The four illustrations provided by the Homeric text are not meant to be exhaustive, but they are very interesting. The mobility of religious personnel, such as prophets, explains the spread of religious techniques and institutions. The mention of physicians is a key to the spread of medical arts. That builders were in demand from country to country explains the diffusion of architectural forms over wide areas.[1] Wandering minstrels account for much of the spread of music and poetry in the ancient world.[2]

Military personnel were also organised into guilds, each with its own speciality. The *maryannu* charioteers were at the top of the military guilds, and appear all over Mesopotamia, Anatolia, Canaan and Egypt. When two armies clashed, members of the same military guilds were to be found serving in both camps. Bowmen and slingers were among the many specialised contingents of the infantry. Sub-divisions were often introduced into the military classifications. For instance, ambidextrous warriors were rated higher than their less versatile colleagues.

The ancient soldiers were not supposed to be flexible to the point of changing their specialities. In this way, they were

[1] Thus Solomon called in Phoenician builders for his Temple and palaces in Jerusalem.

[2] For further details, see my "Ugaritic Guilds and Homeric ΔΗΜΙΟΕΡΓΟΙ," *The Aegean and the Near East: Studies Presented to Hetty Goldman,* J. J. Augustin, Locust Valley, N.Y., 1956, pp. 136-143.

different from modern soldiers who often have secondary as well as primary qualifications and, in keeping with the tempo of modern change, must make adjustments in their military functions. The impression we get from ancient records is that a charioteer warrior never took the reins, while his driver never shot an arrow.[1]

The military guilds were hereditary and enjoyed royal protection in return for service whenever it was needed. Hammurapi's Code regulates military affairs including a Veterans' Bill of Rights to protect the veteran against the loss of his royal endowment (consisting of land and movables) that provided him and his family with economic security. In exchange, the veteran had to serve as a "ready reservist" and rear a son to carry on after him, in the army of the king.

High ranking officers, whose service pleased the king, were often the recipients of royal grants. We have many tablets from Ugarit, whereby the king granted estates to his favourites. It is interesting to note that the king often takes an estate away from someone, to assign it to another.[2] In other words, the king granted land in exchange for satisfactory service. When the king was no longer satisfied with the service of his subject, he would take back the grant and give it to someone more to his liking. Hammurapi's Code, however, in laying down principles, does not reflect such royal caprice, but indicates that the grant can be taken away from the veteran only as a result of chronic and gross incompetence.

Mercenaries were quite common. David and his successors used Cherethite[3] and Pelethite troops for generations. Indeed, such Philistine and similar mercenaries, of Aegean origin, did

[1] Iliad 15: 463-5, 478-483 provides a rare exception. When the archer Teucer's bow string is broken, he carries a spear.

[2] Examples are published in J. Nougayrol's *Le Palais royal d'Ugarit* III, Paris, 1955, pp. 47-53, 58-60, 62-63, etc.

[3] "Cherethite" is the anglicised form of Hebrew *kᵉrētî* "Cretan."

much to spread " Caphtorian "[1] culture in Palestine and throughout the Levantine coast. The great empires also used mercenaries.
It is unnecessary to enumerate the evidence for the employment
of mercenaries by Egypt, Assyria, Babylonia, the Medes and
Persians, etc. It is clear that war brought about cultural interchange not only through invasion and conquest, but also by the
importation of mercenaries. Let us not forget that, from Egypt
to Iran, Greeks (as well as earlier Aegean peoples) were renowned
as mercenaries. Jews were also mercenaries in communities like
Elephantine.

Every student of archaeology soon comes to realise that
artifacts reflecting a specific technique often have wide distribution. We are not referring to accidental, parallel developments,
but rather to the spread of definite schools of manufacture. For
example, in the Roman Empire, two vessels of *terra sigillata* can
be found a thousand miles apart, and yet no one can doubt that
they stem from the same school of ceramic manufacture. Long
before the dawn of writing, we are confronted with essentially
the same phenomenon. At Ugarit, many craftsmen are organised
into guilds administratively for the state. That is to say, they are
related to, and controlled by, the government not through their
locality but through their guild. Potters form one of the numerous guilds of craftsmen. Accordingly, we must account for the
spread of ceramic types in part through the mobility of the
potters. When a community needed a potter, he would be
supplied through the guild. Another community hundreds of
miles away, in need of a potter, might well get him from
the same closely-knit guild. When we multiply this state of
affairs by the number of the guilds (smiths, carpenters, ship-
wrights, sculptors, bakers—to mention only a few of the many
guilds mentioned in the Ugaritic tablets), we get an inkling

[1] " Caphtor " is the land whence the Philistines came to Palestine. Here
we use the term " Caphtorian " to designate Aegean culture broadly.

of how culture was transmitted through the mobility of craftsmen.

The older Codes of Mesopotamia, down to Hammurapi's, show the guild structure of ancient Near East society. But after the impact of the Indo-Europeans, the stratification becomes much more complex. Ugarit has such a plethora of guilds that we suspect the influence of an Indo-European system, akin to the one that later became fossilised as the caste system of India. At the beginning, the system was merely one of professional specialisation, but it became more and more hide-bound and hereditary until guild-classes became castes. It seems that, while the Indo-Europeans did not start the guild system in the Near East, they added considerable impetus to it.

We have noted that religious personnel were organised into mobile guilds. Homeric epic includes prophets among the *dēmioergoí* sought everywhere on the face of the limitless earth. Prophets and priests were, in those days, not so much adherents of a unique cult as professional men who offered their technical services to any employer. To be sure, they might insist on professional freedom, and refuse to act as mere rubber stamps, but their services were for sale within those limits. The Bible reflects the same situation in Numbers 22, where Balak, King of Moab, sought out Balaam from Pathor in Aram along the Euphrates, to secure his professional services for execrating Israel. Balaam had established a wide reputation for pronouncing effective curses and blessings, and Balak felt that a curse upon Israel from the distinguished prophet Balaam might strengthen him against Israel. It is of more than passing interest to note that Numbers 22-24 represents the gentile prophet Balaam as inspired by God; and his utterances, such as " How goodly are thy tents, O Jacob; thy tabernacles, O Israel " (Numbers 24: 5) have remained among the most cherished passages in Scripture throughout Synagogue history.

Two of the priestly guilds occurring both in Israel and Ugarit are the *kôhᵃnîm* and the *qᵉdēšîm*. The *kôhᵃnîm* are represented as legitimate in both traditions; but the *qᵉdēšîm*, while legitimate in Ugarit, came to be outlawed in Israel. In the Bible we can trace how the *kôhēn* guild succeeded in ousting the rival *qādēš* guild in Israel.

The mobility of priests is illustrated in the most amazing way in Judges 17-18. A private citizen, Micah, built and equipped his own sanctuary and appointed his own son as priest, until a Levite, looking for a professional assignment, migrated from Judah to Ephraim where Micah dwelt. Micah appointed the Levite as priest (*kôhēn*) of the family shrine at a salary of ten shekels of silver per year, plus clothing and keep. But later a band of Danite warriors, in need of a priest to provide them with oracles, abducted the Levite and stole Micah's cultic objects as well. They moved, Levite and all, up to Dan in the far north. This tale is important because it shows that priests might go out and seek employment far from home and that priests were so much in demand that they were sometimes worth kidnapping for their professional services. Note that the story brings out the desire to have genuine guild priests, not *ad hoc* appointees.

The importation of cultically-devoted priests from one land to another is illustrated in the account of Ahab's reign, when the Phoenician princess Jezebel, after becoming Queen of Israel, imports Baalistic priests into Israel. Here, however, we run into cultic rivalry which has a more modern ring, and Jezebel's programme led to a violent Yahwistic reaction that ended only with the slaughter of the Baalists under King Jehu.

A quaint example of cultic infiltration is provided by an Aramaic inscription from Teima (Arabia) of about the fifth century B.C.[1] A priest with the Semitic name of Ṣalm-šêzeb

[1] G. A. Cooke, *A Text-book of North-Semitic Inscriptions*, Oxford, 1903, pp. 195-199.

son of a father with the pure Egyptian name of Pet-Osiris, founds a hereditary priesthood for the newly introduced god Ṣalm of Hajam. The community apparently saw nothing strange in introducing the worship of a new god, under a newly established priesthood.

Sometimes cultic centres attracted people from remote areas. Probably the most common cause for such magnetism was an efficacious priesthood, that earned a reputation for helping people in need of practical advice, psychological guidance or medical aid. Cythera began to attract foreigners as early as the Pyramid Age. A stone cup, with the name of a Fifth Dynasty solar temple[1] (*sp-rᶜ*) inscribed in Egyptian hieroglyphs, has been found on Cythera. Early in the second quarter of the second millennium, a Babylonian inscription of Naram-Sin, King of Eshnunna, was dedicated on Cythera " for the life " of that Mesopotamian monarch.[2] The interesting thing is that both of these texts found on Cythera are religious in character.[3] Herodotus (1: 105) relates that the Phoenicians erected a temple on Cythera to the goddess of the heavens. Finally in classical times, Cythera was a great centre of the cult of Aphrodite. The ancient temples were built in the vicinity of Palaiopolis around the middle of the eastern shore. I visited the site in 1958 and found it extensive and promising for excavation. The ancient temples have been largely dismantled, to judge from the beautifully hewn masonry that one finds now and then re-used in the stone walls out in the fields. An intact pithos, found by a local peasant, was three-quarters

[1] Of Pharaoh Userkaf at Abusir.

[2] For the bibliography, see *Journal of Near Eastern Studies* 17, 1958, p. 245. See also G. A. Wainwright, *Antiquity* 18, 1944, pp. 59-60.

[3] This is one of the reasons for believing that both texts were sent to Cythera in antiquity. Modern deception is unlikely because the Naram-Sin text was found on Cythera in 1849 before the decipherment of cuneiform.

excavated at the time of my visit. The Islanders, unlike the Greeks of so many other parts of the country, have no interest in any pre-Christian antiquities and are quite unaware of the ancient importance of Cythera, when Egyptians, Babylonians and Phoenicians came to worship the great goddess there. Ancient cultic installations, carved out of the living rock, can still be seen on a high-place at the north end, near the shore. A well, cleared some years ago, has, at its bottom, ancient statuary, according to my peasant informant, who explained that the water welled up so profusely and suddenly that it became impossible to retrieve the statuettes which were visible. A road had recently been cut through the modern surface exposing ancient stone walls, whose bases have been buried by soil washed down from the heights after the rains. The whole area is covered with ceramics that show the site was occupied in Middle Minoan III (*ca.* 1700-1570), Late Minoan I-III (*ca.* 1570-1100)[1] and subsequently in classical times (5th-4th centuries B.C.).

The problem posed by ancient Cythera has not yet been answered. The Island is rather remote from Egypt and Asia for men to have sailed there, for religious purposes alone. And yet it is hard to discover any more practical reason. Cythera is not remarkable for its natural resources. Was it the last stop on the sea-route before the ancient mariners reached the Peloponnesus (for Laconia is in full view from Cythera)? But then, what was there in the Peloponnesus to attract ships from afar? Probably not the wine and oil, for they were also produced elsewhere in the Levant. It has been conjectured that Greece produced enough lead and tin to attract merchants from the Cuneiform World. (Lead was one of the metals used as a medium of exchange.) Perhaps so. But since ancient mariners liked to hug the shore and engage in island hopping, perhaps Cythera was a major stop on

---

[1] Late Minoan III (*ca.* 1400-1100) is the Mycenaean Age.

the route to the west, possibly ending in Spain. Much remains to be done by way of identifying the sea-lanes in the various periods of antiquity, through showing the periods of occupation of the Mediterranean ports. Meanwhile we must reckon with Cythera as a site where all the evidence so far points to its importance as a religious centre with international attraction.

When Solomon dedicated the Temple in Jerusalem, he is represented as saying to God: (I Kings 8: 41) " And also to the alien, who is not of Thy people Israel, but comes from a distant land on account of Thy fame; (42) for hearing of Thy great name and Thy strong hand, and Thine outstretched arm, he comes to this house to pray. . . . (43) do Thou listen in the heavens, the place where Thou dwellest, and perform all that the alien begs of Thee, so that all the peoples of the earth may know Thy name, to fear Thee like Thine own people Israel, and to know that Thy name is proclaimed over this house that I have built." The thought put in the mouth of Solomon is not anachronistic. Great cultic centres (such as Jerusalem then aspired to become) attracted people from near and far, provided that the people were satisfied. Such shrines functioned around the East Mediterranean long before, as well as long after, the completion of Solomon's Temple in the tenth century B.C. Solomon, who had wide commercial interests, as well as extensive territorial holdings, would naturally want his Temple to command international respect and draw men from the ends of the earth. Such shrines have remained well known throughout the ages. In classical antiquity, the oracle at Delphi was sought within a wide radius. Today Lourdes attracts from every continent people in need of help that they have not succeeded in finding nearer home.

Cythera thus became a centre for Egyptians and Semites and still other people, from Abusir along the Nile to Eshnunna beyond the Euphrates. Such visitors brought their influence to bear on the Aegean, and on returning home, carried some Aegean culture with them.

Our survey of the channels of transmission is far from exhaustive but it should suffice to convey a general appreciation of the many avenues along which international cultural exchange took place.

III

The Cuneiform World

Sumer, the most southerly part of Mesopotamia, is of recent geological formation. The Tigris and Euphrates Rivers deposit a vast quantity of silt each year so that the shore line of the Persian Gulf keeps moving perceptibly southward. At present, the Twin Rivers join to form the Shatt el-Arab, which flows into the Gulf. In Sumerian times, the Euphrates and Tigris emptied into the Gulf separately at points that are now far inland.

Sumer, formed of fertile silt and favoured with an abundance of water from the Rivers, had enormous potentialities requiring only the right human factor to develop them. The Sumerians arrived on the scene, and never was there a better combination of land and people.

Where the Sumerians came from is still disputed. Typologically, the language of Sumer resembles Chinese, which suggests an eastern origin. Some scholars have proposed that the Sumerians came by ship, landing on the north shore of the Persian Gulf. Most authorities maintain that they swept down from the highlands on the east and north. Cultural connections between Sumer and the lands to the north (and north-east and north-west) tip the scales in favour of a land route for the advent of the Sumerians.

While Sumerian wealth and power depended on a richly productive agriculture, Sumerian civilisation from the start was intimately connected with the concept of mountainous terrain and with the arts of the smith and lapidary that are dependent on mines and quarries in the mountains.

The typical temple structure of the Sumerians was the ziggurat, or stage tower with a shrine at the top. It was called the Mountain House and simulated a kind of shrine venerated on mountain tops by the ancestors of the Sumerians, prior to their migration into Sumer. Excellence in the working of stones for seals, and of gold, silver, electrum and copper for jewellery, implements and weapons, indicates early connections with, and exploitation of, the mineral resources of Western and Central Asia. Such a civilisation could not have grown up, from scratch, on the soil of Sumer, without outside connections.

As we have noted, early Mesopotamian pottery, from about 3500 B.C., has links as far afield as peninsular Greece, via Anatolia. Cultural links between Mesopotamia and Greece have persisted, in varying degree, from period to period, ever since.

Shortly after 3000 B.C., the Sumerians developed a system of writing from pictographs. At first the Sumerian script was linear, but it gradually became cuneiform, normally inscribed on clay tablets with a stylus. During the third millennium, Sumerian became a great medium for writing the records of business, law, religion and literature. If we are to measure greatness in such matters by impact on other nations, Sumerian is certainly the world's first great written language and literature. The late Edward Sapir listed Chinese, Sanskrit, Arabic, Greek and Latin as the five great languages of the world, because of their impact on other speech groups. Sumerian ought to be added to the list.

The Akkadians borrowed the Sumerian system of writing and absorbed many Sumerian loanwords into the Akkadian language. Moreover Sumerian remained the classical language of Akkadian culture throughout the 2500 years that Akkadian texts continued to be written in cuneiform. When this script was borrowed by

Impressions from cylinder seals:
(a) Gilgamesh and Enkidu grappling with wild beasts (pp. 50, 51, 70) (b) Presentation scene (p. 145)

Impressions from cylinder seals:
(a) Enkidu fighting the Bull of Heaven by belt wrestling (pp. 50, 51, 70)
(b) Babylonian goddess in a flounced dress (p. 54)
(c) Akkadian heroes fighting a seven-headed monster (p. 190)

the Hittites, the scribes of Anatolia continued to use Sumerian as well as Akkadian word-signs, even though the reader was supposed to pronounce them in Hittite. Sumerian as well as Akkadian words were borrowed into the Hittite language. Wherever Akkadian influence spread (among the Hurrians, Hittites, Elamites, Canaanites and still farther afield into the Aegean and Egypt), the Sumerian impact was felt. While Aramaic was displacing Akkadian in the course of the first millennium B.C., it absorbed a host of Sumerian words from Akkadian and transmitted them to the rest of the Near East. Some got into Arabic and have been carried to the ends of the eastern hemisphere by Islam. Of older date are the Sumerian loanwords in biblical Hebrew.

The greatness of Sumer can be measured in other spheres, too. Its sexagesimal system has reached us via the exact sciences. Our astronomers still divide the circle into 360 degrees with each degree divisible into 60 minutes and each minute into 60 seconds. The division of the hour into 60 minutes of 60 seconds each is also a legacy of Sumer. Whenever we look at a clock, we are reminded of our debt to Sumer.

The achievement of the Sumerians in the art of the jeweller first became fully clear when Sir C. Leonard Woolley unearthed the royal tombs at Ur. I had the good fortune to be a member of the expedition early in 1932, while the tomb-treasures were still emerging from the soil. I had just come from an expedition where most of the finds consisted of pottery, and it is impossible to describe the effect of such a sudden transfer to a site like Ur, where a symphony of colour (gold, carnelian and lapis-lazuli) came to view, wherever we would brush away the soil in the tomb area.

The most characteristic product of Sumerian (and later of Akkadian) art is the seal cylinder. Usually made of stone, the cylinder, often comparable in size with a human finger, bears the artist's work in intaglio. Nearly always, the composition fits into a repertoire of common themes. The main purpose of the cylinder seals was to indicate ownership. Storage jars, and even store rooms, were sealed around the opening with clay over which the seal was rolled completely about the circumference. The need to seal any-size circumference evoked the cylindrical seal which could be rolled for any distance that might be needed. Eventually, the Sumerian cylinder seals were used as signatures by the contracting parties and witnesses on clay tablets.

Graphic art and written literature are two parallel expressions of any civilisation, and for present purposes, they must be treated in relation to each other. They often cover the same subject matter, though with some divergence between the pictorial and written traditions. In ancient Assyria and Egypt, the same historic events are often covered simultaneously by word and in pictures. In Medieval Europe, the unlettered masses who could not read Scripture were able to follow the abundant pictorial versions of Scripture supplied by Church art. (We are now entering a parallel situation, with " comic " or picture book versions of the classics, in which the visual account has made heavy inroads on the verbal.) The interesting fact for Sumer is that pictorial representations of the Mesopotamian classics appear many centuries before our earliest texts thereof. For example, the greatest Mesopotamian classic is the Gilgamesh Epic. Seals depicting scenes from the Gilgamesh Epic are exceedingly common, and begin about 1000 years before the earliest cuneiform tablets dealing with those scenes. Accordingly, the materials out of which the Gilgamesh Epic was fashioned by the second millennium B.C. were circulating orally, and pictorially, around 3000 B.C. For example, the seals, starting in early Sumerian times, depict the heroes (Gilgamesh and Enkidu[1]) grappling with

---

[1] Since some sceptical authors call the identity of these heroes into question, it is well to cite an illustration that is not subject to controversy. The myth of

ferocious beasts. Specifically, Gilgamesh is often shown grappling either with a bull or with the mythological human-
headed Bull of Heaven. In all probability the Gilgamesh Epic
reached the shores of the Aegean by the middle of the second
millennium B.C. Besides, translations of the Epic into Hurrian
and Hittite in Asia Minor reflect its popularity in that part of the
world, and it is hard to imagine how it could avoid circulation in
Greek, perhaps in written but certainly in oral form, in Ionia and
the Aegean islands. The advent of the Gilgamesh Epic to
the Aegean explains the many intimate relationships between
that Epic and the earliest Greek traditions embodied in the
Heracles Cycle[1] and in Homer and Hesiod. Against this background, Sumero-Akkadian bull-grappling takes on special
significance.

Regardless of religious or other ideological content, Sumero-
Akkadian bull-grappling had also its sportive side. This is
abundantly clear from representations showing the beast wearing
a wrestling belt on which the hero secures his hold.[2] We are
confronted by the fact that we can no longer dissociate the major
sport depicted in Sumerian art from the same major sport
depicted in Minoan art. The two schools of bull-grappling have
differences in detail, but they are, nonetheless, reflexes of one
tradition. From the Minoan centre, bull-fighting spread to different parts of the Mediterranean. No one will question that the
different schools of bull-fighting in Spain, Portugal and Southern
France are reflexes of one tradition. By the same token, a common origin for Sumerian and Minoan bull-grappling is indicated

---

Etana who flew heavenward on the back of an eagle, is often depicted (like so
many mythological scenes) on seal cylinders of the Akkad Dynasty.

[1] Cf. B. C. Brundage, "Herakles the Levantine: A Comprehensive
View," *Journal of Near Eastern Studies* 17, 1958, pp. 225-236.

[2] See seal #9 of the " Western Asiatic Seals in the Walters Art Gallery,"
Iraq 6, 1939, pp. 3-34, pls. II-XV.

by historic connections between the two peoples in time and place.

There is a further ramification of bull-grappling that cements the Sumero-Minoan tie-in. The Sumerian Bull of Heaven is an evil monster, partly bovine and partly human in form, slain by the heroes of the Epic. It is hard to dissociate all this from the story of the evil Minotaur, part bovine and part human, slain by the hero Theseus. It is true that the Sumerians represented the Bull of Heaven with human head and bull's body, whereas the later Greek representations of the Minotaur, depict him with human body and bull's head. Textual descriptions such as Plutarch's, state merely that he was partly bovine and partly human. In any case, variations are to be expected in two divergent schools stemming from a common heritage.

In the 24th century B.C., a new dynasty got hold of Mesopotamia. Sargon, of the city of Akkad, established a Semitic Empire that reached out into the Mediterranean. From his time on, southern Mesopotamia came to be known as Sumer and Akkad; Sumer designating the more Sumerian south, and Akkad the more Semitic north. His success marked a turning point in history. From his time down to the present, Mesopotamia became a predominantly Semitic land. Sargon claimed dominion over the entire world; a concept that has plagued mankind ever since.

As we noted above, Sargon's merchants in Asia Minor summoned him to reassert his power there. This implication that his Akkadian Dynasty had connections in Asia Minor from the start is confirmed linguistically. The Akkadian language, though Semitic, has some Indo-European words imbedded in it, from the very beginnings of recorded Akkadian literature. Whereas other Semitic languages express " in " by the prefix *ba-*, and " to, for " by the prefix *la-*, Akkadian is the only Semitic language to express them by *in(a)* and *ana* respectively. Akkadian *in(a)* cannot be dissociated from Greek *en* or Latin and

Minoan bronze figurine; bull vaulting in Crete (p. 54)

Statuette of a Cretan goddess in a flounced skirt (p. 54)

English *in* with the same meaning ("in"). Akkadian *ana* shares some meanings with Greek *ana*. Akkadian *magal*[1] "greatly" is related to Greek *megál-ōs* "great-ly." Sometimes the Sumerian anticipates the Akkadian tie-in with Indo-European; thus Sumerian *a-gar* and Akkadian *ugâru*, meaning "field," cannot be separated from Indo-European *agr-ós* (Greek), *ager* (Latin) and *Acker* (German) "field."[2]

The basic Indo-European vocabulary in Akkadian[3] is due to a process called linguistic alliance. This means only that when two different linguistic groups of people live together, their languages will interpenetrate each other. The above words, embedded in Akkadian and so attested from the first appearance of Akkadian texts, confirm the tradition of the "King of Battle Epic" that Sargon's Akkadian Dynasty had Anatolian connections from the beginning. Since the Akkadian records start around the middle of the third millennium B.C., the formation of the Akkadian language in linguistic alliance with Indo-Europeans in Anatolia must have taken place still earlier.

The western connections of the Akkad Dynasty are indicated in yet other ways. Only one western god, Dagan, obtained an important place in the old Mesopotamian pantheon, and he significantly is the patron god of the Akkad Dynasty. This western god appears in the Linear A tablets of Hagia Triada; he

---

[1] That *magal* is not derived from Sumerian *gal* "great" is indicated by the spelling *ma-ga-al* (A. Ungnad, *Babylonische Briefe*, Leipzig, 1914, p. 329).

[2] Other examples are Sumerian *temen*, Akkadian *tem(m)en(n)u*, Greek *témen-os*; Sumerian *dam-gar*, Akkadian *tamkâru*, Mycenaean Greek *damokor(os)*. These two examples are cultural loans. *Temen* moved with the spread of cultic land uses; and *dam-gar*, with the spread of trade. Like his Mesopotamian prototype, the Mycenaean *damokor(os)* represents the king, and supplies gold, bronze and other commodities (see T. B. L. Webster, *From Mycenae to Homer*, London, 1958, p. 15). E. R. Lacheman made the keen identification of *damakor(os)* with *dam-gar*.

[3] We refer to words like the prepositions rather than the nouns reflecting cultural diffusion.

is Baal's father according to the Epic of Kret from Ugarit; and he is the chief god of the Biblical Philistines.

Still another bond connecting Akkadian Mesopotamia with the Aegean is the goddess that commonly appears on seal cylinders starting in Akkad times, growing in popularity during the Ur III period and becoming exceedingly common during the First Dynasty of Babylon. She wears a flounced dress and holds up her hands, bending her arms at the elbow. In the light of the other tie-ins just pointed out, we are led to compare her with the Minoan goddess with upheld hands and wearing a flounced skirt.[1] Perhaps this goddess reached Crete and Mesopotamia from the intermediate area of Asia Minor. At any rate—as with so much of the evidence—we can no longer go on assuming tacitly that such Mesopotamian and Aegean phenomena are unrelated. The gap has been bridged with the result that we are beginning to see a continuum instead of two unconnected areas poles apart.

Under the Dynasty of Akkad, Mesopotamia launched on a programme of expansionism that carried its arms, commerce and culture towards the ends of the known world. The majestic concept of a World Empire favoured the notion of divine kingship. Kings of the Dynasty, notably Naram-Sin (one of Sargon's successors), often place the sign for divinity before their names, and are depicted in art as wearing the horned crown of godhood. In Greek epic, kings are accorded the titles and honours of divinity. To be sure, since the Pharaohs had been regarded as divine throughout Egyptian history, the concept was nothing new around the East Mediterranean. Nevertheless, it is interesting to note that the early Sumerian rulers did not claim divinity; and,

---

[1] During 1958, Stylianos Alexiou and I expressed the same general conclusion independently. See his monograph Η ΜΙΝΩΙΚΗ ΘΕΑ ΜΕΘ' ΥΨΩΜΕΝΩΝ ΧΕΙΡΩΝ, Heraclion, Crete, 1958; and my concise formulation in *Journal of Near Eastern Studies* 17, 1958, p. 252.

therefore, the concept may have been brought into Mesopotamia by the Akkadians from Anatolia, and may also have persisted in the Aegean from the third millennium into the Mycenaean milieu reflected in the Homeric poems. Spyridon Marinatos (*op. cit.*, p. 134) has rightly pointed out that the concept of "divinely born kings" in Homer reflects the international culture of a Near East of which the Greeks were a component part. He notes in this connection that the Mycenaeans have much more in common with that international complex than with the later classical Greeks (*op. cit.*, p. 126). We may say the same for early Israel, which belonged to the same international complex. The milieu of David and that of Achilles are, as we shall see, closer to each other than either is to the Age of the great Hebrew Prophets, or of Fifth and Fourth Century Athens.[1] The synthesis out of which the early Greeks and Hebrews sprang in the second millennium was already in the making early in the third millennium.

Although the Akkad Dynasty marked the beginning of the end for Sumerian domination, a number of Sumerian revivals were attempted during the following centuries but were doomed to failure by wave after wave of Semitic immigration. The main revival was the Third Dynasty of Ur, in the twenty-first and twentieth centuries B.C. The population in the homeland was becoming more and more Akkadian, but the official written language and institutional structure of the realm was Sumerian. As in the case of all revivals, there were differences between Ur III and the classical past. The chief of state was now a king (*lugal* in Sumerian) instead of merely the human agent (*ensi* in Sumerian) who ruled a city state for the city god. Indeed, Ur III,

---

[1] This is not to deny the continuity of the Greeks since Agamemnon, and another continuity of the Hebrews since Abraham. T. Boman, *Das hebräische Denken im Vergleich mit dem Griechischen*, 3rd ed., Göttingen, 1959, p. 14f., consciously elects to study and contrast the two continuities.

far from being a Sumerian city state, was now an empire. Following the precedent of the Akkad Dynasty, Ur III had commercial colonies far to the north. We have noted why Abraham's birthplace, Ur of the Chaldees, was probably a northern commercial colony named after the Sumerian capital of the Third Dynasty of Ur. The cult of the daughter colony was the same as the cult of the mother city: the moon cult of the god Sin, and his wife, the lunar goddess Nin-gal. Many merchants from the northern Urs entered Canaan for trading purposes and introduced their Mesopotamian moon cult there. It is for this reason that Nikkal (= Nin-gal) was worshipped at Ugarit and even penetrated through Canaan into Egypt.[1] Abraham was not an isolated immigrant, but part of a larger movement from Ur of the Chaldees (and similar communities) into Canaan.

It is from the reign of Ur-Nammu, the first king of Ur III, that we have fragments of the earliest extant lawcode in the world. The urge to regulate society by written ordinances had long been felt in Sumer. An older *ensi* of Lagash, named Urukagina, had written a social reform two centuries earlier. Urukagina's reform consisted mainly of ameliorating fees and prices, in the interest of the common man who had to pay them. Ur-Nammu's lawcode, written in Sumerian, is a more advanced type of document. It is arranged in the classical Mesopotamian form for lawcodes, with prose laws flanked by a poetic prologue and epilogue. The fully developed form of Ur-Nammu's Code shows that it is not a first attempt, but rather rests on a tradition of earlier codes, which may some day be found in Sumerian mounds yet to be excavated.

The importance of the Sumero-Akkadian lawcodes lies in their influence on the later Greeks and Hebrews, via the peripheral areas of Mesopotamian expansionism during the second

[1] See my *Ugaritic Manual*, Rome, 1955, p. 296, #1242.

millennium B.C. Between Ur-Nammu and Hammurapi, two more codes have survived. The earlier is the Eshnunna Code in Babylonian; the later is the Lipit-Ishtar Code in Sumerian. Hammurapi's Code marks the apex of Mesopotamian legal codification, and it is not without significance that precisely at this time, Mesopotamian influence reached out towards its farthest known limits in the West: attaining firm footholds even in the Aegean. Babylonian merchants carrying their native methods of business and law imported their legal system to the lands where Israel and Greece were destined to grow. For this reason Babylonian law can be felt in classical Hebrew and Greek law. For instance, the Hebrew principle of " an eye for an eye, a tooth for a tooth " is anticipated in Hammurapi's Code. And lest this be considered too general a principle to prove anything, we may cite something more specific: The Hebrew legislation (Exodus 21: 28-32) about " the goring bull " (whereby the owner is responsible for the damage to life and limb, caused by the beast after its first offence), is in the tradition of the Mesopotamian Codes, starting with the Eshnunna Code #54 and continued in Hammurapi's Code ##250-252.

We are not to explain the Hebrew parallels as direct copying from the cuneiform codes. We are rather to picture Canaan, on the eve of the Hebrew settlement, as a land in which Mesopotamian law was already entrenched, so that the Hebrews absorbed that legal tradition as an integral part of the Canaanite culture they took over.

In the Greek world, Crete had the reputation of being the most law-conscious area. (Next came Laconia, with its intimate connections with Crete.) The oldest extant Greek code has been found at Gortyn in the Messara, on Crete. It is striking that the Gortyn Code was found specifically in the Messara, which is the part of Crete where Platanos and Hagia Triada are also situated. It may not be a coincidence that the oldest Greek code hails from precisely the part of Crete where Babylonian activity is attested, archaeologically and epigraphically, since the middle of the second millennium B.C.

The commercial colonies in Anatolia attained unprecedented heights during the Old Assyrian period, in the 19th and 18th centuries B.C. Most of our rich documentation comes from the colony of Kanish, now called Kültepe. Other colonies have been found at Alishar and Hattusa. So far, such Assyrian activity seems limited to Central and Eastern Anatolia, but surprises in Western Anatolia are always possible. The Assyrian word for such a colony is *kârum*, literally " port." The term came to be associated with the kind of commercial activity familiar at flourishing "ports," regardless of whether caravans or ships carried the merchandise. The Old Assyrian colonies kept their records in Assyrian. The names of the merchants are mainly Assyrian. Indeed almost everything except the material culture[1] is Assyrian, rather than Cappadocian. Constant commercial interchange was kept up between the Assyrian homeland and the *kârum*. Lead was then used as a medium of exchange, and one of the functions of the Cappadocian colonies was supplying the homeland with sufficient quantities of lead.

The Assyrians were confronted with the problem of coping with the hostility of the native Cappadocian population. Accordingly, they maintained a control over weapons and over the metal from which weapons could be made. Thus the *kârum* had a *rabî kakkê* " administrator of weapons " and a *rabî siparrim* " administrator of bronze," for keeping the natives disarmed.[2]

---

[1] The material culture of a *kârum* is local, not Assyrian. E. Peruzzi's linguistic argument (*Word* 15, 1959, p. 224, n. 34) from the material culture at Hagia Triada is not valid.

[2] J. Lewy, *Journal of the American Oriental Society* 78, 1958, p. 95. Compare I Samuel 13: 19ff., where the Philistines keep Israel disarmed and helpless by monopolising and controlling metallurgy. Much of the Book of Judges

Each Old Assyrian *kârum* served as a centre from which Assyrian civilisation spread into the surrounding Hittite area, with the result that Hittite civilisation became, in many ways, a peripheral form of Mesopotamian civilisation. The best gauge of what took place is the nature of cuneiform Hittite itself. Elements of the non-Indo-European Hattic population peer through the language. The main stratum of the language is Indo-European, with many Sumero-Akkadian loanwords. But far more numerous than the loanwords are the countless Akkadograms, and Sumerograms: i.e., Akkadian and Sumerian words, written as such in the Hittite tablets, but usually meant to be pronounced in Hittite translation. The closest approximations to this in English are the "Latinograms" like "i.e." which we pronounce, not "id est," but "that is." Just as our Latinograms reflect a profound Latin influence on our culture, so too the Sumero-Akkadograms reflect the powerful impact of Mesopotamia on Hittite culture. The vast number of Sumero-Akkadograms indicate quite clearly that the impact was intense quantitatively as well as clear-cut qualitatively. We must recognise this quantitative side, if we are to understand the penetration of Akkadian influence still farther west, into the Aegean. Indeed, the Hittites frequently wrote pure Akkadian tablets, with no trace of their own language. Even in a Hittite text, like the "Apology of Hattusili III," the prologue is written in plain Akkadian with no trace of Hittite.

The cuneiform scribes in Asia Minor transmitted more than the art of writing. In the course of their training, they absorbed

---

reflects a similar situation. Judges 5: 8 states that Israel was disarmed. The warrior Ehud is represented as having to make his own sword (Judges 3: 16). The disarmament imposed on Israel explains why Shamgar had to slay Philistines with an oxgoad (Judges 3: 31) and Samson, with the jawbone of an ass (Judges 15: 15-17). Since their enemies kept them disarmed, they performed their mighty deeds of valour with substitute weapons of the most amateurish sort.

the fundamentals of Mesopotamian law, business, science and literature. In all these fields, the Greeks received a strong exposure to Mesopotamian culture prior to the Mycenaean period, via Hittite Anatolia by land, as well as via Canaan by sea. The miracle of Greece did not happen suddenly. It resulted in part from repeated exposure to the accomplishments of the Assyrians and Babylonians through channels of transmission.

Artistic evidence points to the same conclusions. The Cappadocian seal cylinders have distinctive details, but their subject matter is heavily borrowed from the Ur III and Babylon I styles of Mesopotamian glyptic art.

We know from the exercise tablets of the school for cuneiform scribes at Tell el-Amarna, that the students were trained in Akkadian belles-lettres before they could qualify for an " office job," writing official correspondence. The same held true in Anatolia, where literary texts have been found, including significantly, fragments of the Gilgamesh Epic in both Hittite and Hurrian translation. The cuneiform tradition (unlike the Egyptian hieroglyphic tradition[1]) was bilingual since the days of Sumer and Akkad in the third millennium. This bilingualism was extended, particularly in peripheral areas, to embrace three or four languages, in the more polyglot communities. Hurrian was often added to Sumerian and Akkadian for the scribal curriculum in comparative language study. Trilingual vocabularies in those three tongues have been found at Ugarit, as well as two vocabularies in four languages (Sumerian, Babylonian, Hurrian and Ugaritic). Translation was quite familiar in such communities. The Gilgamesh Epic may well have reached the Aegean in both Akkadian and in translations (perhaps including Mycenaean Greek), during the Amarna Age. We know for a fact that the Akkadian version of the Gilgamesh Epic was read on Palestinian soil prior to the emergence of Hebraic literature

[1] Bilinguals appear only late in Egyptian history.

Victory stela showing Naram-Sin wearing the horned crown of god-hood (p. 54)

Babylonian pottery head of the evil dragon Humbaba (p. 65)

because of an Amarna Age fragment of the Epic found at Megiddo.

Since the Gilgamesh Epic was the major, and most influential, literary masterpiece of pre-biblical and pre-Homeric antiquity, we shall without more ado outline that Epic and point out some of its many effects on East Mediterranean literature.

The Babylonian name of the Epic is " He who Saw Everything " referring to the hero Gilgamesh, who experienced everything and gained wisdom; who " walked a distant road and grew weary."[1]

The title " He Who Saw Everything " would be just as appropriate for the Odyssey as for the Gilgamesh Epic. Odysseus, like Gilgamesh, travelled far and grew weary, becoming experienced and wise in the process.

The Gilgamesh Epic and the Odyssey both recount the episodic wanderings of a heroic city-king, leading to a *nóstos* or homecoming. The partial dependence of the Odyssey on the Gilgamesh Epic is clear from the agreement in a number of specific episodes; not merely from the general over-all scheme shared by both poems.

Gilgamesh was king of the matchless city of Uruk, over which he ruled not only proudly but tyrannically. Like Achilles and Heracles, Gilgamesh was of mixed divine and human parentage. As the goddess Thetis bore Achilles, the goddess Ninsun had borne Gilgamesh. These illustrations of human heroes born by goddesses are well-known, but for some strange reason it has not occurred to biblical scholars that the hero Shamgar, son of Anath (Judges 3: 31; 5: 6), had as his mother the warlike

---

[1] Our translations are made from the cuneiform text in R. Campbell Thompson, *The Epic of Gilgamesh: Text, Transliteration and Notes*, Oxford, 1930, cf. plates. Several additional fragments have been found since 1930. To follow the progress of such discoveries, one should read the periodic reports in journals such as *Orientalia*, *Archiv für Orientforschung* or *Bulletin of the American Schools of Oriental Research*.

Canaanite goddess Anath (now well-known to us from Ugaritic literature).[1] Indeed Anath is more appropriate as the mother of a warrior than the gentler Thetis or Ninsun.

Because of Gilgamesh's tyranny, the people of Uruk cried out to the gods for help. The gods ordered the goddess Aruru to create a being who would divert Gilgamesh from oppressing the people. So she " pinched off some clay, cast it on the plain " and " fashioned the hero Enkidu," powerful and with long hair " like a woman's."

The concept of creation from clay is widespread. Egyptian art often represents the god Khnum fashioning a man as a sculptor makes a figure from clay. Not only does Genesis portray God as fashioning (Genesis 1: 27) man out of earth (Genesis 3: 19), but the book of Job (33: 6) uses the same word as the Gilgamesh Epic for " pinching off " the clay in the creation of a man.

Enkidu's long hair appears on some seal-cylinders confirming his identification in Mesopotamian art. His long hair goes hand in hand with his strength. The emphasis on long hair for heroic men is to be compared with the Minoan insistence on long hair for men. During the heroic age of Israel, from the Period of the Patriarchs through the reign of David, there is the same emphasis on hairiness for the heroic male. The mighty Esau was born ruddy and hairy (Genesis 25: 25), two sure signs that he was destined to be a mighty man. Samson's strength depended on his seven locks of hair, tying in obviously with the Mycenaean style of his Philistine milieu. The last Old Testament reference to the long hair of heroes comes in the reign of David, whose son

[1] While " Anath " never appears as a human name in Israel or Ugarit, Shamgar and two Ugaritic men (Ch. Virolleaud, *Palais royal d'Ugarit* II, Paris, 1957, texts 43: 12 and 61: 6) are called " son of Anath." Could foundlings with heroic aspirations have called themselves " Son of Anath " to enhance their prestige in ancient Canaan? Or was there a guild of warriors (born by Anath priestesses?) called " Sons of Anath "?

Absalom's luxuriant hair proved fatal. There are still other references to the hair of the Hebraic heroes, but they are all in the heroic age, and stop abruptly after David's reign. The same cultural feature appears in Homeric epic, notably in the epithet "long-haired" applied to the Achaeans.[1]

Enkidu lived with the beasts as their friend, protecting them from the hunters. To alienate him from the beasts and to civilise him so that he would confront Gilgamesh in Uruk, a hunter gets Gilgamesh to dispatch a prostitute named Shamhat to change Enkidu and his way of life. So one day, when Enkidu was coming to a waterhole with the beasts, Shamhat sat waiting for him:

> *Shamhat exposed her breasts,*
> *Opened her bosom*
> *So that he took her charm.*
> *She didn't make off*
> *But accepted his love*
> *He took off her clothes*
> *And lay upon her*
> *She treated him, primeval man, to woman's business.*
> *His love inclined over her.*
> *Six days, yea seven nights, Enkidu is in fine fettle and tups Shamhat.*
> *After he is sated with her charms*
> *He sets his face towards his beasts*
> *But the deer see him, Enkidu, and run off.*

Enkidu soon realises he is a changed creature, and no longer trusted by the animals. He goes to the girl, who describes the change that has taken place within him and urges him on to his more worldly destiny:

[1] This topic is documented in my "Homer and Bible," *Hebrew Union College Annual* 26, 1955, pp. 84-85, #99.

You are [wi]se, O Enkidu,
  You are become like a god.
Why should you roam the field with the beasts?
Come, let me lead you to the midst of walled Uruk
  To the holy house, the dwelling of Anu and Ishtar
Where Gilgamesh, perfect in wisdom,
  Like a buffalo holds mighty sway over his people.

All eager, and full of self-confidence, Enkidu is ready to go to Uruk and even challenge the mighty Gilgamesh there, but Shamhat reminds Enkidu of Gilgamesh's superior might, before they head for the city.

Meanwhile, Gilgamesh is apprised by duplicate dreams of Enkidu's arrival. In the first dream, Gilgamesh beholds a star that he is unable to lift or remove, though he is attracted to it as to a woman. He tells the dream to his mother, Ninsun, who interprets it to mean that the star stands for a powerful friend who will never forsake him. The second dream is the same as the first, except that he is unable to lift or remove an axe, to which he is attracted as though to a woman. Duplicate dreams are familiar in ancient Near East records. The dreams of Joseph, where the members of his family are first represented by sheaves, and then by heavenly bodies; and the dreams of Pharaoh, where the years are symbolised first by cows, and then by ears of corn; are familiar examples of duplicate dreams. Throughout antiquity, dreams were regarded as divine messages, which, if correctly interpreted, revealed divine plans and the course of future events.

The theme of comradeship reverberates throughout ancient Near East epic. The devotion between Gilgamesh and Enkidu is paralleled by that between Achilles and Patroclus, or between David and Jonathan. (In such commonplace themes, it is not the topic itself that matters so much as its inclusion in the epic repertoire which is highly selective.)

In Uruk, Gilgamesh and Enkidu grapple with each other, and so impress each other, that the two form a friendship to be devoted to wiping out evil from the face of the earth. Since the evil was envisaged in terms of dragons the heroes had plenty to do, and Gilgamesh was deflected from his oppression.

The first exploit of the two heroic friends is their slaying of the evil dragon Humbaba. Enkidu tries to dissuade Gilgamesh from the hazardous fight, but Gilgamesh is determined to go through with it, reasoning that all men must die, and it will be enough for him to leave behind him a name for bravery and a child to carry on after him:

> *Who, O my friend, has scaled the hea[vens]?*
> *Gods may d[well] eternally with Shamash*
> *But the days of mankind are numbered*
> *And whatever it accomplishes is wind.*
> *Yet here you are afraid of death*
> *With the strength of your heroism failing.*
> *Let me go before you*
> *Let your mouth shout: ' Advance, fear not! '*
> *If I fall, let me establish my fame*
> *(So that men will say:)*
> *' Gilgamesh fell, versus victorious Humbaba '*
> *After my offspring has been born in my house.*

This is the standard of the hero in Homer, too. Achilles, Hector, Odysseus all aspire to (or at least admire) a hero's death that will bring them eternal fame. It is also interesting to note that Greek epic includes the tradition that they have each a son to carry on after them. While the Hebrews came to stress long life, success, and abundant progeny as the blessings reserved for good men, in the heroic age, the standards were more like those in the Gilgamesh Epic, and especially in Homer. Thus David's dirge in 2 Samuel 1 glorifies Saul and his sons (especially Jonathan, the close companion of David) who perished nobly in the flower of their manhood during the Battle of Gilboa.

The swordsmiths fashioned heavy and costly weapons for Gilgamesh and Enkidu, and Gilgamesh declares to the elders of Uruk his intention of proceeding to the cedar forest where Humbaba dwells, of cutting down the cedar of Humbaba, and vanquishing the ogre, boasting:

> *I shall establish an eternal name.*

The elders, however, do their best to dissuade him:

> *The elders of great Uruk replied to Gilgamesh:*
> ' *You are young, O Gilgamesh,*
> *Your heart has carried you away.*
> *You don't know what you might accomplish.*
> *We hear Humbaba is of a strange build.*
> *Who can [fa]ce his weapons?*
> *The forest extends two double-hours*
> *Who can [go do]wn into its midst?*
> *The cry of Humbaba is (like) the flood-storm*
> *His mouth is the Fire god*
> *His breath is Death*
> *Why do you want to do this?*
> *Fighting Humbaba is an unequal battle.*'

But Gilgamesh is resolved to go and slay Humbaba, and the elders advise him to depend on Enkidu for leading him on the perilous journey. The heroes then proceed to Ninsun, Gilgamesh's mother, for her prayers and blessing. She ascends to the roof of the temple:

> *Sets an offer[ing be]fore Shamash and raises her hands, (saying):*
> ' *Why have you set for my s[on] Gilgamesh*
> *Yea, endowed him with a restless spirit?*

Now you have impelled him to go
  On a distant road, Humbaba's place
To head for an unknown battle
  To ride on an unknown expedition
Till the day he goes and returns
  Till he reaches the cedar forest
    Till he slays the mighty Humbaba
And wipes out from the land every evil that you hate.'

This passage is of interest on many counts. The divine mother, concerned for her restless son, anticipates the concern of Thetis for her son, Achilles. Like Ninsun, so too Thetis appeals to a great god to aid her mortal son. The roof ritual of Ninsun is attested also in the Ugaritic Epic of Kret, who similarly offers sacrifices on the roof and lifts his hands heavenwards. This Gilgamesh passage also brings out a major difference between such older Near East epic and the later tradition brought in after the Indo-European impact. Heroic valour is portrayed in terms of vanquishing dragons of evil. There is no trace of valour in a war fought for the regaining of a beautiful heroine such as we find in the Ugaritic Epic of Kret, the Iliad and in both of the great Indic epics. The theme of romantic love, hinging on the importance of the individual woman, seems to be an Indo-European innovation in Near Eastern literature. In any case, it is lacking in early Egyptian and early Mesopotamian literatures.

The heroes beat their way to Humbaba, and slew him though he begged to be spared, offering them not only his cedars, but his own person as their slave.

Thereafter, Gilgamesh dressed so handsomely that the goddess Ishtar was attracted to him and offered him her hand in marriage:

He washed off his dirt, and cleaned off his grime
  He shook out his hair over his back

67

He threw off his foul things
  Put on his pure things
He changed in to a fringed cloak
  Tied on a sash
Gilgamesh donned a crown.
The great Ishtar raised an eye toward the beauty of Gilgamesh
(Saying): ' *Come to me, Gilgamesh, you be my spouse.*
  Present me with your fruit.
You be my husband
  And I'll be your wife.
I'll hitch for you a chariot of lapis and gold
  With wheels of gold and diamond horns . . .'

A proposal of marriage by a goddess to a mortal is remarkable enough. For the mortal to reject the proposal, as Gilgamesh does, makes the incident still more worthy of saga. Interestingly enough, this theme recurs in Greek epic; for Odysseus rejects the proposal made to him by Calypso. Gilgamesh turns down Ishtar, asking her rhetorically: "What spouse [have you loved] forever?" He then reminds her of her seamy marital history:

> *For Tammuz, the spouse of your y[out]h*
>   *Annual weeping have you decreed for him.*
> *You loved the coloured allalu bird*
>   *But you smote him and broke his wing*
>   *So he stays in the forest crying,* ' *My wing!* '.
> *You loved the lion, perfect in strength*
>   *But you dug twice seven pits for him.*
> *You loved a famed war horse*
>   *The whip, the spur and the scourge you decreed for him*
>   *Seven double hours of running you decreed for him*
>   *Drinking fouled water you decreed for him*
>   *You decreed weeping for his mother, Silili.*

> *You loved the pastor of the herd*
>   *Who constantly piled up for you the ashes (of sacrifice)*
>   *Daily he slaughtered kids for you*
>   *You smote him, turning him into a wolf*
>   *So that his own shepherds drive him off*
>   *And his dogs bite his legs.*
> *You loved Ishullanu, your father's gardener*
>   *Who constantly brought you dates*
>   *Daily making your table bright.*

The poem goes on to state Ishtar's proposal of marriage to the hapless gardener, who turns her down because of her bad marital record. Gilgamesh, ending his recital, rebuffs the goddess with the statement:

> *You would love me but treat me like them.*

Resolving on revenge for the affront, Ishtar goes to her father, Anu, the head of the pantheon, for permission to destroy Gilgamesh by means of the Bull of Heaven, a powerful creature depicted as a human-headed bull. And lest Anu should raise an objection to granting Ishtar's extreme request, she threatens to turn the order of things topsy-turvy.

Anu reminds Ishtar that the slaying of the hero will bring on a seven-year famine, whereupon Ishtar assures Anu that she has laid up a seven-year supply of food. The notion that prolonged drought or famine will follow the death of a hero appears, as we shall note in Chapter v, in both Ugaritic and biblical literature. In Ugaritic literature, the land where Aqhat fell as a victim to Anath's machinations, is cursed with seven (or climactically, eight) years of drought marking the same time span as the Gilgamesh Epic.

The laying up of stores to neutralise the effects of a seven-year famine is, of course, familiar from the story of Joseph in Egypt.

Joseph, like Ishtar, anticipates the seven years of famine by storing up an adequate supply to tide the population over.

The battle between our two heroes and the Bull of Heaven is of interest for the history of bull grappling along lines delineated above. Enkidu grasped the bull by the horns, and after the heroes had slain it, they cut out its heart and placed it as an offering before Shamash: the god who detests evil.

The victory distressed Ishtar, who complained of Gilgamesh for killing the Bull of Heaven. In return, Enkidu heaved the right leg of the Bull of Heaven at her: a grievous insult which sealed his fate. The singling out of this particular act as a heinous affront, reverberates in the Odyssey (20: 299; 22: 287-291), where Ctesippus' hurling of an ox foot is represented as a terrible insult that cannot go unavenged.

The gods decide that Enkidu must forfeit his life. Enkidu thereupon curses the various agents that had been instrumental in alienating him from nature and forcing upon him the career that was now sealing his fate. His final curse is directed at Shamhat, the lass who civilised him and led him to Uruk. But Shamash rebukes Enkidu, reminding him that Shamhat had made a hero of him, and that it is no small honour to live and die as a hero:

> *Why, O Enkidu, do you curse Shamhat, the harlot,*
> *Who caused you to eat food fit for gods*
>> *And caused you to drink wine fit for kings*
>>> *And caused you to wear princely garb*
>>>> *And caused you to have good Gilgamesh as comrade?*
> *And now, Gilgamesh, your brother and friend*
>> *Has caused you to lie on a great couch*
>>> *On a well-appointed couch he has caused you to lie*
>> *He has made you sit on a throne of ease*
>>> *The throne on the left*
>>>> *So that the [rul]ers of the earth kiss your feet*

He will make the people of Uruk [we]ep and wail for you
For you he will fill with grief men [who had been gay]
After you(r death), he will cause his body to wear (long) hair
[He will dre]ss in the skin of a lion and roam the pl[ain].

The need to be mourned may be well nigh universal. It figures in the texts and art of the ancient world. Specifically, the mourning for a dead hero by his surviving comrade is singled out in both Greek and Hebrew epic; for David mourns for his friend Jonathan, and Achilles, for Patroclus.

Another parallel with Greek lore is the wandering of Gilgamesh in a lionskin, which Burr Brundage compares with Heracles wearing a lionskin as he roams.[1]

On hearing the rebuke of Shamash, Enkidu cancels his curse of Shamhat by blessing her.

A dream provides Enkidu with a preview of Irkalla, the dismal abode where even heroes must spend a dreary eternity, much like the Greek concept of Hades, and the Hebrew concept of Sheol:

. . . to the house of darkness
  The dwelling of Irkalla
To the house whose enterer never goes out
  On the road whose going is without return
To the house whose inhabitants are deprived of light
Where dust is their food
  And mud their nourishment
Clad like a bird with wing-garments
And they see no light
  But dwell in murk.

Enkidu sees himself ushered into the dreary abode of the dead, where Ereshkigal rules as queen, attended by a goddess who

[1] *Journal of Near Eastern Studies* 17, 1958, pp. 226-7.

functions as her recorder. As Enkidu enters, the recorder asks:

> *Who has brought this fellow here?*

The death of Enkidu fills Gilgamesh with both grief and fear. On the one hand, he mourns for his friend; on the other, he dreads the prospect of death for himself:

> *Gilgamesh, for Enkidu his friend,*
> *Weeps bitterly and roams the plain (saying):*
> *' Shall I not die like Enkidu?*
> *Trembling has entered my body*
>   *I fear death, I roam the plain.*
> *To the side of Utnapishtim, son of Ubara-tutu,*
>   *I have taken the road, and shall go swiftly . . .'*

Utnapishtim, the Flood hero, had not only been saved from the Deluge, but won immortality to boot. Gilgamesh, therefore, resolved on going to him in order to find out how a mortal can evade death. The way was perilous, but Gilgamesh is now resolved to make the journey, no matter how great the hazards.

En route to the distant abode of Utnapishtim, Gilgamesh comes to Mount Mashu, where a scorpion-man and his wife dwell. The hybrid scorpion-man is depicted on many seal-cylinders. On seeing Gilgamesh,

> *The scorpion-man calls to his wife:*
> *' The body of him who has come to us is flesh of the gods.'*
> *His wife answers the scorpion-man:*
> *' He is two-thirds god and one-third human.'*

And therein lies the tragedy of Gilgamesh, who aspires to the immortality of his divine component, but must die because of the part of him that is mortal.

Gilgamesh tells the scorpion-man of his aim to reach far-off Utnapishtim, and is informed that the road is long, dangerous and beset with darkness. But at the end of the road is a bright land full of wondrous fruit trees.

Along the way, Gilgamesh is reminded that his mission is in vain. Even Shamash, whom Gilgamesh had served so well, tells the hero that his quest for immortality is hopeless. But Gilgamesh presses onwards, and en route, comes to the tavern run by Siduri, the divine ale-wife (for in Babylonia, taverns were run exclusively by women). He poured out his heart to her and implored her to help him:

> *Enkidu, whom I loved so much . . .*
> *And who underwent all hardships with me,*
> *Has gone to the fate of mankind.*
> *Day and night I wept over him*
> *And gave him not over for burial . . .*
> *Seven days and seven nights*
> *Until the worm fell from his nose.*
> *Now that he is gone, I have not found immortality.*
> *I keep wandering like a hunter in the midst of the plain.*
> *Now, O ale-wife, I look at your face!*
> *Let me not see the Death that I dread!*

Also the ale-wife tried to dissuade him from his wild-goose chase, reminding him of the actual order of things, and of the satisfactions that are within the grasp of mortals:

> *You will not find the immortality that you seek.*
> *When the gods created mankind*
> *They ordained death for mankind*
>   *Immortality they kept within their own grasp.*
> *As for you, O Gilgamesh, let your belly be full*
>   *May you rejoice day and night*
>   *Establish gladness every day*
>   *Day and night dance and play*

May your clothes be clean
  Your head be washed
  May you be bathed in water
Watch the little lad who holds your hand
Let your wife rejoice in your bosom
  This is the business [of mankind].

This advice of Siduri expresses both the pessimism and pleasure-seeking sides of the ancient East. Man could not aspire to immortality in a universe where the gods had reserved it for themselves. The consolation that remained for man was, therefore, the enjoyment of earthly pleasures: food, drink, merriment, the physical amenities, a lad to support one in his cups[1] and conjugal happiness. The quest of pleasure is at least realistic, whereas the quest for eternal life is against the divinely established order. True enough, Utnapishtim had divinity conferred upon him; but that special favour was granted under unique circumstances and constitutes no precedent for the rest of us.

Gilgamesh, however, insists that Siduri direct him on the way to Utnapishtim. She tells him of the perilous journey, including the Waters of Death, over which Utnapishtim's boatman, Zur-Shanabi,[2] would have to ferry him.

Siduri, upon hearing from Gilgamesh that he had slain Humbaba, lions and the Bull of Heaven, asked why such a hero looked so ill. Gilgamesh's enumeration of his triumphs is to be compared stylistically with Anath's enumeration of hers in Ugaritic literature. Gilgamesh's poor appearance and sadness of heart anticipate Odysseus' state after his adventures. Gilgamesh answers Siduri, telling her that his bad state is due to grief for his

---

[1] While the Gilgamesh Epic does not explicitly say so, other ancient Near East literatures state that a son holds his parent's hand to support him while intoxicated. Cf. the Ugaritic Epic of Aqhat and Isaiah 51: 17-18.

[2] Also called Ur-Shanabi.

friend who has perished. It will be recalled that Odysseus' inability to save his companions from death is singled out as a major blow to the hero.

Subsequently, Zur-Shanabi also asks Gilgamesh why he looks so ill and is also told that the death of Enkidu is the cause. The boatman agrees to ferry Gilgamesh across the Waters of Death to the distant Utnapishtim. Gilgamesh helped accomplish the voyage by punting with a pole.

When Gilgamesh beheld Utnapishtim, he found the Flood hero to be so much like himself, that his hopes to achieve the same immortality were buoyed up:

> *Gilgamesh spoke to him*
> *To Utnapishtim, the Distant:*
> *' I look at you, Utnapishtim,*
> *Your figure is not different*
> *You are like me*
> *Yea, you are not different*
> *You are like me.*
> *My mind had fancied you as a wager of battle*
> *[But instead] you lie [on] your side, recumbent on your back.*
> *[Tell me] how you came to stand there*
> *And found immortality in the assembly of the gods.'*

Utnapishtim proceeds to narrate the whole flood story in order to show Gilgamesh that it took a unique set of circumstances, such as will never be repeated, for the gods to assemble and confer immortality on Utnapishtim. The flood story itself is of the greatest interest because of the light it sheds on the Mesopotamian background of the biblical Deluge.[1]

---

[1] George Smith's discovery in 1872 of this Babylonian parallel to the Genesis flood story inaugurated the era of ancient oriental parallels to the Bible (see L. Deuel, *The Treasures of Time*, World Publishing Co., Cleveland and New York, 1961, p. 133).

Utnapishtim speaks to him, to Gilgamesh:
' *Let me reveal to you, O Gilgamesh, a mystery,*
  Yea, a secret of the gods, let me tell you.
Shurippak,¹ a city that you know,
  Situated [along] the Euphrates . . .
That city is ancient, and gods are in its midst.
Their hearts impelled the great gods to cause a flood.'

Utnapishtim goes on to enumerate some of the gods of the
pantheon that made the baleful decision. It appeared to the ancient
Mesopotamians (and to so many others of their contemporaries)
that the gods were essentially evil. How else is one to explain the
endless troubles that befall us? The good god is exceptional.
Ea is often depicted as the deity friendly to mankind. Here it is
Ea who keeps faith, in letter but not in spirit, with his fellow gods;
but actually helps the human Utnapishtim by divulging the
secret plans of the gods. He does this by formally addressing, not
Utnapishtim personally, but the building in which Utnapishtim
lives:

(Ea) repeats the word (of the gods) to (Utnapishtim's) reed hut:
' *Reed hut, reed hut!*
  Wall, wall!
Reed hut, hear!
  Wall, perceive!
O man of Shuruppak, son of Ubara-tutu,
Tear down the house
  Build the ship.'

House walls built of reeds could be removed and converted
into the hull of a vessel. Reed shipbuilding was common in
Mesopotamia, but not in Israel. The fact that the text of Genesis

¹ Usually " Shuruppak " (with *u*, not *i*, as the second vowel), but here
with *i*.

6: 14 still contains the word for reeds[1] in connection with the building of the Ark is traceable to the Babylonian background of the biblical Deluge. Ea goes on to advise and instruct Utnapishtim:

> *Abandon wealth, seek life*
> > *Scorn possessions, keep alive the soul.*
> *Take aboard the ship the seed of all living*
> *The ship that you are to build*
> *Shall be of measured specifications*
> > *Its width and length shall be equal* . . .

Utnapishtim assures the god that he will follow his instructions but asks how he can keep the secret from the people. Ea tells him to announce that the earth god Enlil is hostile (which is true enough), and so he must depart for the Sea in the ship he is building. Ea also instructs him to deceive the people by saying that a rain of *kibati* will come. The people will take this to mean the rain will bring them " wheat "; but actually it will bring them " misfortune," for *kibati* has both connotations. Such deception, on the part of gods and heroes, is paralleled in Hebrew[2] and especially Greek literatures, notably in the Odyssey (where not only Odysseus, but also his patron deity Athena, glory in being deceptive).

The ship was completed and laden with supplies in seven days, during which the craftsmen were wined and dined by Utnapishtim, who relates:

> *[I caused] the craftsmen [to drink] (wine) like river water*
> > *So that they made a festival like New Year's day.*

Then treasures and living creatures were brought aboard:

---

[1] The consonants *qnym* should be read *qānim* " reeds."
[2] Note especially the reciprocal deception permeating the stories of Jacob and Laban. For divine deception, see I Kings 22: 23.

[With whatever I had, I] loaded her
 I loaded her with whatever silver I had
 I loaded her with whatever gold I had
 I loaded her with whatever living creatures I had
 I took aboard all my kith and kin
 The game of the plain, the beasts of the plain
 I took aboard all the craftsmen.

It is to be noted that Utnapishtim takes aboard treasures in spite of Ea's telling him to abandon them. Mesopotamian civilisation was unthinkable without gold, silver and other metals. Note, too, that craftsmen were considered as special species, much like the kinds of animals. In a society where people were grouped according to hereditary functions into guilds, carpenters were, so to speak, as different from smiths, as one species of game from another.

Shamash set the time and the Deluge came. Utnapishtim tells how he entered the vessel and shut the doors:

I looked at the nature of the weather
 The day was terrible to behold.
 I entered the midst of the ship and shut the door.
 For running the ship, I turned the vessel with its equipment over
 to Puzur-Amurri[1] the sailor.

The text describes the terrible storm, which frightened even the gods. In their destructiveness, the gods had apparently forgotten that if the human race perishes, there will be no one left to serve the gods and supply them with sacrifices of food and drink.

The gods were afraid of the Deluge
 They cringed and ascended to the heaven of Anu

[1] This Amorite name, built into the Mesopotamian Deluge Story, points to West Semitic influence.

The gods cowered like dogs, crouched against the outer doors
Ishtar cried like a woman in travail
  There moaned the mistress of the gods good at the cry.

The undignified behaviour of the gods is reminiscent of virtually every ancient pantheon: whether in the refined epics of Homer, or the cruder Egyptian story of Horus and Seth. Ishtar's epithet *ṭâbat rigmi* "good at the cry" anticipates Homer's epithet of Menelaus: "good at the (war) cry."

At the end of seven days, the Deluge came to an end. It is to be noted that reckoning time (whether days or years) in sevens, occurs not only in Mesopotamia, but also in Ugaritic, Hebrew, and Greek epic traditions. Accordingly, the institution of the seven-day week, which has reached the West through the parallel East Mediterranean channels of Hellenistic usage and of the Hebrew Creation account in Genesis, is widespread in the ancient East. The ship had landed on a mountain (quite as in the Genesis tradition), where it remained for another seven days. Utnapishtim determined whether the earth was dry enough for debarkation by sending out a series of birds (much as Noah did). The first bird, a dove; and the second, a swallow, returned because they could find no spot on which to light. By the time the third bird, a raven, was dispatched, the earth had dried sufficiently so that it did not fly back to the ship. Utnapishtim thereupon narrates:

I let out (my passengers) to the four winds, I poured out libations
  I set up sacrifices on the mountain peak,
    I fixed twice seven sacrificial vessels.

The expression "twice seven" for "14" is of interest. Not only is *dìs heptá* "twice seven" so used in Greek ritual contexts,[1] but it is likely that the dual of "7" in early Hebrew literature should be

[1] e.g., Herodotus 1: 86.

rendered " 14 (times) " and not " sevenfold " as all the translations would have it.[1]

Like Noah, Utnapishtim celebrates his emergence from the ark by sacrificing. As God smelled the sweet savour of Noah's offering (Genesis 8: 21), so too

> *The gods smelled the savour*
> *The gods smelled the good savour*
> *The gods gathered like flies over the libator.*

Blame is now heaped on Enlil, in the assemblage of the gods, for his role in attempting the destruction of mankind:

> ' *Let the gods come to the sacrifice*
> *But let Enlil not come to the sacrifice*
> *Because he heedlessly established the Deluge*
> *And numbered my people for destruction.'*
> *As soon as Enlil arrived*
> *He beheld the ship and was furious*
> *Filled with wrath over the Igigi gods (and asked):*
> ' *Has any soul escaped?*
> *No man was to live through the destruction.'*

One of the gods, Ninurta, divulged Ea's role in saving a remnant of the human race. Ea thereupon mollified Enlil so successfully that Enlil conferred divinity on Utnapishtim and his wife. In Utnapishtim's words:

> *Enlil boarded the ship*
> *He took my hand, he took me up*
> *He raised up and caused my wife to kneel by my side.*
> *He touched our foreheads, standing between us and blessed us:*
> ' *Previously Utnapishtim has been human*
> *But now Utnapishtim and his wife are like us, the gods.*

[1] Cf. *Ugaritic Manual*, p. 84.

Let Utnapishtim dwell far off at the mouth of the Rivers.'
So they took me and let me dwell far off at the mouth of the Rivers.
But now, who will assemble the gods for you,
  So that you might find the life that you seek?

Utnapishtim's dwelling place at the mouth of the Rivers anticipates the location of El's residence in the Ugaritic tablets, at the
mouth of the Two Rivers. The apotheosis of the human pair is
paralleled not only in any number of famous Greek apotheoses,
but also in the canonical Hebrew tradition, starting with Enoch
(Genesis 5: 24). The early traditions of Israel had much more
of this sort of thing; but they have been toned down, and in
many cases eliminated, in the Old Testament. Pseudepigraphic
literature preserves many such features from pre-Canonical
antiquity.[1]

The reader should note that this kind of apotheosis is quite
different from modern doctrines of personal immortality.
Modern doctrine brings such salvation within the grasp of all
men. Not so in the ancient material we are surveying. There,
such phenomena are to be viewed as exceptions, not as pre-
cedents. Indeed they are worthy of saga precisely because they
run counter to the order of things. It will be noted that Utnapishtim reminds Gilgamesh that a unique set of circumstances
occasioned a convocation of the gods resulting in the apotheosis.
No one, not even Gilgamesh, has any reason to assume that

---

[1] e.g., in the Genesis Apocryphon found at Qumran, the racy description
of Sarah's physical beauty and of her adventures while abducted from her
husband, hark back to the same ancient school of literature as Homer's description of Helen's pulchritude and abduction. Rabbinic lore about the Bible
(collected by Louis Ginzberg, *Legends of the Jews*, 7 vol., Philadelphia, 1909-
1938) also contains material from the ancient East Mediterranean, sometimes
rooted in the second millennium, as we shall have occasion to illustrate. The
genuineness of such elements is due in large measure to the fact that classical
rabbinism developed in the East where Greek was spoken and the pagan classics
(especially Homer) and lore were fostered as a living, unbroken tradition.

another such convocation will ever take place for conferring immortality on him.

The next section of the Epic portrays Utnapishtim as telling Gilgamesh to remain awake for a week. The idea seems to be that if anyone hopes to avoid the sleep of death, he ought at least be strong enough to fight off ordinary sleep for a week. But sleep quickly overcame Gilgamesh, who proceeded to slumber for an entire week. To prove to him on awakening that he had really slept a whole week, the wife of Utnapishtim had baked bread for him every day, with notations written on the wall to record the daily loaves. On waking

> *Gilgamesh says to him, to Utnapishtim, the Distant:*
> ' *Sleep had scarcely come over me*
> *When you quickly touched and roused me.*'

But Gilgamesh, told to count the loaves, noted the successive stages of mould which proved that he had slept the entire week. (The use of mouldy bread to indicate the passage of time recurs in the biblical Book of Joshua 9: 5-12, where the Gibeonites convince Joshua that they came from afar because of the mouldy state of their hardtack). Again, the inevitability of death is brought home to Gilgamesh who cries out to Utnapishtim:

> . . . . . . *Where can I go?*
> *The Snatcher has seized my [heart];*
> *Death sits [in] my bedroom;*
> *And wherever I set [my foot], there lurks Death.*

The despair of Gilgamesh evokes pity in the heart of Utnapishtim, who instructs Zur-Shanabi to let Gilgamesh wash off his grime, and supply Gilgamesh with a garment that will remain new and show no signs of wear until he comes home to Uruk. The ritual washing that gives a man a fresh start, crops up (as we have seen above) in other literatures, including the Iliad and the

biblical Book of Micah. The garment that doesn't wear out
appears in the biblical narrative of Israel's wandering for forty
years in the wilderness, en route from Egypt to the Promised
Land (Deuteronomy 8: 4; 29: 4).

> *Zur-Shanabi took him and brought him to the bath*
> *He washed away his filth with water like snow*
> *He cast his films and the sea carried (them) off*
> *So that his body appeared good.*
> *He renewed his head[band]*
> *He put on a garment: the dress of his nakedness*
> *Till he should go [back to his city]*
> *Till he should arrive on his way*
> *[The garment would show no wear]*
> *But remain quite new.*
> *Gilgamesh and Zur-Shanabi rode on the ship*
> *They launched the ship [on the waves] and rode off.*

A recurrent theme in eastern life is the bestowing of gifts.
This has found a place in the ancient literatures, particularly in
the case of heroes on the eve of their departure for home. The
Israelites were laden with gifts by the Egyptians on the eve of the
Exodus.[1] Odysseus was showered with gifts on the eve of his
departure for home, in the land of the Phaeacians. Without such
gifts, homecoming for the weary traveller would be repre-
hensible, as the Odyssey clearly states.[2] In Egyptian literature,
the Serpent showers gifts on the Shipwrecked Sailor who is
about to sail back home. In keeping with this motif, the wife of
Utnapishtim says to her husband:

> *Gilgamesh has come here, tired and weary.*
> *What will you give him so that he may return to his land?*

[1] Exodus 3: 21-22; 12: 35-36.
[2] "Homer and Bible," pp. 72-73, ⧺⧺65-66.

On hearing this, Gilgamesh brought the ship close to the shore with his punting pole, and Utnapishtim revealed to him the secret of a wondrous plant at the bottom of the sea. Its name is "The Old Man Becomes Young," for when eaten it rejuvenates the old. This is not quite the same as immortality or apotheosis, but might well be prized as the next best thing. By tying stones to his feet, Gilgamesh dived to the bottom, plucked the plant, untied the stones and came to the surface with the precious plant of youth. Instead of eating it then and there, Gilgamesh plans to take the plant back to Uruk, where in his old age he will be able to eat it and become young again. But on the way back to Uruk, a serpent robbed him of the precious plant:

> *Gilgamesh saw a well whose waters were cool.*
> *He went down into its midst and washed in the water.*
> *A serpent sniffed the scent of the plant*
> *And came up [out of the water] and carried off the plant.*
> *When he returned, it had sloughed its skin.*
> *Then Gilgamesh sat, weeping*
> *the Tears flowed upon his cheeks.*

Man's enemy, as in the Genesis narrative, is the serpent. Here he robs Gilgamesh of his last hope to evade the ravages of old age. The serpent's shedding its skin was taken by the ancients to signify its rejuvenation. Gilgamesh pours out his heart to Zur-Shanabi, the boatman:

> *[For] whom, O Zur-Shanabi, have my hands grown weary?*
> *For whom is my heart's blood spent?*
> *I have accomplished no good for myself*
> *But I have benefited the Lion of the Ground.*

The "Lion of the Ground" is the *kenning* for the serpent. Epic poetry tends to use such conventional (and often extravagant) epithets for persons, creatures or even things.

Gilgamesh and Zur-Shanabi continued their journey and at last arrived in Uruk.

> *Gilgamesh says to Zur-Shanabi, the boatman:*
> ' *Go up, Zur-Shanabi, walk on the wall of Uruk.*
> *Examine the terrace*
>   *Look at the brickwork*
>   *To see whether its bricks are not baked*
>   *And whether the Seven Sages did not lay its foundations.*
> *One* sar *is city, one* sar *is garden, one* sar *is meadow;*
>   *(plus) the area of Ishtar's Temple*
> *Uruk is composed of three* sars *and the temple area.*'

Thus ends the eleventh tablet of the Gilgamesh epic. In a universe where man cannot achieve immortality, or even rejuvenation, civilisation at least offers something in which man can take pride. The unit of Sumerian society was the city-state, much as in Greece. Even as the walls of Troy were of divine construction, so were the foundations of Uruk laid by legendary Sages in a shadowy past. Of the greatest interest is the ideal of city planning, whereby Uruk was divided into three equal areas—urban, garden and meadow—plus the temple precincts. The city was thus self-sufficient with dwellings, farms and grazing land, plus the cultic centre that regulated the economic, social and other major facets of communal activity.

The twelfth and final tablet of the Gilgamesh Epic is quite different from the rest of the Epic, and some scholars have been inclined to regard it as an inorganic appendage. While much remains to be explained, it is safer to view the twelfth tablet as part of the Epic as the Mesopotamians themselves did. Enkidu descends to the Underworld, where he is interviewed on the *post mortem* welfare of the various categories of the dead in Hades. This theme crops up in the Odyssey, where Odysseus interviews Achilles (among others) in Hades. (For a description of the inmates of Hades, see also Ezekiel 31 and 32.) The concept of Hades itself is a cultural feature shared by the Hebrews and Greeks with the Mesopotamians. (The Egyptians, who preferred to believe in a happy afterworld, stand apart in this regard.) The Babylonian Irkalla, the Hebrew Sheol[1] and the Greek Hades are all reflexes of the same idea: a gloomy underworld where the good and bad alike dwell after death. If one leaves sons on earth who sacrifice to him, one's lot in the Underworld is better than a childless person's. The way in which one has lived and died also affects one's welfare below. But at best there is no joy in the afterlife. The close parallelism in detail (including the verbal descriptions) leaves no doubt that Hades and Sheol are simply the Greek and Hebrew words for one and the same idea that filtered into both traditions from a common source: possibly from Mesopotamian religion and story. As we have noted, the discovery of a fragment of the Gilgamesh Epic at Megiddo, from about the Amarna Age, shows that the text was known in Palestine prior to the emergence of Israel as a nation. In Anatolia, en route to Greece, the Epic was known not only in Babylonian, but in at least two translations: Hurrian and Hittite. Accordingly, the Greek and Hebrew parallels to the Gilgamesh Epic cannot be attributed completely to chance; the spread of the Epic into Israelite territory and towards the Aegean, prior to the heroic ages of the Hebrews and Greeks, is attested physically by clay tablets.

The Adapa Legend deals with a theme familiar from the Gilgamesh Epic: a hero's futile quest for immortality. Like Adam, Adapa had obtained knowledge or wisdom, but not immortality. Summoned to heaven, Adapa was told by Ea that he would be offered the bread of death and the water of death

---

[1] This Hebrew word means " asking," referring to the inquiring of the dead through witchcraft; cf. I Samuel 28: 16 where the root of "Sheol" expresses Saul's inquiring of Samuel's ghost. The Greek *puthésthai* " to inquire (of the dead) " is used in a similar context in Odyssey 11: 50.

there. Ea instructed him not to partake of either. But as it turned out, the bread of life and the water of life were offered to him; yet, following Ea's unfortunate advice, he refused both and lost his chance to win eternal life. The discovery of this text at Tell el-Amarna, in Egypt, shows its wide distribution far from the homeland.

Another literary text found at Amarna is the myth of Nergal and Ereshkigal, gods of the Underworld. The story goes that Nergal, among the gods assembled in heaven, had failed to show respect to the subterranean goddess, Ereshkigal, through her messenger. She therefore summoned Nergal with intent to kill him. But Nergal, perceiving her intentions, stationed his hench-men at the fourteen gates of the Underworld and assaulted Ereshkigal:

> *In the midst of the house, he grabbed Ereshkigal*
> *By her hair; he dragged her down from the throne*
> *Onto the earth to cut off her head.*
> *' Don't kill me O my brother!*
>   *A word let me tell you! '*
> *Nergal listened to her; his hands dropped.*
> *Weeping, she relented (and said);*
> *' You be my husband*
>   *Let me be your wife!*
> *Let me give you kingship over the wide earth*
>   *And put the tablet of wisdom in your hand.*
> *You be the lord*
>   *I'll be the lady.'*
> *Nergal hearkened to this utterance of hers*
> *He seized her, kissing her and wiping away her tears*
> *(Saying): ' What! You have desired me since months past till now! '*

This last scene is paralleled in the Odyssey (10: 293-7; 320-347). Odysseus threatens to slay Circe with his sword with the result that she becomes terror-stricken and offers him her love.

" The Descent of Ishtar into Hades " is interesting in subject matter and attractive in presentation. The central theme is the descent and death of the life-goddess Ishtar, in the Underworld. Because of this, all the reproductive processes on earth come to a halt. She is finally revived through the water of life, and returns to earth so that reproduction starts anew. Her descent through the seven gates of the Underworld and subsequently her return upward through the seven gates, links the fertility motif to the system of seven, familiar from other Near East traditions (e.g., Old Testament and Ugarit) in which periods of famine or abundance occur in seven-year cycles.[1]

The Underworld is called " The Land of No Return " and is described thus: (Ishtar went)

> *To the dark house, the dwelling of Irkalla*
> *To the house whose enterer cannot go out*
> *On the road whose going has no return*
> *To the house whose enterer is deprived of light*
> *Where dust is their nourishment*
> *Yea, their food is mud*
> *They behold not light*
> *They sit in darkness*
> *They are clad like a bird*
> *With a feathery garment.*

Arriving at the first of the seven gates of the Underworld, Ishtar orders the gatekeeper to open and makes dire threats if he fails to let her in:

> *O gatekeeper, open your gate!*
> *Open your gate so that I may enter.*

[1] See *World of the Old Testament*, pp. 98-99. Cf. also " the seven years of Baal (dIM) " in line 29 of the Alalakh text published by S. Smith, *The Statue of Idri-mi*, British Institute of Archaeology in Ankara, London, 1949, pp. 16-17.

If you don't open the gate so that I cannot enter
I shall smash the door
　And break the bolt
I'll smash the threshold
　I'll wreck the doors
I'll bring up the dead that devour the living
　The dead shall outnumber the living.

Reluctantly, Ereshkigal, the Lady of the Underworld, permits her gatekeeper to let Ishtar enter, but only in accordance with the decrees of the Lady of the Underworld, where one can only enter naked as one is born.

He let her enter the first gate, he stripped her
　He took away the great tiara of her head.
　' *Why, O gatekeeper, have you taken away the great tiara of my*
　　　head? '
　' *Enter, my Lady, such are the decrees of the Mistress of the Earth.*'
He let her enter the second gate, he stripped her
　He took away her earrings.
　' *Why, O gatekeeper, have you taken away my earrings?* '
　' *Enter, my Lady, such are the decrees of the Mistress of the Earth.*'
He let her enter the fourth gate, he stripped her
　He took away her breast ornaments.
　' *Why, O gatekeeper, have you taken away my breast ornaments?* '
　' *Enter, my Lady, such are the decrees of the Mistress of the Earth.*'
He let her enter the fifth gate, he stripped her
　He took away the belt of birthstones on her waist.
　' *Why, O gatekeeper, have you taken away the belt of birthstones on*
　　　my waist? '
　' *Enter, my Lady, such are the decrees of the Mistress of the Earth.*'
He let her enter the sixth gate, he stripped her
　He took away her bracelets and anklets.

' *Why, O gatekeeper, have you taken away my bracelets and anklets?* '
' *Enter, my Lady, such are the decrees of the Mistress of the Earth.* '
He let her enter the seventh gate, he stripped her
He took away the undergarment of her body.
' *Why, O gatekeeper, have you taken away the undergarment of my body?* '
' *Enter, my Lady, such are the decrees of the Mistress of the Earth.* '

When Ishtar came into the presence of Ereshkigal, the latter had her smitten with sixty diseases, affecting every part of her body. The eclipse of Ishtar, by sympathetic principles, stopped the reproductive processes on earth. Sexual functioning ceased among mankind as well as animals. The gods became concerned and worked out a plan to restore Ishtar to life, so that fecundity might return to the world. The benevolent god Ea fashioned a creature to be sent to Ereshkigal and, after getting her in a good mood, the creature extracts from her the promise to give him the flagon containing the water of life. The water of life is sprinkled on Ishtar, who is revived and ascends through the seven gates, receiving at each the articles that had been taken from her there. Restored to life, Ishtar rejoins her beloved Tammuz, and the text ends with their reunion accompanied by rites for the dead, with the invocation that the dead may rise and smell the incense. Accordingly, it seems that the text aims not merely at guaranteeing reproduction among the living, but also the after-life of the dead. Just as Ishtar rose from the dead, so too can our dead, because of her precedent. This is the typical use of myth in religion and magic. Myth provides the precedent for inducing the same result for us, here and now.

The Mesopotamians produced a Creation poem called Enuma Elish (" When on High "). It was read every year in connection with the Akitu or New Year Festival to signalise the

re-establishment of order: cosmic and local. Just as the text tells
of the creation of the universe, the supremacy of Babylon, and
the unrivalled kingship of Marduk, the god of Babylon, the
reading of and dramatic ritual associated with the Enuma Elish
signified the stability of the universe and nation for the coming
year. The reign of the King of Babylon was to be renewed on
every New Year Festival, by his grasping the hands of the
Marduk idol.

The Creation epic of Babylonia is quite different from the
Genesis account. And yet, some details are shared by the two
traditions. For example, the goddess of the primordial Deep
(* Tihâm-at) occurs as Tiâmat prior to Marduk's creation of the
universe, and as T^chôm before God's creation of the universe. In
both accounts, a supreme god injects order into a chaotic " pre-
historic " state of affairs. Neither account is a creation *ex nihilo.*

Rebellion and fighting among the gods evoked the role of
Marduk, who put an end to chaos among the gods. Jewish
pseudepigrapha and legend, nurtured subsequently in Christian
circles, preserve similar memories modified into the revolt of the
angels. This has been suppressed from the canonical creation
account because a pantheon is ruled out by monotheism. And
yet, the old polytheism has left its traces in the Genesis narrative;
e.g., God's saying " Let us make man in our image " (Genesis 1:
26).

It is characteristic of the theogonies that younger gods eclipse
their older predecessors. Marduk is a young god who achieves
kingship over the pantheon. It is interesting to note that while
Hebrew tradition identifies Yahweh with Elohim (the universal
and monotheistic principle), Ugaritic represents Yawe (a shorter
form of Yahweh) as a younger god; none other than El's son.[1]

---

[1] See *Ugaritic Manual*, p. 272, #806. The short form of the divine name
(*Yaw* reduced to *Yô*) appears in the name of the mother of Moses (*Yô-kébed*
" Jochebed ").

In the main Ugaritic school of thought, it is the younger god Baal who wins the kingship and enjoys more glamour than his father Dagan or than El himself; and the younger goddess Anath who outshines El's wife Asherah.

Theogonies, with younger gods eclipsing the older ones, may crop up independently in many parts of the world, and as such, would find no place in this study. We are here concerned with related, not with unrelated, parallels. We therefore turn our attention to a Hittite tradition of kingship in heaven which H. Güterbock has rightly compared with the Greek tradition that has come down to us in the Theogony of Hesiod.[1] The Hittite text relates that once Alalu was king of the gods, and Anu (the Mesopotamian god of heaven) rebelled against him and seized the kingship. Subsequently, the god Kumarbi bit off and swallowed the genitals of Anu and wrested the kingship from him. Before Anu left the scene, he informed Kumarbi that the swallowed genitals had impregnated him with three gods, including the Storm God, who would displace Kumarbi. Thus we get a series of four successive kings of the Hittite pantheon: (1) Alalu, (2) the heaven god, Anu, (3) Kumarbi (who spat out deities, including his successor) and (4) the Storm God. Hesiod records a Greek tradition paralleling the last three of these four kings of the pantheon. Uranus is the heaven god corresponding to Anu. His son, Cronos, who emasculates and displaces him, corresponds to Kumarbi. Cronos swallows his own children, except Zeus, who later makes Cronos spit them out. Again, Cronos corresponds to Kumarbi who spat out deities. Zeus, lord of the storm, corresponds to the Hittite Storm God, as the final and actual king of the pantheon. It is the details that demonstrate the relationship between the two traditions.[2]

[1] H. Güterbock, *Kumarbi: Mythen vom churritischen Kronos*, Zürich & New York, 1946.

[2] See O. R. Gurney, *The Hittites*, Pelican ed., London, 1952, pp. 190-192.

The place of the Hittites in the evolution of Western Culture is important for evident reasons. First, the geographical location of Asia Minor made it the landbridge between the Semitic World and Greece. The impact of the Semitic Akkadians upon the Hittites is plainly so strong that we can readily understand how there was enough of a Mesopotamian component in Anatolian culture for it to carry over into the Aegean. Cuneiform Hittite texts are not only written in the script of Mesopotamia, but are full of Sumero-Akkadian logograms and loan-words; so much so that the interpretation of Hittite texts comes more easily to Assyriologists than to Indo-Europeanists. Accordingly, the Mesopotamian element in Anatolia was qualitatively and quantitatively equipped to move still farther westward and leave its mark on Europe during Minoan and Mycenaean times.

The Hittites carried their composite culture (partly through their conquests that extended in every direction) from the Aegean to Babylon, from the Black Sea to Canaan.

The Canaanite tie-ins with the Hittites are numerous. To take only one specific point that is clear from written evidence, the Hebrew word for "hand" is used to designate a "monument" or "memorial stone"; the same usage is found in Ugaritic. But the Hebrew has a highly specialised meaning for "hand"; namely, "a victory stela" such as David set up along the Euphrates to mark the farthest border of his conquests (1 Chronicles 18: 3). Hattusili III[1] uses the word for "hand" in exactly this sense of "a victory stela." His scribe employs the Sumerogram šu (=Akkadian *qâtu* "hand"), but neither šu nor *qâtu* are so far known to have this meaning of "victory stela" in Sumerian or Akkadian. "Hand" in that sense is a feature of the West embracing the Canaanite and Hittite spheres. Indeed, we could call that sphere simply "Hittite," because Syria and

[1] Apology 2: 30.

Palestine were actually called Hattu (Hittite Land) by the Mesopotamians because of the Hittite influence there.

A Hittite enclave flourished around Hebron in the Patriarchal Age. Genesis 23 portrays Abraham buying a plot of land from Ephron, the Hittite, in the presence of the whole Hittite community there because land could not be sold to an alien unless the community sanctioned the sale. The transaction, moreover, is according to Hittite law, rather than Hebrew or Mesopotamian law. The issue raised during the dickering before the sale has nothing to do with haggling over price, though this had usually been read into the text by moderns in spite of the clear wording. The issue is whether Abraham will be permitted to buy only the corner of the estate containing the cave for burying his dead, or whether he will have to buy the whole estate in order to get the cave. In Hittite law, a property owner continues to render feudal obligation on land until he sells all of it. Thus the issue is clear: Abraham wanted the burial plot without assuming feudal obligations; but Ephron, the Hittite, insisted that Abraham buy all or nothing. Since Abraham had on his hands a corpse requiring burial, he had no time for protracted negotiations; instead he yielded and bought the land on Ephron's terms. The inclusion of the trees on the land, in the statement of the sale, is also typical of Hittite law.

Early Mesopotamian law does not reflect the institution of levirate marriage. Levirate marriage signifies that a woman acquired as a wife belongs to the husband's family even after his death, to the extent that she continues to serve as wife for another man in his family. Usually the other man is her brother-in-law (=Latin *levir*), but in Hittite law, her father-in-law is eligible, too. Levirate marriage is widely attested among the ancient Indo-Europeans, including the Indians, Hittites, Greeks and Romans. Moreover, the institution is prominent in the ancient Semitic World only in the wake of the Indo-European invasions that took place during the second millennium B.C.; e.g., at Nuzu, Ugarit, in the lawcodes of the Assyrians and Hittites, and in the Bible. The older cuneiform codes show no trace of it, down to and including Hammurapi's Code.

The Bible mentions the Hittites among the early inhabitants of Palestine, and states that intermarriage between Hebrews and Hittites took place. Ezekiel (16: 3) goes so far as to tell the Jerusalemites that they are a hybrid people; their father, so to speak, is Amorite, and their mother, Hittite. We need not be surprised, then, to find in Genesis 38 a narrative with close Indo-European parallels sociologically. The story goes that Tamar marries one of Judah's sons who dies, and is, therefore, married to another son of Judah, who also dies. Tamar is entitled to be the mother of the heir through some other member of Judah's family, but Judah withholds his third son from her. She is driven to the expedient of posing as a veiled prostitute, and thereby gets Judah (her father-in-law) to impregnate her. The text declares that Tamar was within her rights, so that we have a tie-in with the Hittite Code which reckons with the father-in-law as eligible in the levirate succession. But there is yet another remarkable " Indoid " parallel. When Tamar is found to be pregnant, but Judah does not yet know he is the man involved, he prescribes that Tamar be burnt alive; and her own father indeed turns her out to be burnt. In India, there are traditionally two ways of disposing of widows—through levirate marriage (*niyoga*) or burning (*suttee*). Both seem to be reflected in Genesis 38 (*mutatis mutandis*—for suttee in India in effect prevents infidelity, whereas in Genesis 38 it is intended to atone for apparent infidelity).

One of the most remarkable documents of ancient Anatolia is the *Apology of Hattusili* III. Though a son of King Mursili, Hattusili was not in line to succeed his father. And yet he did manœuvre into position and wrest the throne for himself. To justify himself he composed this *Apology* showing how he had been wronged, and how he and the goddess Ishtar entered into a covenant, whereby she protected him and advanced his career in return for his devotion to her and for his elevation of her to the foremost place among the gods. The relationship between the king and the protecting deity is of a piece with the personal Covenant relationship between the Patriarchs and Yahweh, in which human devotion is matched by divine protection. Greek heroic literature is replete with illustrations of such covenant relationships between a particular man and a particular deity. Anchises and Aphrodite are such a pair; Odysseus and Athena are another. Like Hattusili and Ishtar, those pairs too illustrate covenants between a man and a goddess.

When Hattusili, after the military success of his youth, scored his first great victory as a man, he tells us that, at that time, " Ishtar called me by name."[1] This is a striking parallel to the Hebrew terminology whereby the Deity calls " by name " the Messiah, who is the Deity's favoured human king. Note that God calls Cyrus, the Messiah (Isaiah 45: 1) by name (vv. 3-4), guaranteeing future victories (vv. 1-3) quite as Ishtar called on Hattusili by name and vouchsafed victories for him. This Hittite parallel should be incorporated into the collateral evidence for the study of Messianism.

The full importance of the Hittites is yet to be realised. Among the many avenues of approach is the study of historical writing. Already in the second millennium, Hittite historiography rose far above anything that Pharaonic Egypt and ancient Mesopotamia were ever to produce. Egypt and Mesopotamia never got beyond the annal stage of recording history. The Hittites achieved the highest level of historical writing prior to the Hebrews and Greeks. We can now surmise why it was the Hebrews and Greeks who first emerged as the historians of the West. Both of them started their historiographic careers on Hittite substratum.

[1] Apology 2: 44.

The Cuneiform World

It is no accident that Herodotus, the Father of History, came from Anatolia. The seeds of historical writings were planted by the Hittites back in the second millennium throughout their sphere of influence, spanning Halicarnassus and Zion. We may further note that those seeds took root, not inland, but along the Palestinian and Ionian shores of the Mediterranean, where men had developed more cosmopolitan attitudes.

IV

Egypt

The people of Egypt have from time immemorial regarded their land as the gift of the Nile. Wherever the River's waters reach, the soil is fertile. Beyond, there is only desert.[1]

The Land, almost sealed off from the rest of the world, is ideally suited for nurturing a distinctive civilisation. It is only at the north and south ends of the long, narrow country that Egypt is open to outside influences. The far south has always been open to Black Africa. The Delta (or Lower Egypt) has always been part of the Levant or East Mediterranean. Upper Egypt, as the long area in between is called, has therefore been the most distinctive part of Egypt. It is the usual centre of nationalism, and because of its dry climate, where papyri and other organic material are well preserved, most of what we know archaeologically of ancient Egypt is from there. This has its unfortunate side, because it was precisely the Delta that had direct contact by land with Canaan, and by sea with the Greeks, Phoenicians and other East Mediterranean peoples. The relative dearth of ancient remains in the Delta is in part responsible for the general underestimation of Egypt's role in the birth of Western Civilisation. From other sources, however, we have sufficient evidence to delineate

---

[1] For orientation on ancient Egypt, see Wm. C. Hayes, *The Scepter of Egypt*, I-II, Harper, New York, 1953-1959; and J. A. Wilson, *The Culture of Ancient Egypt*, Phoenix Books, U. of Chicago Press, 1956; and Sir Alan Gardiner, *Egypt of the Pharaohs*, Clarenden Press, Oxford, 1961.

Egypt's role in broad outline and to fill in many of the details as well.

The Nile Valley has a long prehistory, attested by simple artifacts that need not be surveyed here. Historical beginnings lie in the fourth millennium at approximately the same time as in Sumer. A few Mesopotamian elements in early Egypt suggest the priority of Sumer.[1] But this in no way alters the fact of Egypt's great and distinctive individuality.

The people of Egypt embody a number of racial strains, of which the primary element is probably akin to the Semitic subdivision of the White Race. But all such racial definitions have to be discounted somewhat, because our evidence, and indeed our concern, are not with physical criteria, but with culture. We know that the ancient Egyptian language has as its main stratum the same linguistic heritage familiar to us from the Semitic languages. So when we speak of the Semitic affinities of the Egyptians, we have language rather than human physique in mind. (To-day, the black Arabic-speaking Muslims of the Sudan are Semitic in language and religion, despite obvious racial differences from the other Semitic Arabs.)

The protohistoric beginnings of Egyptian culture lie in the last centuries of the fourth millennium. It was then that the first attempts at unifying the whole valley are attested. It was then that the traditional system of writing, traditional symbolism, the canons of Egyptian art, and so forth, were firmly established to last for over three thousand years, deep into Roman times, when the simple Greek alphabet displaced the cumbersome native script and Christianity supplanted the native paganism.

The clearest index of what happened around 3000 B.C. is the slate palette of Narmer, who is depicted as Pharaoh of a United Egypt. On one side of the palette, Narmer wears the high

[1] H. Frankfort, *The Birth of Civilization in the Near East*, Doubleday (Anchor), Garden City, New York, 1956, pp. 121-137.

" White Crown " of Upper Egypt; on the other side, he wears the flat " Red Crown " of Lower Egypt. On both sides, he is victorious in battle, either about to bash in the head of a fallen foeman or accompanying the banner-bearers of his army in the presence of rows of decapitated enemies. The King is already represented as a conquering falcon (i.e., Horus, the god of kingship), and as a mighty bull, demolishing the walls of an enemy city with his horns. The classical Egyptian titulary, which includes " Horus " and " Mighty Bull," is thus anticipated in this protohistoric palette. Indeed, the palette is an eloquent witness of the establishment of Egyptian culture in its principal features. Some of the ideas reflected in it are related to phenomena found outside Egypt, too. For instance, the image of the King as goring the foe with horns crops up in the Bible, where the Prophet Zedekiah gives iron horns to Ahab for vanquishing the Aramean foe.[1]

In Egyptian memory, the first king of the First Dynasty was Menes, under whom Upper and Lower Egypt were united. The culmination of early Egyptian history is called the Pyramid Age, when Dynasties III-VI of the Old Kingdom ruled the Nile. It was then that the first monumental stone buildings were erected; and the Pyramids are, incidentally, the only surviving Wonder of the Seven Wonders of antiquity. To secure the immortality of the deceased Pharaohs, the Pyramid Texts were written. They are spells rather than literature and therefore do not come within the scope of this book. That other literature was then written is fairly certain; for instance, Egyptian tradition clearly ascribes some wisdom literature to the Old Kingdom. The Westcar Papyrus tells wondrous tales of the Court of Cheops, who built the great Pyramid at Giza.

Already in the third millennium, Egyptian influence extended beyond the confines of the Nile Valley. Byblos became the

[1] I Kings 22: 11.

centre of a strong Egyptian outpost with a flourishing temple. The stone cup found on Cythera (bearing the Egyptian inscription *sp-r^c*) probably reflects cultic relations between the shrines of the great Aegean goddess (=later Aphrodite of Cythera) and of the great Egyptian sun-god Re. In any case, it attests contacts between Egypt and Cythera (which is within sight of the Peloponnesus) in the Pyramid Age. The cultural prestige of Egypt was enormous, and it should not surprise us to find Egyptian literary, as well as political, commercial and cultic influence in and around the East Mediterranean.

The eclipse of the Old Kingdom was followed by a Dark Age known as the First Intermediate Period. Then came a renaissance under the xIth and xIIth Dynasties called the Middle Kingdom:[1] the classical age of Egyptian language and literature. For the first time in world history, Egypt then produced a written literature for enjoyment. The Pyramid texts were magical and religious in nature, for guaranteeing the eternal existence of the Pharaohs who had died. Even the wisdom literature was designed for living the good and successful life, rather than art for art's sake. Mesopotamia always retained a certain grimness in its literary texts, of which most were religious in character. Even the Gilgamesh Epic, which is essentially a secular epic, deals with too serious a problem to be called entertaining. Man's futile quest for preserving the life of his friends and himself can hardly be called literature designed for pleasure. But Egypt, by the early second millennium, had developed the art of the short story for providing entertainment. Middle Kingdom tales, like the Tale of Sinuhe, or the Shipwrecked Sailor, are eminently successful attempts to give the reader pleasure. They are completely un-

---

[1] A standard date for the Middle Kingdom is 2050-1800 B.C. (Wilson, *Culture of Ancient Egypt*, p. 319). It is likely, however, that Egyptian chronology, prior to the expulsion of the Hyksos around 1570 B.C., will have to be reduced. Carbon-14 tests are not yet sufficiently refined to be of much help for such early periods.

encumbered with propaganda, moralising, religion, or weighty problems.

It goes without saying that other people, outside Egypt, must also have developed folktales for diverting each other. But such tales remained oral. The Middle Egyptian stories are the first written, secular literature created for enjoyment. We owe the writing of those stories to the Egyptian concept of the afterlife. The Egyptians were a simple folk who wanted to have as good a time as possible in the next world, which they fancied could be a quite literal continuation of this world at its best. One of the pleasures of this world worth continuing in the next was enjoying good stories. For this reason, papyri inscribed with diverting tales were placed in tombs with the dead. As far as we know, the Egyptians were the pioneers in writing this branch of belles-lettres, and they thus set the example which spread abroad and eventually contributed to the composition of antiquity's greatest masterpiece of entertainment literature: the Odyssey.

The finest piece of Egyptian narrative literature is the Tale of Sinuhe. That the Egyptians themselves also thought so is reflected in the fact that several copies of the text have come to light, ranging from the xiith to the xxth Dynasties. The Tale is typically Egyptian in its love of the Nile Valley and all that went with it. All men tend to love their own country, but many nations have an inclination to migrate when opportunities are available abroad. The Lebanese, Greeks, Swiss or Scots are all proud of their land and way of life, but many of them migrate and settle abroad. Not so the Egyptians, from antiquity to the present. The *nóstos* or homecoming of Sinuhe is even more typical of Egyptian social psychology than Gilgamesh's or Odysseus's of Mesopotamian or Greek psychology.

While the Tale of Sinuhe, like the epics of Gilgamesh and Odysseus, deals with episodic wandering that ends in a *nóstos*, the Egyptian narrative unfolds in simple prose; not epic poetry.

In this regard, Hebrew saga goes solidly with the Egyptian, versus Babylonian and Greek epic. The Hebrew-Egyptian tie-in is not purely accidental. Israel and Egypt are adjacent and in antiquity there was considerable human contact between them. Accordingly, the narrative styles of Egyptian and Hebrew have not only a general similarity, but often agree in specific detail. This is particularly the case in the Biblical stories of Joseph and the subsequent sojourn of Israel in Egypt.

The courtier Sinuhe was with Sesostris I, son of Amenemhat I (founder of the xiith Dynasty), on an expedition in Libya. It was then that Amenemhat died, and the narrator tells us that the palace family and entourage went into mourning, laying their heads upon their knees: a gesture of mourning practised also in Israel and at Ugarit.

The death of the king meant the possibility of intrigue and usurpation, especially since Sesostris was far off in Libya. So the loyalists at the palace sent messengers to Sesostris bearing news of Amenemhat's death and urging him to return to the palace at once. On getting the secret message, Sesostris hastened towards the palace without even informing his army. But Sinuhe learned that things were not running smoothly, by chancing to overhear someone apprising one of the royal princes of the situation. Sinuhe was frightened, as courtiers often are when there is a palace shake-up. Furtively, Sinuhe crossed northern Egypt and headed for Canaan. Around the Isthmus of Suez, he was about to faint from thirst and said to himself: " This is the taste of death." But in the nick of time, he heard the sound of cattle and saw bedouin with them. The sheikh of the tribe recognised Sinuhe, whom he had once met in Egypt. He gave him water and then cooked some milk for him. Sinuhe stayed with the tribe a while, before pressing onwards towards Phoenicia.

The Tale, which we shall presently survey, continues with Sinuhe's adventures in Syria, prior to his happy homecoming.

We have hinted at the similarity with the epics of Gilgamesh and Odysseus. It remains to point out that the closest parallel is the narrative of the Patriarchs in Genesis. In prose style, the Hebrew and Egyptian schools of literature appear closer and closer, the more we contrast them with the poetic epic traditions. The geographic locales are moreover the same: wanderings by land throughout Canaan and the Delta. Abraham, a Semite, wandered into Egypt and returned to his promised land: Canaan. He also married an Egyptian, Hagar, who bore him a heroic son, Ishmael. Burial in his own land is important in the narrative of Genesis. Jacob migrated to Egypt where he died, but his burial in Canaan figures prominently in Genesis. Sinuhe's tale is the same in reverse. He is an Egyptian who wanders in Canaan, where he weds a chieftain's daughter who bears him fine sons. Yet, he abandons the woman and does not reckon with her sons as the continuation of his line; cf. Abraham's dismissal of Hagar and Ishmael. Sinuhe's yearning to be buried in his beloved land of Egypt matches the same theme in the Patriarchal Narratives. The mummification of Jacob and Joseph leaves no doubt as to the Egyptian influence on the Genesis tales.[1]

The Tale of Sinuhe tells of his wandering from land to land, including Byblos, where there had been an Egyptian settlement and Temple for a long time. Then he spent a year and a half in Qedem, where a Syrian prince induced him to enter his service. When the Prince says to Sinuhe: "You will be well-off with me, you'll be hearing the Egyptian language," we are to understand that Egyptian individuals and groups perpetuated their ancestral culture, including the use of their own language, while engaged in careers on Canaanite soil. In fact, the story goes on to state that other Egyptians who knew Sinuhe were among the Prince's entourage. When the Prince asks Sinuhe: "Why, then, have

[1] Note that Sinuhe is successful in Canaan but buried in his native Egypt, even as Joseph is successful in Egypt but buried in his native Canaan.

you come here?" (for he had already invited him to remain), he is not being impolite but is asking the natural question that one asked of strangers, exactly as in the Ugaritic and Homeric epics. Sinuhe replied that he had run up no bad record, but that an illogical fear had impelled him: "I do not know what brought me to this region. It was the plan of God." Note that Sinuhe does not speak of some particular god of Egypt, but of the universal God. Whenever we find men of different religious backgrounds meeting each other in an international age, they have arrived at the conclusion that above national, local and particularistic deities, there is the one God who rules the universe. Joseph and Pharaoh, therefore, speak of "God" without any need of explanation. Amazingly enough, the Bible itself attributes the inspired word of God to Pharaoh Necho, while describing the virtuous successor of David (none other than Josiah) as too misguided to recognise God's word from the mouth of Necho.[1] Sinuhe's attribution of his exile and vicissitudes to God's plan is matched by Joseph's statement about his dislocations.

Sinuhe goes on to praise the new Pharaoh, Sesostris, and assures his Canaanite audience that benefits will accrue to every land that is loyal to him. Such a statement makes sense only if Syria was then an Egyptian sphere of influence.[2]

The Prince gave the hand of his eldest daughter in marriage to Sinuhe and entrusted him with the fertile border province of Yaa. "It produced figs and grapes. Wine was more plentiful than water there. It abounded in honey and olive oil. All kinds of fruit were on its trees. Besides, there were barley and wheat and countless cattle of every species. Great privileges devolved upon me because of the love shown me. He made me chief of a tribe among the best of his land. I was supplied with rations

---

[1] 2 Chronicles 35: 20-24 (N.B. v. 22).
[2] This does not mean that Egypt monopolised Syria as a sphere of influence. Interpenetrating spheres of influence were the norm.

consisting of liquor and wine daily, as well as cooked meat, roast fowl, not counting desert game, for such was caught in traps for me and put in my presence, besides what my hunting dogs fetched. . . . There was milk in all that was cooked. I spent many years. My sons grew strong, each ruling his tribe." Sinuhe boasts that his character was as noble as his fortune was good, for he was hospitable to all and generous and helpful to those who were in need.

Soon Sinuhe was commander-in-chief of the Prince's army, and scored victories on all sides, winning land, animals and all sorts of booty. He so gained the love of the Prince that the latter put him in charge of his household, much as Pharaoh was to do with Joseph.

The crowning victory of Sinuhe's career was scored over a Syrian chieftain who challenged him to a duel. The chieftain let fly his arrows against Sinuhe who evaded them. Then as the chieftain made for Sinuhe, Sinuhe shot an arrow through his neck. " He cried out and fell on his nose. I slew him with his own battle-axe, and on his back I yelled out my battle cry."

The feature of hacking the enemy with his own weapon recurs in David's victory over Goliath. The shouting of the war cry of victory is not unusual; e.g., it is familiar to us from the Gilgamesh Epic (where Enkidu prematurely boasts that he will shout in Uruk); cf. also the Homeric epithet " good at the (war) cry " to which we already alluded.

Sinuhe grew richer from the chieftain's spoils, as well as more famous than ever from the victory. For all this, Sinuhe thanks God: " God has so done to show His mercy towards one against whom he had been angry and caused to wander in a foreign land. To-day his (i.e., Sinuhe's) heart is joyous."

> Once a fugitive fled
> Now there are reports of me in the palace.

Once a straggler dragged along, a victim of hunger
  Now I give bread to my neighbour.
Once a man left his land because of misfortune
  Now I shine in robes of linen.
Once a man ran, for want of anyone to send
  Now I'm rich in slaves.
My house is beautiful, my domain is large. They mention me in the
  palace.

And yet, Sinuhe was not happy in his lot. Despite all his success, he lived in exile and longed to return to the Egyptian court: "O God (whoever you may be), who destined this flight, be merciful, restore me to the court. Mayhap you will grant me to see once more the place where my heart has never ceased to be. What can mean more to me than to be buried in the land where I was born? Come to my rescue!"

His prayers were answered. Pharaoh and the members of his immediate family sent messages to the aging Sinuhe welcoming him home. The text includes the royal letter summoning him back to enjoy the favours and honours of the Egyptian court until his death when he would be buried in princely fashion among the princes of Egypt. The text goes on to give Sinuhe's grateful reply.

Sinuhe took only one day to put his Syrian house in order before leaving it, for all time, behind. He made over his property to his children, appointing his eldest son as head of the tribe with all that went with it: slaves, flocks, harvested fruits and all the fruit trees. Then he headed south until he reached the Egyptian frontier where the commandant sent a message to Pharaoh informing him of Sinuhe's arrival. His Majesty sent a party to fetch Sinuhe and to provide him with gifts for rewarding the Syrians who had brought him to the border.

A well-equipped boat, with servants who prepared bread and

beer aboard, brought him to the palace, where he was received with every kindness. The splendour of His Majesty was too much for Sinuhe who swooned in his presence and afterwards could hardly say a word with composure.

The Queen and the royal children were amazed to see Sinuhe dressed as a bedouin and had to be assured that it was really he. The King announced that Sinuhe was to be a noble in the court. Thereafter, the royal children led Sinuhe to a house of one of the princes. Installed there, Sinuhe enjoyed every luxury and comfort. His reconversion from barbarian to Egyptian was effected with a shave, coiffure, fine linen cloths, fine oil, and a bed to sleep on. To put it succinctly in the words of Sinuhe: "I gave back the sand to those who dwell thereon."

Sinuhe was equipped handsomely to spend his old age in ease. He now had a country estate with plenty of servants. The palace supplied his meals. In anticipation of death, he got a stone pyramid, fully equipped with priests and a gold-covered statue of himself, with a skirt of fine gold.

The tale ends with Sinuhe's expression of gratitude: "Never has so much been done for a commoner. And I am the object of royal favours until the day of death arrives."

The Tale of Sinuhe is not only among the oldest examples of secular literature; it is eminently successful in telling an interesting story entertainingly. With artistic economy of expression, it provides atmosphere and depicts what is in the mind of the hero.

Another Middle Kingdom story is about a Shipwrecked Sailor. A prince, just returned from a mission and about to report to the Pharaoh, is apprehensive of His Majesty's reaction. To comfort and counsel him, a companion tells him to have self-confidence and to report to the King with aplomb, for "the mouth of a man can save him; his word can render people favourable towards him." The Egyptians put great store on a ready tongue and a well-told story. The companion thereupon tells of his own adventures, when he was shipwrecked on a wondrous isle.

He had set out with 120 sailors, the pick of Egypt. They were brave to the extreme, because though they could foretell any storm, they set sail and ran into a hurricane. The ship was wrecked. The Egyptian text tells us " it died " using the same word recently found in a Ugaritic letter mentioning a shipwreck.

All aboard perished except the narrator who was washed ashore on an island where he lay alone and faint for three days. Then he got up to forage for food and found the island unbelievably fertile. " I found there figs and grapes, wondrous vegetables of all kinds. . . . There were also fish and birds there." The shipwrecked sailor ate his fill and had to abandon what he could not carry, for everything was there in superabundance. He then kindled a fire with a fire-stick and offered sacrifices to the gods.

Suddenly the trees cracked and the earth quaked. He buried his face, and when he mustered enough courage to uncover it, a huge serpent with gold-covered members and eyebrows of lapis-lazuli stood before him and asked: " Who brought you here, who brought you here, little one? Who brought you here? If you delay in telling me who brought you into this isle, I'll cause you to see yourself reduced to ashes and become something that nobody sees any more." The sailor was beside himself and could not answer coherently, so the serpent, without hurting him, carried him in his mouth to his lair where he ordered him (this time without threats) to tell his story. Respectfully, the sailor told his tale:

" I was going to the mines on a mission of the King, aboard a ship 120 cubits long and 40 wide. One hundred twenty sailors got aboard, from the elite of Egypt. Whether they scanned the sky or scanned the land, their heart was braver than lions. They could announce a storm before it came and a tempest before it broke. Each of them vied with his comrade in courage and strength, and there was not a misfit among them. A storm broke while we were on the Great Green, before we could reach land. They continued to navigate, but the storm got worse, raising a wave of eight cubits. A beam of wood struck me violently. Then the ship died and of those who were aboard, not one survived except me. And here I am in your company. I was then carried to this isle by a wave of the Great Green."

So far the narrative is a story within a story. Now the serpent goes on to tell his own tale, which is a story within a story within a story. This interweaving of narratives is one of the simple forerunners leading up to the intricate artistry that we admire in the construction of the Odyssey.

The serpent introduces his autobiography by predicting that in four months a boat, manned by Egyptians known to the Sailor, would arrive to carry him back to his country where he would die in his own town; the only happy ending to any Egyptian's life. The serpent then tells how he had been happily surrounded by his family, when suddenly a star fell and burned up every one of them, leaving griefstricken, as the sole survivor, only the serpent who was telling the tale. He closes his speech with this admonition: "If you are strong, control your heart, and you will again hug your children in your bosom, you will kiss your wife and see your home. This is worth more than anything else. You will get back to the country where you lived among your brethren."

The grateful Sailor then declares that he will tell the Pharaoh of the Serpent's greatness and see to it that precious gifts, such as incense, will be sent to him. But the Serpent reminds him that such gifts from Egypt are unnecessary, because the Serpent's domain in Punt produces and exports those precious commodities. The Serpent goes on to predict that after the Sailor has departed, the island will disappear into watery billows. This detail is of considerable interest, for it agrees strikingly with the predicted disappearance of the land of the Phaeacians, after Odysseus' departure. Indeed, the whole Tale of the Shipwrecked Sailor is to be compared with the episode of the wondrous land of the Phaeacians on which Odysseus was shipwrecked. The general agreement becomes more impressive as we note the specific details that tie in.

The boat came as predicted, and the Serpent wished the Sailor *bon voyage*: " Back to your home in health, in health, O little one! May you see your children! Make my name good in your town. This is all I ask of you." While the Serpent can scarcely be called a heroic figure, he is reflected as desiring a good name in human memory, rather than worldly possessions, somewhat in the manner of the epic heroes.

The Serpent sent the Sailor on his way with a great cargo of precious gifts, thus assuring him a triumphal homecoming.

The Sailor concludes his narration by telling that he reached the Pharaoh, gave him the gifts and was awarded a high position at court. But the poor fellow who has been listening takes little comfort, for it is he, not the story teller, who has to face an ominous audience in the palace.

The two Middle Egyptian stories that we have reviewed were composed and written down during the first half of the second millennium, long before the Mycenaean Age in which the earliest memories of Homeric epic are rooted. The Story of Sinuhe deals, like the Odyssey, with the episodic wanderings of a hero, climaxed with a *nóstos* (" homecoming "). But, unlike the Odyssey, Sinuhe travels by land. The Shipwrecked Sailor anticipates a specific episode of the Odyssey, and, like the Odyssey, deals with sea travel. However, the locale is the Red Sea, not the Mediterranean. In Late Egyptian literature, various strands of Sinuhe and Shipwrecked Sailor were combined with a shift of scene to the East Mediterranean, resulting in the Misadventures of Wenamon: a composition that in many ways anticipates Homer's Odyssey, as we shall note below (after we complete our survey of the Middle Egyptian texts).

The longest surviving piece of Middle Egyptian literature is known as the Eloquent Peasant. The Egyptians loved high-flown speech, with all its conceits and floweriness. This tale brings out the Egyptian's twofold ability of telling a narrative directly and simply, and, at the same time, of glorying in extravagant rhetoric. There was a peasant who left his oasis with his donkeys laden with goods that he hoped to sell along the Nile. His wife supplied him with provisions and also kept enough for herself and the children during his expected absence. En route, a rascal named Jehuti-nakht cast covetous eyes on the Peasant's donkeys. Since cultivable land is so precious in Egypt, the paths were very narrow. The Peasant had to conduct his beasts along such a path between water, on one side, and a grain field, on the other. In order to filch the donkeys, Jehuti-nakht created a pretext by laying a garment across the path, so that to avoid treading on the garment, one of the donkeys veered towards the grain field and helped himself to a mouthful of barley. The rascal then declared that he would seize the offending donkey. The Peasant replied that he knew the owner of the land to be a man of high principle who would not allow such injustice to be perpetrated on his estate. The rascal replied that no one listens to a poor man and proceeded to give him a beating and rob him of his donkeys. The Peasant could do nothing but complain loudly. Jehuti-nakht in vain tried to silence him. After ten days of complaining without getting any satisfaction from Jehuti-nakht, the Peasant went to the residence of the virtuous land-owner to complain. The latter, Rensi by name, happened to be leaving his house to go down to his official boat which he used (as Egyptian administrators were wont) for business. Hearing the Peasant's complaint,

Rensi tried to find out the facts, but the officials tried to cover up for Jehuti-nakht out of class solidarity. Yet, Rensi kept an open mind, and the Peasant continued his complaints and turned for justice to Rensi as "the father of the orphan, husband of the widow, brother of the abandoned wife, and garment of him who has no mother." The speech of the Peasant was so eloquent that Rensi told the Pharaoh: "My lord, I have found one of those peasants, who really speaks beautifully. He has been robbed by a man in my service and has come to complain to me thereof." The King decided that they would maintain silence and let the peasant keep complaining so that his eloquent speeches could be recorded in writing, as well as afford them maximum pleasure as listeners. The King was humane enough to request that Rensi make sure that the Peasant's wife and children were provided for, because he knew that such peasants came to the Valley when supplies at home were quite low. The King added: "See to it that the Peasant himself gets supplies. You will then watch that they give him provisions without letting him know that it is you who have given them to him." So Rensi saw to it that the Peasant and his family were supplied with enough to eat and drink.

The device of the Pharaoh and Rensi is essentially the same as that of Joseph, who humanely keeps his brothers and their family supplied while enjoying the act that he obliges them to put on, including speeches that he thus draws out of them.

The bulk of the composition consists of the nine eloquent complaints of the Peasant. In them, he admonishes Rensi to uphold the principles of justice and charity, for only thereby can a man—no matter how wealthy and highly placed—achieve satisfaction in this world and eternal life in the next. The Peasant is respectful, but pulls no punches. He asks the lordly Rensi: "Will you be a man of eternity?"

After delivering the nine speeches, the Peasant is afraid that he will be the worse off for them. But the ending is happy. Rensi tells him that he has been detained intentionally. For a moment, the homesick Peasant is dismayed and asks: " Must I then eat your bread and drink your [beer] for ever? " To which Rensi replies: " Stay just a little while so that you can hear your pleas." The scroll is then brought and read off to them. Thereafter, it is sent to the Pharaoh who treasures it above all else in the land and tells Rensi to decide the case. The decision is, of course, in the Peasant's favour and against Jehuti-nakht. The Peasant is prepared for his return home, enriched by the heavy damages imposed upon the villainous Jehuti-nakht.

The classical age of the Middle Kingdom was rudely terminated by invaders from Asia, known as the Hyksos, in the seventeenth century B.C. The Hyksos included Indo-European charioteers, whose horses introduced enough speed to revolutionise the art of war and change the course of ancient history. The Hyksos ruled a World Empire for perhaps a century.[1] Though they conquered Egypt, they established their capital at Avaris in the northwestern part of the Delta, centrally located for the capital of an empire embracing holdings in Egypt, Western Asia and the East Mediterranean. Regularly, the Pharaohs claim dominion over the Two Lands (i.e., Upper and Lower Egypt). In the Hyksos Age, the plural of " Lands " (instead of the dual) may appear in this formula, reflecting the fact that for the Hyksos, Egypt was viewed as part of a larger empire.[2]

The Hyksos Pharaoh Khayan has left monuments, one of which was found at Knossos, and another turned up through a

[1] The Hyksos occupied Egypt for about a century until they were expelled around 1570 B.C. In spite of their importance relatively little is known about the Empire of the Hyksos. This is to be attributed to the accidental character of archaeological discovery, and the difficulty in interpreting the scattered evidence now available.

[2] See E. Meyer, *Geschichte des Altertums*, 2nd ed., 1909, I, 2, p. 295.

dealer in Baghdad.[1] While such evidence does not prove the existence of an empire exercising absolute sway over the whole Near East, it does suggest a political entity, controlling Egypt (Lower Egypt more firmly than Upper Egypt) and Palestine, with spheres of interest reaching out as far as Mesopotamia and Crete. Though the precise character and extent of the Hyksos Empire during the seventeenth and early sixteenth centuries B.C. cannot yet be defined, its existence is beyond question, and it doubtless contributed to the channels of cultural transmission during Babylon I times: a critical period forming the backdrop of the great Amarna synthesis.

Resistance against the Hyksos invaders gained momentum in Upper Egypt, where Hyksos control was tenuous. From there the local rulers of Thebes organised the military strength that succeeded in ousting the Hyksos from Egypt around 1570 B.C., thereby establishing the native Eighteenth Dynasty over the Two Lands. The Hyksos had taught the Egyptians the need for horse-drawn chariotry. With this new means of warfare, the Eighteenth Dynasty was able to usher in the Empire Period of Egyptian history that reached its height under Thothmes III,[1] who conquered Palestine and Syria up to the Euphrates River. His conquests form the setting of an Egyptian tale called The Taking of Joppa.

The story goes that Thoth, a general of Thothmes III, undertook the capture of Joppa. In those days, it was almost impossible for any army to take a well-fortified city (for the Assyrians were yet to develop the techniques of breaching strong city walls) and so Thoth had to resort to stratagems of one sort and another.

The opening part of the papyrus tells how Thoth was enter-

[1] Khayan's hieroglyphic inscriptions include monuments at Gebelein in southern Egypt, at Gezer in Palestine, the stone lion from Baghdad, the alabaster jar lid from Knossos, and a cylinder seal in Athens (Wilson, *Culture of Ancient Egypt*, p. 162).

[1] Ca. 1502–1448 B.C.

taining the Prince of Joppa, who asked to see the mace of Thothmes III. Thoth not only showed him the mace, but murdered him with it. Slaying guests was worthy of saga, precisely because it ran against all the laws of hospitality. However extenuating the circumstances, the murder of guests was not sanctioned among any nation of antiquity. For that very reason, it appears in the epic repertoire; cf. Odysseus' slaughter of the wooers who were guests in his halls, Jael's murder of her guest Sisera and Jehu's murder of the Baalists, who had been invited by him to attend services in a Temple.

The next stratagem was to fill two hundred baskets with one soldier each. Every soldier was provided with equipment needed for capturing the city, once they were brought inside. Then by beguiling the authorities of Joppa with the false report that Thoth had capitulated to the Prince of Joppa, the baskets with their fatal cargo were admitted into the city. The Egyptian troops then captured Joppa for the greater glory of the Pharaoh.

For our investigation, the most significant feature of The Taking of Joppa is the capture of a city by the ruse of getting concealed troops therein. This is essentially the Trojan Horse motif,[1] even though our Egyptian ruse is more closely paralleled in the tale of Ali Baba and the Forty Thieves.

The Empire Period brought Egypt into the age of internationalism that produced the great East Mediterranean synthesis. Pharaohs of the Eighteenth Dynasty contracted marriages with Mitanni princesses. An international language, Babylonian, now served as the means of communication from Mesopotamia to Egypt, including also Canaan, Anatolia and the islands of the East Mediterranean. A collection of about four hundred documents, known as the Tell el-Amarna letters, found at Akhetaton,[2]

[1] Mercenary troops frequently transmitted such military lore from land to and.

[2] Akhetaton is the ancient name of Tell el-Amarna.

the capital of Amenophis IV, preserves the diplomatic correspondence between the Pharaohs (Amenophis III and IV), on the one hand, and the rulers of Western Asia, on the other. These letters, reflecting the nature and extent of international give-and-take, show how the heritage of Semite, Hurrian, Indo-European, Egyptian, Minoan and other ethnic elements of the Near East funnelled into the Amarna Order, out of which proto-Israel and proto-Hellas emerged.

A large proportion of the Amarna letters deal with Phoenician relations, reflecting the prominence of that important maritime people in the East Mediterranean.

Ugarit, on the north shore of Syria, has long been known from the Amarna Letters. But since 1929, the French expedition there, under Claude Schaeffer, has unearthed a mass of texts and monuments that has made of Ugarit a cornerstone in reconstructing the origins of western culture (see Chapter V). The Ugaritic tablets mention Egyptian residents, and Egyptian inscriptions have been found there.

During the Empire Period, Egypto-Aegean relations are clearly attested both in Egypt and in the Aegean. The Egyptian term " Keftiu " corresponds to " Caphtorians." Caphtor (which is mentioned in Akkadian, Ugaritic and Hebrew texts) designated the Aegean World, whose hub was Crete.[1] The influence of Egyptian and Minoan art on each other is unmistakable.

The new international order witnessed the penetration of

[1] Most scholars would pinpoint Caphtor as Crete, though it has been proposed to localise it elsewhere in the East Mediterranean ranging from Cythera (so E. Weidner) to the southern coast of Asia Minor (so G. A. Wainwright, of whose valuable publications on the subject, we may note "Early Tin in the Aegean," *Antiquity* 18, 1944, pp. 57-64; N.B. p. 61, n. 23). Sea people, like the Caphtorians, were on the move. Accordingly we should not try to localise their land too narrowly. Originally " Caphtor " may have designated some specific and limited region in the East Mediterranean, but the solution of this moot question lies beyond the scope of this book.

classes of people across political boundaries. For example, the fighting charioteers, known by the Indo-European name of *maryannu*, appear in Egypt as well as all over Western Asia. The *Apiru* also appear all through Western Asia and Egypt throughout the second millennium B.C.

Since the Amarna Age was one in which men of such different origins and backgrounds came into contact, it was inevitable that the spirit of the Age should produce an over-all universal religion to run parallel with the local religions that flourished in the component parts of the Order. Egypt was divided up into districts called "nomes." Each nome had its own cult and among the inhabitants of the same nome, it was the provincial cult that satisfied the average Egyptian's religious needs. However, since Old Kingdom times, the Re cult had become the universal religion of life, straddling all the nomes and eclipsing their local religions. Some compromise had to be made with the deeply entrenched localisms. For instance, Amon the ram-god was the main deity of the capital, Thebes. He was fused with Re, to form Amon-Re, who thus became the universal god of what aspired to be a World Empire. The biblical tradition is quite clear in representing the Hebrews and other nations as being in complete agreement on the validity of Elohim,[1] the God Who transcends all cults and rules the Universe. Under Amenophis IV, who changed his name to Ikhnaton, solar monotheism went too far for Egyptian sensitivities. It involved a revolution in religion, art and even language that strained Egypt beyond its capacity for change. With the death of Ikhnaton, the counter-revolution came on and restored religion and art more or less to their former state. However, his language reform (whereby the

---

[1] " Elohim " happens to be the Hebrew designation for the One God. In Akkadian texts from Ugarit, the same God is called *ilâni*: the exact Akkadian equivalent of Elohim. He was called by different names in different languages, but sophisticated citizens of the Amarna Order knew that the various names all referred to the same Deity.

classical Middle Kingdom Egyptian was supplanted by the contemporary New Kingdom Egyptian as the written language) was there to stay.

It cannot be overstressed that Egyptian developments were not in isolation during the Amarna Age. Its monotheism was in the air internationally. Geographically, Egypt was a lateral area in the Amarna Order; off to the southwest and exposed to the rest of the Amarna Order only via the Delta. Palestine, however, was the hub of the Order, forming the land-bridge between Asia and Egypt, and situated along the shores of the Mediterranean. It should come as no surprise, therefore, that the monotheistic spirit of the age took permanent root in that hub which has come to be known as the Holy Land. Palestine was sufficiently international to digest universal monotheism and make of it a permanent factor in the future of mankind; Egypt could not digest it because of deep nationalistic institutions.

The Amarna Age marks a decline in Egyptian power abroad. From that time on, Egypt experienced a number of revivals, but in general it may be said that Pharaonic Egypt went into a decline and never again equalled the splendours of the Pyramid Age, Middle Kingdom or Empire Period. And yet the early centuries of decline are precisely the era when Egypt was a major part of the synthesis that evoked the earliest literatures of Israel and Greece. For this reason, Late Egyptian literature (as the following compositions are called) is of prime importance in our investigation.

Around the 13th century B.C. was composed The Tale of the Two Brothers. For present purposes, it is only the plot of the first part of the composition that interests us. The story goes that two brothers lived together. The older one, Anubis, was married. The younger, Bata, was not. In accordance with the fratriarchal elements of society, Bata served his older brother faithfully. But Anubis's wife tried to seduce Bata, and when he resisted her advances, she accused him of trying to rape her. This theme is familiar from the biblical story of Joseph and Potiphar's wife, and from the Homeric account of the virtuous Bellerophon and the lecherous Anteia. It is accordingly part of the ancient East Mediterranean repertoire.

By far the most important of the Late Egyptian stories for the history of Greek epic is The Misadventures of Wenamon. The manuscript itself dates from the tenth century, but it relates to events during the early years of the eleventh century when Egypt's claim to prestige abroad had already become a painful anachronism.

Wenamon was sent to Phoenicia to get lumber for repairing, or replacing, the sacred boat of Amon. En route, he stopped at Dor, near the Carmel Coast of Palestine, where the Aegean folk known as the Tsekel were in control. This ties in with the biblical account, which does not list Dor among the cities captured by the Hebrew tribesmen of the Conquest.[1] It will be remembered that the tale of Wenamon is set in the biblical period of the Conquest and Judges. The coast of Canaan remained largely in the hands of the Phoenicians and Aegean folk such as the Philistines and Tsekel.

At Dor, one of Wenamon's own crew robbed him of the gold and silver he needed for defraying the costs of the expedition. Wenamon complained to the local ruler, but the complaint fell on deaf ears because, as the ruler retorted: " The thief who robbed you is yours; he belongs to your ship! " Yet, the ruler offered to try to locate the thief.

Wenamon proceeded to Tyre. En route he managed to lay his hands on some silver through skulduggery that was later to plague him. Next, he reached Byblos where the ruler rudely told him by messenger, " Get out of my port! " every day for twenty-nine days. For consolation, Wenamon had little except his

---

[1] See Joshua 17; 11-22 and Judges 1: 27.

statue of " Amon of the Road " that he carried with him for
protection.

The deadlock was broken when one day, while the Prince of
Byblos was sacrificing to his gods, a priest of his was seized by a
fit of ecstasy. The hieroglyph referring to the priest depicts a
man quivering all over. Such fits are familiar to us from the
ecstatic prophets of ancient Israel; e.g., those among whom Saul
" prophesied." The Byblian ecstatic was inspired to declare this
oracle to his prince:

> *Bring the g[o]d up!*
> *Fetch the envoy in charge thereof!*
> *It is Amon who has sent him.*
> *It is he who has caused him to come!*

Note that the oracle consists of two verses, each with two parallel
hemistichs. Poetry is also the regular medium for oracles in
Hebrew, Greek and other ancient Near East literatures.[1]

Meanwhile, poor Wenamon had found another boat bound
for Egypt and was ready to board it with " Amon of the Road,"
and give up his mission as futile. But then the harbour master
came requesting him to stay till the morrow on orders of the
Prince. Wenamon replied: " Aren't you the one who keeps
coming to me every day and says: ' Get out of my port!' And
now aren't you saying ' Stay this ni[gh]t ' in order to let the ship
I've found depart so that you can come once more and tell me
' Get out '." But the Prince was firm and commanded all concerned to see to it that Wenamon remained.

On the morrow, the Prince sent someone to conduct Wenamon up from the shore to the palace. One of the finest examples
of the terse Egyptian way of indicating atmosphere is the following description of the prince sitting in his chamber with his back

---

[1] This goes hand in hand with the belief that poets were divinely inspired
(e.g., " by the Muse or Apollo " to give a Homeric formulation).

to a picture-window overlooking the sea. In Wenamon's words: "I found him sitting in his upper chamber, his back turned to a window, with the waves of the great Syrian Sea rolling up to his neck." The Egyptian artists may not have applied the principles of perspective, but the Wenamon text shows a full appreciation of perspective in the world as we see it.

There follows a dialogue between the Prince and Wenamon, in which the Prince asks a number of embarrassing questions. For instance, when Wenamon is asked for his credentials, it turns out that he left them with the authorities in the Delta. When the Prince inquires: "On what kind of mission have you come?" Wenamon answers: "I have come in quest of the wood destined for the great and splendid ship of Amon-Re, King of the Gods. Your father supplied it; your father's father supplied it; and you'll do it too." To this the Prince replied: "Sure, they supplied it! And if you give me the (pay) for doing it, I'll supply it. Of course, my forebears carried out the mission, but the Pharaoh had sent six ships laden with the wares of Egypt, which were unloaded in their warehouses. But what do you bring me?"

The Prince of Byblos makes it perfectly clear that he is not subordinate to any Egyptian master, although he expresses respect for the culture of Egypt and reverence for Amon. Wenamon took up the religious aspect of his case, instead of dwelling on the financial (which was all too weak at that point), stressing that the earlier Pharaohs had paid only worldly goods, whereas if the Prince respects the god's need for the lumber, he will give the Prince something much better: life and health. Yet, Wenamon was realistic enough also to dispatch a request to Egypt for gold, silver and other valuables to serve as payment. The Prince's messenger carried the request to Smendes and his wife, Tentamon —the rulers in the Delta—and came back to Byblos in the spring with the requested payment. The Prince was satisfied and sent a crew into the forest to fell the timber. Then he told Wenamon to take the timber and depart with a warning not to delay because of any fear of the sea. He added that some Egyptian emissaries once tarried seventeen years in Byblos until indeed they died there. Then with sardonic humour, he offered to have their grave shown to Wenamon who, however, begged to be excused.

Wenamon's concern was now how to get the timber to Egypt. Apparently what he feared was not so much storms at sea, but piracy. He tried to persuade the Prince to provide a fleet to get him and his cargo safely to Egypt, which Amon would requite by adding fifty years to the Prince's destined lifespan.[1] Wenamon was certainly resourceful with his tongue.

An ominous sight confronted him in the harbour. Eleven vessels were there, belonging to hostile Tsekel, apparently those from whom Wenamon had seized silver to replace what Wenamon's own crewman had stolen at Dor. The Tsekel were demanding his arrest. In anguish, Wenamon sat and wept. The Prince's secretary asked what ailed him, and Wenamon replied: " Don't you see the migratory birds that, for the second time, are going down to Egypt? See them going towards the marshes. But how long am I to stay, abandoned here? For can't you see those people who are coming back to arrest me? "

It was sad enough for any Egyptian to be away from home for the second year and, to make matters worse, he was faced with personal arrest and failure of his mission at the moment when success had seemed imminent. News of Wenamon's plight brought tears to the eyes of the Prince who, to console Wenamon, dispatched to him wine, a sheep, and an Egyptian singing girl with these instructions: " Sing for him. Don't let his heart take on cares."

The mention of the Egyptian singing girl in Byblos is an

[1] That a god can add an extra period to a ruler's destined lifespan, appears also in 2 Kings 20: 6, where God extends Hezekiah's fated lifespan by fifteen years.

important reminder to us that professional entertainers carried words and music from land to land in the area under investigation. The wandering minstrel is familiar to us from Homer. There, however, we get the impression (although the text doesn't explicitly say so) that the minstrel and his audience are always Greek. The Wenamon text, however, plainly states that the Phoenician Prince had the Egyptian *artiste* among his retinue.[1]

The next morning the Prince went with his guard to the Tsekel to inquire about their intentions. They plainly declared that they had a score to settle with Wenamon. The Prince refused to arrest the envoy of Amon, but he reminded the Tsekel that what they did on the high seas was their own business. With that, the Prince sent Wenamon off to sea. The wind blew his ships ashore on Cyprus, where the people wanted to kill him. But he appealed to the Princess of the City, first hailing her and asking her entourage: "Isn't there any among you who understands Egyptian?" One of them answered: "I understand it." Then Wenamon declared that Cyprus was famed the world over for its justice. He states his case against the hostile Cypriotes, and the Princess begins to give him a kindly answer, when the extant part of our manuscript ends abruptly.

We have noted that Middle Egyptian literature included (1) the theme of the wandering hero (Sinuhe) who at last comes home; and (2) the theme of the Shipwrecked Sailor who returns home after an amazing adventure on a magic isle in the Red Sea. In Wenamon, the two themes are fused with a shift of scene to the East Mediterranean. These Egyptian literary developments unmistakably foreshadow the Odyssey. The entertaining nature of the Odyssey is the culmination of a trend that we can so far trace only in Egypt: written literature for pleasure's sake.

[1] To cite another example of importing foreign singers: Sennacherib tells us in his Annals that Hezekiah sent him male and female singers as gifts from Jerusalem to Nineveh.

Wenamon and Odysseus are men on a mission, beset with frustrating obstacles, sailing the East Mediterranean, yearning for their native soil year after year. The happy ending of Wenamon must be the *nóstos*, just as with Sinuhe, the Shipwrecked Sailor and Odysseus. In scope, form and artistry, Wenamon and the Odyssey are, of course, poles apart; the one is in the pithy, prose tradition of Egyptian stories; the other is a long epic in hexameters. The one remains a minor composition; the other a masterpiece of world literature. But unfavourable comparisons serve no useful purpose. We should not lose sight of the fact that however humble, the Misadventures of Wenamon paved the way for Homer's Odyssey.

Among the remaining literary compositions of Egypt, we single out a twelfth-century manuscript that tells of the Contendings of Horus and Seth, for inheriting the divine kingship of Osiris. The story is quite vulgar and depicts the pantheon as behaving in a way that the modern man cannot square with divinity. But the modern student must not make the mistake of thinking that the ancient easterner had any difficulty in reconciling the notion of divinity with carryings on that included chicanery, bribery, indecent exposure for a laugh, and homosexual buffoonery. Crude foibles are attributed to the gods, not only in Egyptian, Babylonian, Ugaritic and Hittite texts, but even in Homeric epic.

Horus, the son of Osiris, is equated with the forces of good; Seth, brother of Osiris, is equated with the forces of evil. After all manner of contests, ordeals and legal bickering, Horus wins out to succeed Osiris in divine kingship. (Every historic Pharaoh claimed to be Horus incarnate.[1])

Some of the notions incorporated within the text are of interest. When letters are exchanged among the gods, Thoth is

---

[1] Except for a brief interlude during the Second Dynasty when the Pharaoh was identified with Seth.

regularly the scribe. Indeed, far from being ominiscient, the gods are as ignorant as mortals and are constantly being duped because of their ignorance. Moreover, the gods are illiterate except for the divine scribes, of whom we know only Thoth by name.

To get Seth to admit that Horus should inherit the office of his father, Isis appears as a pretty young woman to Seth, who becomes enamoured of her. She fabricates the story that her husband, a shepherd, had died and now a stranger wanted to defraud their son of the flocks. Seth replied: " Shall the flocks be given to the stranger, while the son of the father of the family is on hand?" Thereupon Isis transformed herself into a bird, flew up and perched herself on a tree and said to him: "Weep for yourself. It is your own mouth that has said it; your own authority that has judged you. What more do you want?" Thus Seth was tricked into defending the claim of his opponent Horus, the son of Osiris. This device of inventing a case to get a person to condemn himself is familiar from 2 Samuel 12: 7, where the Prophet Nathan puts David in a position where he can tell him: " Thou art the man " worthy of the death penalty that David had decreed for Nathan's fictitious character.

One of the odd incidents in the story is the offence that Isis gives to her son Horus, so that he cuts off her head and turns her into a headless flint statue. Scholars suspect that the incident is etiological—explaining a natural rock formation that resembled a headless woman. In any event, we are to compare the punishment of Lot's wife and perhaps Niobe: who were turned into mineral effigies.

The main theme of the Contendings of Horus and Seth (i.e., divine kingship) is a central motif in much early religious literature: the *Enuma Elish* of Babylonia, the Baal and Anath Cycle of Ugarit, the Hittite Kingship in Heaven myth and Hesiod's Theogony. Most important of all, of course, are the enthronement Psalms (e.g., 24: 7-10) of the Old Testament referring to

God's kingship. So basic was this theme that strict monotheism had to yield; for without other gods, Yahweh could not be king of the gods. Whence expressions like " Who is like thee among the gods, O Yahweh? " (Exodus 15: 11).

The international character of East Mediterranean culture is reflected by the intrusion of Canaanite gods into the Egyptian pantheon during the Empire Period. Astarte and Anath appear in the Contendings of Horus and Seth. Astarte and the Canaanite sea-god Yamm are the main figures in another Late Egyptian text, probably dating from the early part of the 19th Dynasty during the last years of the 14th century.

Contacts between Egypt and the rest of the East Mediterranean were so numerous and strong that the literary influence of the time-honoured Egyptian culture must have been powerful on the other ethnic groups in the area. Hebrew narrative prose style is heavily indebted to the Egyptian. In subject matter, we have noted tie-ins between Egypt, on the one hand, and Israel and Greece, on the other. The reason that the full contribution of Egypt to East Mediterranean literature is not yet realised, is the scholarly attitude. Once the nature of the problem is more widely appreciated, the rate of progress in evaluating Egypt's role will be stepped up.

V

Ugarit : Link between Canaan and the Aegean

Ugarit was discovered by the merest accident. The name of the site had long been known from the Amarna Letters, but its actual location on the map had remained a mystery until, in 1928, a Syrian peasant ploughed into a Mycenaean tomb. The authorities in the Department of Antiquities looked into the matter and a French expedition was soon at work on the mound that turned out to be Ugarit. In 1929, clay tablets in a new script were unearthed and published. In the following year, the Ugaritic script was deciphered by three scholars independently: H. Bauer, E. Dhorme and Ch. Virolleaud. It is to Virolleaud that we owe the publication and pioneer interpretation of nearly all the texts.

Ugarit is of unique importance for reconstructing the origins of Western Civilisation. The reason is reflected in the nature of the discovery that called attention to the site in 1928. A Mycenaean tomb in the vicinity of a Semitic port meant that the area was one in which the people of Canaan and the Aegean had commingled.[1] The archaeological finds at Ugarit brought this out quite clearly, and comparative archaeologists soon used those finds for studies of Mycenaean civilisation embracing Crete, the

---

[1] As of now, Ugarit is the closest link between Canaan and the Aegean. There is always the hope that still closer links will be found, especially on Cyprus or along the southern coast of Asia Minor. [Since the writing of this note, the hope has been fulfilled, on Crete. See the Postscript to Chapter vi.]

Peloponnesus and other parts of the Greek sphere. The late Miss H. L. Lorimer, in her notable book, *Homer and the Monuments* (London, 1950), went further: she drew heavily on the archaeological finds at Ugarit for illuminating problems arising from the text of Homer. However, she did not make a single reference to any of the Ugaritic texts, even though it seems obvious in retrospect that if the art of Ugarit is related to the text of Homer, the epics found at Ugarit ought to be still more directly related to the epics of Homer. The long delay in recognising this important fact was due to the circumstance that Semitists, and not Classicists, deciphered and interpreted the Ugaritic tablets. Those Semitists were admirably equipped for pointing out biblical parallels, but most of them were unconcerned about the Greek side of the problem.

The scribes of Ugarit required an educational system to train them from the bottom up. The simplest school texts found there are ABC tablets listing the letters of the local alphabet in their fixed, invariable order.[1] The Phoenician alphabet of twenty-two letters is derived from the longer Ugaritic ABC of thirty letters. Contrary to the strict alphabetic principle,[2] the last three letters of the Ugaritic ABC are appendages so that twenty-seven remain for our consideration. Five sounds in the repertoire of twenty-seven came to converge with other sounds because of soundshifts in standard Phoenician. The remarkable fact is that when those five sounds are eliminated, the remaining twenty-two letters appear at Ugarit in precisely the same order as they are still preserved in the Hebrew alphabet. The traditional order of the

---

[1] The texts are collected in my *Ugaritic Manual*, Rome, 1955. More recently discovered Ugaritic texts are being published by Ch. Virolleaud *Palais royal d'Ugarit* II (Paris, 1957) and V (in press).

[2] i.e., " one and only one symbol for each distinctive sound." We might add that the Phoenician or Hebrew alphabet reckons only with consonants. The Ugaritic alphabet, however, has three different aleph signs (*'a*, *'i*, *'u*) depending on which vowel follows the aleph.

Greek alphabet reflects its Phoenician origin. The Latin ABC is only a step further removed. Accordingly, whole blocks of letters (such as *j, k, l, m, n, o, p, q, r, s, t*) appear in the same fixed order in the Latin, Greek and Hebrew alphabets. When an extra letter appears in Ugaritic (as in *l, m, ḏ, n*) the order of the letters that survive into Hebrew is always the same (for the Ugaritic *ḏ* is one of the five letters rendered unnecessary by the soundshifts mentioned above).

It stands to reason that the community that provides us with the most primary form of the ABC so far discovered should be of exceptional importance for the study of the cultures associated with the development and use of the ABC in the East Mediterranean. Aegean influences contributed to the Ugaritic ABC. Then the Ugaritic ABC gave rise to the Phoenician-Hebrew ABC,[1] which in turn was borrowed by the Greeks. The centrality of Ugarit in the basic elements of East Mediterranean culture impresses itself on us again and again.[2]

Ugarit was a city in the hands of a West Semitic community. By water, it joined Western Asia to the Mediterranean. It lay between the Hittite Empire and Canaan. It had enclaves of Assyrians, Hurrians, Hittites, Egyptians, Aegean folk and other foreigners. The polyglot nature of the community is mirrored

---

[1] This statement is based on the fact that typologically the Ugaritic ABC is older than the Phoenician ABC. However, both forms of the alphabet were in use simultaneously during much of the second millennium B.C., and according to information that has reached me, letters of the Phoenician type (i.e., not cuneiform of the Ugaritic type) have been discovered on antiquities said to date from the 18th century B.C. If this is true, we need not be surprised if still earlier documents turn up in the Ugaritic script.

[2] In his unpublished doctoral dissertation at Brandeis University, Michael Astour makes the important observation that *Sapuselátōn* (recorded in Pausanias 2: 25: 10 as the earlier name of a place in the vicinity of Epidaurus) reflects Ugaritic *šapš+'ilat*—"Sun+goddess." In all other Semitic languages the Sun is *šam(a)š* with *m*; only in Ugaritic does the *p* appear. It is also worth noting that the Sun is a goddess at Ugarit; contrast Mesopotamia, etc., where the Sun is a male deity.

in the vocabulary texts, whereby the scribal students learned to translate Ugaritic words into Sumerian, Akkadian and Hurrian. The two main scripts were the Akkadian syllabary and the Ugaritic alphabet: both written in cuneiform with a stylus on clay. The normal language for business, law and diplomacy was Akkadian; the normal language for religion, literature and local administration was Ugaritic. Hurrian was also used not infrequently for rituals and incantations. A few tablets in Cypro-Minoan attest the intimate connections with Cyprus. Egyptian and Hittite hieroglyphs round out the repertoire of scripts found at Ugarit.

The Ugaritic tablets come from the Amarna and Ramesside Ages (ca. 14th-12th centuries B.C.) in which the traditions of both the Hebrew Patriarchs and the Trojan War are rooted. More than any other excavated site, Ugarit was the meeting place of Semite and Indo-European; a cosmopolitan city where a literature was produced reflecting the varied heritages of the component parts of the population. Ugaritic literature, therefore, anticipates basic aspects of the earliest Hebrew and Greek literatures, providing a historic backdrop for both, as we shall bring out later in this chapter.

The poetry of Ugarit is so close to Hebrew poetry that it has cleared up a mystery of long standing. It used to be thought that classical Hebrew was linguistically the creation of " primitive " Hebrew tribesmen, and that it was a sort of miracle for such tribesmen to produce a polished literature from the very start. It turns out that the Hebrews found in Canaan a highly polished literary medium, now attested by the Ugaritic myths and epics. The distinctive contribution of the Hebrews is the content of the Bible rather than the literary medium which they found waiting for them upon their advent in Canaan. In the Old Testament, the Hebrews never call their language " Hebrew " or " Israelite," but quite correctly " the language of Canaan."

For twenty years after the first discovery of the Ugaritic tablets, a vast number of biblical parallels were pointed out by many scholars in many lands. In comparison, the Greek parallels went virtually unnoticed. Meanwhile, I had been noting literary resemblances between Ugaritic and Greek epic. In the briefest way, I mentioned the relevance of Ugarit for the study of Homer, in a publication of 1941. World War II interrupted my studies, but the break enabled me to return to them in 1946 with a fresh outlook instead of depending on "authoritative" attitudes. In gathering the Homeric parallels to Ugaritic literature and collating them with the biblical parallels to Ugaritic literature, a striking fact impressed itself upon me: there was a notable overlap that could not be accidental. The two-way parallels unmistakably linked Homer and the Bible. The most important of these parallels had to do with the central theme of the Kret Epic. King Kret (named after the eponymous ancestor of the Cretans) had lost Hurrai, his only wife destined to bear him the children who would carry on his line. Accordingly, he mustered an army and marched to the land where she was being held, and recovered her so that the divine promise of predestined progeny could be fulfilled.

This theme is completely lacking in the older literatures of the ancient East, including the Gilgamesh Epic and the Middle Egyptian Romances. On the other hand, the Helen of Troy motif is central in Indo-European epic, both in Greece and India. I refer to the hero who must recover his destined wife from her abductors. The divine promise of progeny through the destined wife is central in early Hebrew literature from Abraham and Sarah on, though this too is alien to the older Near Eastern literatures, such as the Gilgamesh Epic or the Egyptian stories. Moreover, the biblical narratives[1] themselves assumed a new aspect because of the Ugaritic parallels. The destined bride of

[1] See Genesis 12: 15; 20: 2; 26: 8-10.

Abraham was twice wrested from him, once by the King of Egypt and once by the King of Philistine Gerar. (The latter king, or one of his subjects, also came close to wresting Rebecca from Isaac.) But the hero Abraham retrieved the destined mother of his royal line, both times. In other words, the Helen of Troy motif permeates the Patriarchal Narratives of Genesis, but no one noticed it because ingrained attitudes kept our Greek and Hebrew heritages in water-tight compartments. Ugarit, being new and not part of our traditional heritage, was able to bridge the gap between Homer and the Bible. We shall note more of these triple parallels (Ugaritic, Hebraic and Greek) in this and the following chapters.

I pointed out a group of Ugaritic and other Near East parallels to Greek epic in the *American Journal of Archaeology* 56, 1952, pp. 93-94. It had an immediate effect among classicists, one of whom wrote an article accepting twelve of my fifteen parallels. [1] I continued my investigations and published a number of articles, culminating in a detailed, but over-compact monograph called *Homer and Bible*.[2] Its results, including my thesis that the Kret Epic is an " Ur-Ilias " (as regards the Helen of Troy theme) in Semitic dress, were incorporated by T. B. L. Webster in his important book *From Mycenae to Homer*, London, 1958. Meanwhile, the Nestor of biblical scholars, Professor Otto Eissfeldt, in a review article of my *Introduction to Old Testament Times*, indicated his deep understanding of the subject and its significance for classical and biblical studies.[3]

As we have already observed, the whole subject of early Greco-Hebrew relations is touchy. While a galaxy of Classicists, Orientalists and Bible scholars have understood and elucidated

[1] F. Dirlmeier, "Homerisches Epos und Orient," *Rheinisches Museum für Philologie* 98, 1955, pp. 18-37.

[2] See the review of it by A. Lesky, *Gnomon* 29, 1957, pp. 321-325.

[3] O. Eissfeldt, " Recht und Grenze archäologischer Betrachtung des Alten Testaments," *Orientalistische Literaturzeitung* 49, 1954, pp. 101-8.

various aspects of the problem, the academic rank and file tend to shun this kind of topic. It would be overoptimistic to expect at this time a universal understanding of the role of Ugarit in linking early Greek and early Hebrew literature. The subject is not for those who have developed a mental block before they examine the evidence. Nor have we any right to demand that every student of antiquity be perceptive in the field of comparative culture.

Ugaritic literature is divisible into two main categories: epics about men and myths about gods. The myths have few, if any, human characters in them; but the epics, while dealing with mortals, portray the gods as dealing with the human *dramatis personae* and affecting their destiny as in all epic: Mesopotamian, Greek, Indic, Teutonic, etc., and in the heroic saga of Israel.

We start our survey of the Ugaritic texts with the epics, for it is they (rather than the myths) that link the oldest classical literatures of Israel and Greece. Both of the Ugaritic epics (known as the Epic of Kret, and the Legend of Aqhat) are of unusual interest for the backdrop of our oldest traditional literatures. Of the two, the Kret text holds first place because it is the earliest known example of the Helen of Troy motif, and, as such, is of prime importance for the background of the Iliad.

. The scribes of Ugarit called the text " Kret " after the hero: a king, whose very name shows Cretan affinities. He had betrothed his rightful wife by paying the dowry, but she departed. The word for " departed " is never used as a euphemism for " died." Nevertheless, until I pointed out the Helen of Troy theme in this text, *tbᶜt* " departed " was taken to mean that Kret's wife had died, and that the heroine of the Epic was, therefore, another woman. The element of romantic marriage whereby (no matter how polygamous the society, nor even the household of the hero himself) there is only one woman who counts in his life, is generally alien to the earlier literatures of the Near East. It comes in with the advent of the Indo-Europeans and appears at Ugarit and in the Bible (from Abraham to David) as well as in the Iliad.

Kret's loss of his destined bride confronted his royal line with the threat of extinction. So

> *He entered his chamber and wept*
>> *While repeating words, he shed tears.*
> *His tears were poured like shekels earthward*
>> *Like fifth-shekels on his couch.*
> *While weeping, he sighed*
>> *While shedding tears, there was moaning*
> *Sleep overcame him*
>> *And he lay down in a deep sleep*
>>> *And he was disturbed, and in his dream El descended*
>>>> *In his vision the Father of Man*
> *And he drew near while asking Kret:*
> ' *Who is Kret that he should weep?*
>> *Or shed tears, the Good One, Lad of El?*
> *Does he desire the kingdom of the Bull, his father,*
>> *Or sover[eignty like the Father of Ma]n?* '

Kret replies that he wants only his destined bride to bear him the progeny to carry on his line.

El then instructs Kret how to retrieve his bride. First he tells him how to be ceremonially fit and how to offer sacrifices and prayers that will win divine aid. Then El predicts how things will turn out once his army is prepared and marches to Udum (Edom) where the bride is being withheld by the local royal family. El instructs Kret to reject all her father's offers to buy him off and deflect him from his purpose, but to insist on getting the bride. (In typical epic style, the instructions and predictions are repeated virtually verbatim when Kret fulfills them. For this reason, it is possible to restore virtually all the broken words in either the first or second section.) El instructs Kret:

> *You shall wash and rouge yourself*
> *Wash your hands to the elbow*
> *From your fingers to the shoulder.*

Ritual washing is all but universal, but painting oneself for ritual fitness is not so well known. The colour for males is red over a vast geographical area, as we shall note in a later chapter. El goes on to tell Kret:

> *Enter into the shade of a tent*
> *Take a lamb in your hand*
> *A lamb of sacrifice in your right hand*
> *A lambkin in both hands.*

El further instructs Kret concerning offerings of bread and of a bird, and proceeds to the following libations and other rituals:

> *Pour from a cup of silver, wine;*
> *From a cup of gold, honey.*
> *Go up to the top of the tower;*
> *Ride on the shoulders of the wall.*
> *Lift your hands heavenward;*
> *Sacrifice to the Bull, your father, El;*
> *Win over Baal with your sacrifice,*
> *Dagon's son, with your offerings.*

The details of the above passage are of interest. Hebrew law makes a point of forbidding burnt offerings with honey.[1] The Ugaritic passage suggests that the Hebrew prohibition was in opposition to native cultic usage. The Kret text continues:

[1] Leviticus 2: 11.

Then Kret shall go down from the roof
To prepare food for the city,
Wheat for the community.
He shall bake bread of the fifth,
Even hardtack of the sixth month
Until (the host) is supplied.
Then the army shall go out
My supplied army.

The emphasis on the quartermaster's task, within a religious framework, is matched in Exodus. In both accounts the baking of a bread supply on the eve of a great military movement is considered worthy of saga and finds a place in the epic repertoire. The Jewish custom of eating unleavened bread to celebrate the Exodus is based on the Hebrew text. The Ugaritic passage helps us set this feature of the Passover narrative in its wider international framework.

Kret is to muster an army of " three hundred myriads ": three million men who will cover the steppe like locusts. El orders Kret to march with this mighty host:

Go a day and a second
A third, a fourth day
A fifth, a sixth day.
Behold, at sunrise on the seventh
You will reach Udum the Great
And Udum the Small.

Six days of activity climaxed by a specially significant seventh day is familiar from the Creation Account in Genesis, and is repeated often in the cuneiform literatures, Homer and the Bible. The reference to Udum the Great and Udum the Small is paralleled by the reference to Hubur the Great and Hubur the Small.[1]

[1] Hubur is the name of Kret's city.

Sennacherib similarly tells us that he captured Great Sidon and Small Sidon. The " Great " city was the metropolitan area, while the Small city was the citadel or fortified temple-palace area. Since the Small city was the best defended and contained the most sacred area as well as the treasures, it was regarded as the more important.

The relation of the small to the large city varies at different sites. In the case of the Phoenician coastal cities, the small city is the offshore island, while the great city is the metropolitan area on the mainland (so Tyre and Sidon). Elsewhere the small city is often the acropolis located in the midst of the metropolitan area. In some cases (like Hazor and Carchemish), the small city is near the edge of, but within, the walled great city. In the Ugaritic texts, the small city appears as the second, or climactic, element. Since, as we have noted, the small city contained the most important structures, treasures and defences, we can understand why the great city is less important than the small.

Udum is a city whose name is connected with Edom. If Kret's home city of Hubur is in the vicinity of Ugarit, the general vicinity of Edom fits the requirements of the Kret Epic quite well, because the Phoenician cities of Sidon and Tyre are situated midway as we shall see. Moreover, the Philistine Pentapolis is called the habitation of Kret in Zephaniah 2: 6 and the Wady Krit in 1 Kings 17: 3 may also attest the fame of Kret in Palestine.[1] In other words, just as the Ugaritic Legend of Daniel and Aqhat provides the story of Daniel in Ezekiel 14: 14, the Ugaritic Epic of Kret provides the story of Kret (var. Krit) in Zephaniah (and 1 Kings 17: 3, 5).

A problem arises concerning the apparent lack of a mound to

[1] Points like this must be examined in the original Hebrew; translations obscure the issue. Krit appears as " Cherith " in English; while Kret in Zephaniah 2: 6 is generally mistranslated as a common noun. The ancient Hebrew text of Zephaniah 2: 6 has only the consonants KRT, which were later supplied with vowels as if those consonants were a Semitic root.

mark the site of a notable city such as we may assume Udum to have been. In the first place, we must admit that since still more famous cities (such as Akkad) have not yet been identified, this one may await discovery, too. But I would suggest still another possible explanation. The Minoan tradition of city planning did not reckon with city walls. Knossos, Phaistos, Mallia and the other Minoan towns are unwalled. Now it might be argued that islanders relied on the sea for protection, but I think this approach is unrealistic. Crete itself was fragmentised into various political entities that might be mutually hostile in various sectors at various times. Without concerning ourselves with origins, we know that Minoan cities were unwalled. It is human to persist in tradition long after the tradition has become obsolete. For example, Spartan institutions were close to those of Crete, and nowhere is this more striking than in the absence of a wall around Sparta. The Greek mainland consisted of city states hostile to, and often warring with each other. Yet Sparta continued to go on without a wall.

Scholars have generally concluded that the absence of walls around the Minoan cities indicates a peaceful way of life. I question this. The Spartans were so warlike that they counted on their men to defend the city; their soldiers were their " wall." The Philistines from Caphtor, akin to the Cherethites[1] of Crete, were also warlike. I suggest therefore that the same tradition of an unwalled Udum may account for the absence of a mound to mark the site.[2] That the Negev was capable of supporting numerous communities is clear from fairly numerous remains of the Byzantine period in the area.

To go on with the narrative of the Kret text: Kret and his

[1] " Cherethites " is the English Bible form of *Krētîm*, as " Cretans " are called in Hebrew.

[2] Without a wall to retain the debris, an ancient ruin will not result in a mound. I have given the basic facts of " dirt archaeology " in the opening chapters of *Adventures in the Nearest East*, Phoenix House, London, 1957.

army were to occupy the land around Udum, apparently while King Pebel would sleep for an entire week.[1] But on the seventh day, Pebel would wake up on hearing the neighing of his steed, the braying of his ass and the barking of his dog. The repertoire of the domestic animals is not without interest. The ass had been the riding animal from remote antiquity in the Near East. Among the Semites, it had not yet been rivalled by the horse. However, the Indo-Europeans had already introduced and used the horse to draw the war chariot. If we contrast the Patriarchal Narratives with the Epic of Kret, we note in the latter (but not in the former) the horse.[2] Even more striking is the dog in the household of Pebel (and, as we shall see, of Kret, too). All through the Old Testament, the dog is a detested animal, not to be admitted to the home. The dog has retained this wretched status down to the present among the Arab nomads and peasants. The favoured position of the dog in Ugarit—placing him in the palaces of kings—connects the Epic of Kret with the Mycenaean world as reflected in Homeric Epic, depicting the dog in the palaces of Priam and Odysseus.

Pebel (as predicted by divine revelation) would send a delegation of two emissaries to offer gifts to Kret on condition that he go home and relinquish his claim on his destined bride, Hurrai:

[1] Cf. Gilgamesh's sleeping for a week. It is interesting to compare Jonah (1: 5-6) who went to sleep on the ship while all the crew were desperately trying to avert shipwreck. Jonah, like Pebel, slept during a noisy crisis that would have kept any normal person awake.

[2] This statement is in accordance with the traditional vocalisation of the Hebrew text. However, the Greek translation of Genesis 14: 11, 16, 21 (dealing with Abraham's warfare) thrice takes the Hebrew word RKŠ not as *rᵉkûš* " property " but as *tèn híppon*=*rékeš* " horses, chariotry," bringing the milieu of the Patriarchal Age closer to that of the Ugaritic epics, wherein the riding animal is the donkey, but the horse was used in battle. I am tentatively inclined to take the Septuagint as correct because it twice takes RKŠ as " property " (Genesis 14: 12, 16) carefully distinguishing the property of Lot from the (chariot) horses of the kings.

The message of King Pebel:
' *Take silver and yellow gold,*
   A portion of her estate and perpetual slaves,
      Three horses (and) a chariot from the yard of a handmaid's son
Take everything, O Kret!
And depart, O king, from my house;
   Be distant, Kret, from my court!
Do not besiege Great Udum and Small Udum.
Udum is a gift of El;
   It's a present of the Father of Man.'

But Kret was to refuse these terms and insist on getting back the girl, saying:

What need have I of silver and yellow gold,
   A portion of her estate and perpetual slaves,
      Three horses (and) a chariot from the yard of a handmaid's son?
You must yield what is not in my house.
Give me the Lass Hurrai
Fairest of the harem[1] of your firstborn,
Whose beauty is like Anath's beauty,
   Whose loveliness is like Astarte's loveliness,
Whose brows are lapis lazuli,
   Whose eyes are bowls of marble.

. . . .

For El has granted in my dream—
   In my vision, the Father of Man—
A boy born of woman to Kret,
   E'en a lad to the Servant of El.

Kret woke up upon the completion of the divine message. There was no doubt as to its meaning and authenticity:

[1]Or "family."

> *Kret awoke; 'twas a dream.*
> *El's servant; 'twas a theophany.*

On awakening, Kret did as the god had directed him and began the march towards Udum at the head of his mighty host. On the third day

> *He arrived at the shrine of Asherah of the Tyrians,*
> *Even of the Goddess of the Sidonians.*
> *There Kret of Tha^c made a vow:*
> *' By the life of Asherah of the Tyrians,*
> *Yea of the Goddess of the Sidonians!*
> *If I may take Hurrai to my house,*
> *Yea cause the girl to enter my court,*
> *I shall give twice her price in silver,*
> *Even thrice her price in gold.'*

This vow, as we shall see, was followed by the success of the mission; but Kret apparently failed to fulfil his promise to the Goddess, bringing sorrow on himself and his realm.

Kret then proceeded from Phoenicia to Udum, arriving at Udum after four more days' march. The itinerary suggests that south Phoenicia (where Tyre and Sidon are located) lies about midway between Kret's city and Udum.

At Udum everything happened as predicted. Pebel tried to buy Kret off, but Kret was not to be deflected from his resolve, and he insisted on getting the fair Hurrai as his bride.

At this point we may recapitulate how the Epic of Kret illuminates the very core of our literary heritage from both Israel and Greece. Kret's recovery of his abducted bride is related to the Helen of Troy motif appearing in the Iliad. Helen's story is so famous that we are all too apt to assume it is universal. Actually it reflects a striking innovation brought in by the Indo-Europeans to the Near East. The older literatures, such as the Gilgamesh

Epic and the Middle Egyptian novelettes, show absolutely no interest in romantic love or the theme of the destined bride. Sex, to be sure, plays a role, but devotion to an individual heroine is totally lacking. The Helen of Troy motif is an integral part of the royal epic in the Amarna/Mycenaean sphere. In one form or another, it had to appear in virtually any royal epic of the Age. This embraces the Patriarchal Narratives as well as Greek and Ugaritic epic. Genesis makes it perfectly clear that Abraham is a king, somewhat in the manner of the Mycenaean kings. He is called a king,[1] and the divine promise to him assures that the royal line will issue from him. The Septuagint and New Testament,[2] as well as Rabbinic literature,[3] never lost sight of the royal status of the Patriarchs. But for reasons that seem perverse in retrospect, the Genesis narratives have, in the mainstream of postbiblical Jewish and Christian tradition, been detached from world literature so that the secular and literary and historical aspects of the Patriarchal Narratives became obscured. The abductions of Sarah and Helen were not previously compared because the scholars who knew both Greek and Hebrew literatures kept the sacred Hebrew text sealed off from the profane Greek text. The facts of history do not warrant any such barrier, however. Ugarit, where Mycenaean and Canaanite influences met, makes it perfectly clear that no such gulf separates Homer from Bible. The rewinning of Helen, Sarah and Hurrai are three reflexes of one and the same cultural impulse.

The rest of the Epic of Kret, in so far as it has survived, is

---

[1] The Septuagint calls Abraham a king in Genesis 23: 6.

[2] Which derives Jesus, the last "King of the Jews," from Abraham, the first "King of the Jews," in the opening chapter of Matthew. The purpose of the genealogy is hardly to establish the Jewishness of Jesus which was never challenged, but rather his kingship which was questioned.

[3] e.g., Job (who according to Midrash was Esau's grandson and Dinah's husband) is repeatedly called a king, and possesses a throne (L. Ginzberg, *Legends of the Jews* II, 1910, pp. 225, 231, 237).

written on tablets whose arrangement is not certain. I am inclined to start with text #128 dealing with the marriage of Kret
and Hurrai. Whether it is the original marriage that took place
prior to the events in the main tablet that we have just discussed,
or the remarriage after Kret brought Hurrai home from Udum, is
debatable. But the marriage is noteworthy in any case because of
the circumstances that attend it. El, the head of the pantheon,
came to the wedding and blessed it. Since King Kret passed for
El's son, it was only fitting that El should attend, even as the gods
of Olympus attended the marriage of Peleus with the goddess
Thetis. Text #128 represents Baal inducing El to bless the royal
couple:

> *And Aliyan Baal declared:*
> *' (Before you) depart, O Latpan,[1] god of mercy,*
> *Will you not bless Kret of Thaᶜ*
>   *Nor beatify the Good One, lad of El? '*
> *El takes a cup in his hand,*
>   *A bowl in his right hand*
> *And verily El blesses [   ];*
>   *El blesses Kret [of Thaᶜ,*
>   *Even blesses] the Good One, lad of El:*
> *' The woman you take, O Kret,*
>   *The woman you take to your house,*
>   *The lass you make enter your court*
> *Will bear you seven sons*
>   *And an eighth daughter, Octavia.*
> *To you she will bear the lad Yassib,*
> *Who will suck the milk of Asherah,*
>   *Yea suckle the breasts of the Virgin [Anath],*
>   *The wetnurses [of the Good and Gracious Gods].'*

The divine blessing over a cup of wine permeates the religious

---

[1] Latpan is the same as El.

thinking of the ancient Near East. In fact, it is typical of the seal cylinders of the Third Dynasty of Ur, which frequently depict a seated deity so blessing a standing devotee, in what is usually called a " presentation scene" but might better be termed a " benediction." The purpose of marriage throughout antiquity was procreation, specifically the providing of a son and heir. This was particularly important in royal circles because of the succession to the throne. The ancients believed that in addition to the biological requirements, divine blessing was necessary for progeny. The emphasis on divinely promised progeny permeates the royal epic of Ugarit and Israel. It appears in both of the royal Ugaritic epics, and it pervades early Hebrew saga, starting with the divinely promised Isaac.

The birth of seven sons to a hero is a recurrent theme. In the Gilgamesh Epic, it is stated that the *post mortem* welfare of a man who has left seven sons behind him to look after his interests is the best available in the Underworld. Accordingly, among Job's abundant blessings are seven sons. Jesse's seven[1] (or climactically eight[2]) sons may be tinged with this motif, too. Alongside the sons, there is named the heroic daughter, Octavia, a younger child, who despite her youth and sex, is destined for a leading role, eclipsing her older brothers. In a Patriarchal society, in which the oldest son should become the leader, it is all the more worthy of saga to highlight the success of the young and of the girls. Job's (like Baal's) sons are nameless; but Job's (and Baal's) three glamorous daughters are named in the tradition. Canaanite epic glories in telling about interesting women, especially those who eclipse their male associates. In Judges 4 and 5, Deborah and Jael surpass Barak and all their other male contemporaries. This attitude may possibly explain the prominence given in Greek epic to the Amazons, the peers of men in battle.

The fact that the crown prince, Yassib, is to be suckled by the

[1] I Chronicles 2: 13-15.   [2] I Samuel 16: 10-11.

145

goddesses, fits in with the widespread doctrine of divinely nurtured kings. The Pharaohs are often depicted as the young Horus sucking the breasts of Isis. At Ugarit there is an ivory panel on the royal bedstead, depicting the young princes sucking the breasts of a goddess. The same fiction is attested also in Mesopotamia; and perhaps once in the Old Testament.[1] In Homer, kings are often called " divinely nurtured," perhaps referring to their having achieved divine kingship through sucking the milk of a goddess.[2]

After a break in text #128, there is a fragmentary account of the sons and daughters to be borne by Hurrai. It is noteworthy that the youngest (who is a daughter) is divinely destined to be elevated to the status of firstborn.[3] It is interesting to compare the genealogies of ancient Israel which confront us with another girl who was elevated over her brothers to become " sororarch,"[4] if we may coin such a feminine counterpart of " fratriarch."

Text 128 then relates that the gods who blessed the marriage and predicted the progeny that would ensue, went home:

> *The gods bless and go;*
> *The gods go to their tents,*
> *The generation of El to their tabernacles.*
> *And she comes to term and bears him one son,*
> *And she comes to term and bears him two sons.*

---

[1] Isaiah 60: 16.

[2] Though it is also conceivable that they had been fed ambrosia by the gods.

[3] For the elevation of a younger child to the position of fratriarch over the firstborn, see 1 Chronicles 26: 10.

[4] A man's sororarch is called "his ruling sister" in 1 Chronicles 7: 18. The Hebrew ('*ăḥôtô ham-môléket*) is clear. None of the translations reflect the plain meaning of the original because the social institution is not generally understood.

> *Behold in seven years*
> *The sons of Kret were as she (Asherah) had promised,*
> *Also the daughters of Hurrai were, too.*
> *So Asherah remembered his vow,*
> *Yea the Goddess, [his promise].*
> *And she lifted her voice and shouted:*
> *'Look, now!*
> *Since Kret has changed his vow*
> *I shall break [mine, too].'*

Failure to fulfil his vow to the deity could only bring retribution upon Kret. It is characteristic of all branches of ancient literature that there are no happy success stories without suffering. The virtuous have their lapses; the great have their downs as well as ups; and even the laws of nature have their exceptions. It is this flight from the ordinary that makes the content of the literature " worthy of saga." Kret, the son of El, is a model hero and loved by the gods; yet he brings misery on himself by a conspicuous breach of character. The same can be said of Achilles and Moses, *for the same reason.*

At this point, there is a break in the text and what follows is a feast prepared on Kret's orders by Hurrai. It is part of the epic repertoire to specify that the hero bids his wife to make the repast. Just as Kret is described as ordering Hurrai to prepare the feast, so too Abraham orders Sarah, and Menelaus orders Helen to do so. The fact that a man may tell his wife to make dinner for guests is wellnigh universal, and in any case banal. What interests us here is that this feature forms part of the epic repertoire. Mediterranean literary usage highlighted it; contrast modern literary usage which has little or no place for it in traditional poetry or in prose belles-lettres.

> *Aloud he calls to his wife:*
> *'Hear, O Lady Hurrai!*

Cook the sleekest of thy fatlings;
  Open a flagon of wine;
Invite my seventy bulls
  My eighty stags
Even the bulls of Great Hubur and Little Hubur.'

While it is always possible that the text is to be taken literally (fantastic as the animal guests seem to us), it is likely that the animals are simply honorific titles for the grandees of Kret's realm. Compare the Pharaonic title *kꜣ nḫt* "mighty bull." Amos 4: 1 refers to the ladies of Bashan as the "kine of Bashan"; and David refers to Saul or Jonathan as a stag (2 Samuel 1: 19). Homer, too, refers to a swift warrior as a stag.[1] The strength of the bull and the fleetness of the deer makes the animal epithets quite appropriate. Note, too, that the feast is built around meat and wine, quite as in the Homeric tradition. Fruits and vegetables (however much they were eaten in daily life) play no role at the festive board.

The epic calls for many standard types of repetition. In this case, the fulfilment of Kret's command by Hurrai is described in the same words, with the single change of the imperatives to three feminine singular forms of the narrative present:

Lady Hurrai hearkens
  She cooks the sleekest of her fatlings;
    She opens a flagon of wine.

Such repetition characterises Ugaritic, Greek and Mesopotamian epic. It occurs in Hebrew, but is sharply reduced in keeping with the Hebraic tendency towards conciseness: a feature which Hebrew shares with Egyptian.

The text goes on to tell how Hurrai welcomes the guests:

[1] "Homer and Bible," pp. 104-5, #171.

148

> *She brings his bulls into his presence;*
>   *His stags she brings into his presence—*
> *The bulls of Great Hubur (and) Little Hubur.*
> *They come into the house of Kret.*

The guests are seated and Hurrai does the honours:

> *She stretches her hand into the cauldron;*
>   *She sticks the knife into the meat,*
> *And Lady Hurrai declares:*
> *' I have invited you to eat, to drink;*
>   *Kret your lord has a feast.'*

The fragmentary sequel tells of weeping at the feast, doubtless because Kret has been stricken by the offended Asherah.

Text 125 tells of the unhappy household, cringing like dogs in the palace of the gravely ill Kret. The threat of death made Prince Ilhu, a son of Kret, wonder about Kret's divine status:

> *In thy life, O our father, we'd rejoice;*
>   *In thine immortality, we'd be glad.*
>
> . . . .
>
> *How can it be said that Kret is El's son,*
>   *The scion of Latpan-and-Holiness?*
> *Or can gods die?*
>   *The scion of Latpan not live?*

This question must arise in any society that accords divine status to mortals. A close counterpart can be found in the Iliad where Zeus allows his own son, the mortal Sarpedon, to perish like other men.

Kret counselled his son to refrain from grief and to summon his sister Octavia, who apparently had the power to help Kret surmount his crisis:

149

And Kret of Tha^c declared:
' My son, do not weep for me—
  Do not mourn for me.
Exhaust not, my son, the well of your eye,
  Nor the brain of your head with tears.
Summon your sister Octavia.

. . . .

She will weep and mourn for me.

. . . .

Tell your sister Octavia:
" Kretan has sacrificed a sacrifice
  The King has poured a libation ".'

The sacrifice is the same as a feast. In fact, all meals where a beast was slaughtered for food were both feasts and sacrifices simultaneously. Gods and mortals each received their share of the common feast. This was not a fiction confined to poetry, but an accepted idea in real life. The sympathy and aid of Octavia were evidently regarded as capable of effecting Kret's cure. In text 128, Hurrai was seen in a similar role. Since doublettes are a built-in feature of the tradition, both feasts, each graced by a heroine, are part of the basic story. One feast marks the approach of Kret's fall; the other precedes his restoration. The variant of Kret's name, " Kretan," is interesting because the suffix -*ân* is usually added to the stem " Kret " in the Hagia Triada tablets. The addition of -*ân* to other names that also occur without the suffix is known in both Ugaritic and Hebrew.

Ilhu goes to Octavia, summoning her to the sacrifice. She asks how long Kret has been sick, and her brother Ilhu replies:

> It's three months that he has been ill
> Yea four that Kret has been sick.

The rest of tablet #125 is partly fragmentary and partly repeats the content of the beginning of the tablet. Tablet #126 relates that the rain of Baal had been withheld so long that

> The bread was spent from their jars,
> The wine was spent from their bottles,
> The oil was spent from [their containers].

Famine has struck the land because of the King's sin, exactly as David's realm was punished for his sin. Homer relates that the well-being and abundance of a land depends on the conduct of its sovereign.[1]

The cure of Kret became the concern of gods as well as men, and the pantheon, headed by Latpan (=El) himself, enter the scene. The help of certain lesser deities is required for their specialised services. Among these deities is Ilshu, the carpenter of Baal's house, and Ilshu's wife, the carpentress of the goddesses.

> And Latpan, god of mercy, declares:
> ' Hear, O carpenter of the god, Ilshu,
>   Even Ilshu the carpenter of Baal's house
>   And your wife, the carpentress of the goddesses
> . . . . '

The fragmentary state of the text prevents us from knowing all the details in the story of Kret's cure, but col. v of tablet #126 makes it clear that El recites an incantation inviting any god to exorcise the demon of disease from Kret's tormented body. On finding that no god volunteers to perform the exorcism, El himself agrees to do the job, apparently by invoking the spell that

[1] See "Homer and Bible," p. 65, #43.

had in the cosmic past been used to quell Tannin, the primordial
monster of evil:

> And Latpan, [god of mercy, declares:
> ' Who] among the gods [will cast out the disease]
> By exorcising the de[mon?'
> None among the gods] answers him.
> He declares a [second and third time]:
> ' Who among the [gods will cast out] the disease
>   By exorcising [the demon]?'
> None among the gods ans[wers him].
> He declares [a fourth] and fifth time:
> '[Who among the gods] will cast out the disease
>   By exo[rcising the demon]?'
> None among the gods answers him.
> He declares a sixth and seventh time:
> '[Who] among the gods will cast out the disease
>   Exorcising the demon?'
> None among the gods answers him.
> So Latpan, god of mercy, states:
> ' Sit, O my sons, on your seats
>   Yea on the thrones of your lordships.
> I myself will perform the magic
>   I shall indeed stay the hand of the disease
>   Exorcising the demon.'

The text goes on to tell how an effigy was shaped from mud and
the spell of Tannin proclaimed. Magic makes use of these two
elements: the physical act and the verbal spell. We cannot re-
construct all the details of the magical procedure in this text. But
we can safely say that the effigy represented the demon afflicting
Kret and that the spell that had of old subdued Tannin terrified
the demon into fleeing from the body of King Kret so that the
latter was restored to health.

Text #127 tells how a female agent called "Remover" attended Kret as he returned to health. After washing him

> *She opened his appetite to eat,*
> *His desire to dine.*

The word for appetite is "soul" (*napš-*), which we translate "appetite" because of the requirements of the context. The same word for "soul" is used in the sense of "appetite" in Hebrew. Egyptian, Hebrew, Ugaritic and other Near East languages have several words for various aspects of "soul." The Egyptians speak of the *ba, ka, sekhem* and still other souls. The Hebrews speak of *néfeš, rûᵃḥ, nᵉšāmāh* and still other souls. At Ugarit, we find *brlt* beside the more familiar *napš-* and *rûḥ-*. Accordingly, when we read in the *De Anima* of Aristotle of the four souls, including the appetitive soul, we are dealing not with a creation of Greek philosophy but rather with the Aristotelian development of a basic East Mediterranean concept whose intricacy is already attested in the Pyramid Texts of the third millennium.

After "Remover" has banished the prospect of Kret's death and restored his appetite for food, Kret

> *Lifted his voice and shouted:*
> *' Hear, O Lady Hurrai!*
> *Cook a sheep that I may eat,*
> *A lamb that I may dine!'*
> *Lady Hurrai hearkens.*
> *She cooks a sheep so that he eats,*
> *A lamb that he dines.*
> *Behold a day and a second,*
> *Kret returns to his court;*
> *He sits on the throne of kingship*
> *On the dais, on the seat of sovereignty.*

It is part of the epic repertoire to feature the rebelliousness of the Crown Prince against the heroic king. There is no ground for questioning the historicity of Absalom's rebellion against David; but the emphasis given to it in the Scriptural account doubtless stems from the traditional treatment of royal epic. In the epic of Kret, his son, the Crown Prince Yassib, is impelled by his inward parts (much as the spirit within one's shaggy breast impelled many a Homeric hero) to challenge his father's kingship and request Kret to yield the throne to him instead:

> *The lad Yassib departs,*
>   *Into his father's presence he enters.*
> *He lifts his voice and shouts:*
> *' Hear now, O Kret of Thaᵉ*
>   *Listen and let thine ear be attentive.*
> *Are you ruling* effectively
>   *Or governing* fittingly ?
> *You have let your hands fall into negligence;*
>   *You have not judged the case of the widow*
>   *Nor adjudicated the cause of the broken in spirit.*

. . . .

> *In front of you, you do not feed the orphan*
>   *Nor in back of you, the widow.*
> *Since you are a brother of the sickbed,*
>   *Yea a companion of the couch of disease,*
> *Get down from the throne that I may rule—*
>   *From your sovereignty that I may sit thereon.*

The virtue of kings was measured by their effectiveness in rescuing the weak from the strong. Widows and fatherless children were especially vulnerable in ancient societies. Accordingly, the protection of these two categories of unfortunates was the test of a king's beneficence.

Whether Yassib did not know that his father had been cured and restored to fitness for kingship, is not clear from the text. In any event, Kret heaps a mighty curse on his son for making so presumptuous a request:

> *O my son, may Horon break—*
> *May Horon break your head—*
> *Astarte-name-of-Baal, your pate!*

We have only part of the Epic of Kret but that is enough for delineating its significance. It gives us the story of a personage known only by name in the Bible. It provides the background we need for seeing in the Patriarchal Narratives a royal epic, of a specific type calling for progeny secured through divine help from the destined wife who must be retrieved from her royal captors. More than any other known text, it bridges the gap between Homer and the Bible most strikingly in the Helen of of Troy motif, but also in countless details. No future first-hand account of world literature can afford to neglect the Epic of Kret as a landmark supplying the backdrop of Hebrew and Greek classics in the East Mediterranean of Amarna-Mycenaean times.

The other legendary epic, in which mortals are portrayed (albeit in direct contact with the gods, much as in Homer and the Bible) is called the " Aqhat " text in Ugaritic. It concerns a virtuous royal father named Daniel mentioned in Ezekiel 14 as a righteous man of old, who like Noah and Job, survived a great catastrophe together with his progeny. Scholars were quick to recognise that this Daniel has nothing to do with the hero of the Book of Daniel, but with a remote figure in Canaanite lore. The name Daniel is appropriate for a superman, exemplary in justice; for *dan* means " to judge "; and *el*, " a god." The Ugaritic text portrays him dispensing justice, defending the widow and fatherless in the gate. Aqhat may well be the Ugaritic form of the same name that appears in Hebrew as Q^ehāt (English " Kohath," son of Levi).

Daniel had a wife, Danatai, and a model daughter, Pughat. The name of the latter is borne by one of the two heroic mid-wives in Exodus 1: 15. The Hebrew form is anglicised as " Puah." The use of names is significant because as a culture changes, its repertoire of personal names changes. It is only in pre-monarchic Israel that we find several of the Ugaritic names, including Abram, Israel, Moses, Kohath, Puah,[1] etc.; these names are not borne by subsequent Old Testament people, though some of them came back into use during post-Old Testament periods of revival.

Daniel longed for a son to discharge the filial duties for him in this world and in the afterlife. The Ugaritic emphasis on securing through divine aid a long awaited son belongs to the same Canaanite tradition as the Old Testament stories leading up to the birth of Isaac, Joseph, Samuel, etc. Lest the reader imagine that concern with the birth of a son be universal in literature, he should reflect on the fact that *every* Old Testament example is before the monarchy. That it remained a factor in real life is beside the point. We are concerned rather with the standard of what was worthy of saga. Preoccupation with the birth of a son is part of the repertoire of what was worth recording down through the period of the Judges and Samuel, but not there-after.

Our tablets begin with Daniel regaling the gods with food and drink at a shrine where he resorted to incubation in order to get a revelation assuring him of the birth of a model son. The use of incubation is familiar to us also from Kret's and Abraham's obtaining a divine promise of offspring. Daniel went through

[1] Spelled *abrm, yšril, mt, aqht* and *pǵt* in Ugaritic; though *abrm* could also correspond to biblical " Abiram."

the rituals for a week, and on the seventh day, Baal (as also in the Kret Epic) took favourable notice of him with a view to fulfilling his desire for a son. Baal took pity on Daniel

> *Who has no son like his brethren*
> *Nor a root like his companions*

and urged the gods who were being wined and dined by Daniel to

> *Bless him to the Bull, God, my Father,*
> *Strengthen him to the Creator of Creatures*
> *So that his son may be in the house*
> *A root in the midst of his palace.*

In other words, Baal gets the gods to intercede with El (the head of the pantheon) on Daniel's behalf. " Bull " is the epithet of El even as Yahweh has animal epithets, including *'ābîr* of Jacob (Genesis 49: 24; Isaiah 49: 26; 60: 16; Psalm 132: 2, 5) or of Israel (Isaiah 1: 24). God was worshipped as the golden calf in the wilderness, and we further compare the cultic bull calves at the Yahwistic shrines at Bethel and Dan.

The son was to have a number of specified virtues. He was to see that his father received full attention religiously to assure him an optimum afterlife. Thus the son was to erect a memorial stela to him in the shrine and offer incense to gratify his soul. In this world, the son was to steady his father when the latter was in his cups

> *Holding his hand in drunkenness*
> *Carrying him when sated with wine.*

There was no temperance movement in the heroic age. Canaanite heroes ate and drank copiously, even as their Homeric (or later Viking) counterparts. This Ugaritic passage is one of many that have opened the eyes of modern scholars to the plain meaning of long misunderstood biblical texts. Thus this passage shows that the plain meaning of Isaiah 51: 17-18 implies that the Hebrews too considered it a comfort of parenthood to have sons to steady the drunk parent, even if the latter be the mother.

The model son was to render still other service, like keeping the father's house in repair and cleansing the father's blood-stained clothes after battle:

> *Plastering his roof on the day of mud*
> *Washing his clothes on the day of wounds.*

It may be noted that the rain not only showed whether the roof leaked and needed repair, but the mud after the rain provided the material for plastering the roof.

After divine assurance of the birth of a model son, Daniel impregnated his wife, and it was only a matter of time for the son to be born. On receiving the assurance, Daniel

> *Cracks a smile and laughs*
> *Sets his feet on the footstool*
> *Raises his voice and shouts:*
> *' Let me sit and rest*
> *So that my soul may repose in my breast*
> *For a son will be born to me like my brethren*
> *Yea a root like my companions.'*

After giving expression to his satisfaction on the promised birth of the model son,

> *Daniel reaches his house*
> *Daniel gets to his palace*
> *The Kosharot enter his house*
> *Yea, the swallows, the daughters of shouting.*

The Kosharot are songstresses, comparable with the Greek Muses. In Ugaritic, they attend joyous celebrations, gladdening them with song. They are mentioned in Psalm 68: 6, where the text should be translated "(God) brings out prisoners with the Kosharot," meaning that when God rescues the unfortunate, he frees them not into a cold, unfriendly world, but into one of joyous song. Like many biblical passages, this one was not understood until the discovery of Ugaritic literature.

Daniel slaughters an ox and proceeds to wine and dine the Kosharot for a week. After seven days, the Kosharot depart. The fragmentary text tells of the couch and the passing of months.

After the son, Aqhat, is born, the god of craftsmanship brings a wondrous bow as a gift for Aqhat, who is destined to become a mighty hero, successful in the chase. The god arrives with the bow as Daniel, who is a ruler, dispenses judgment in the city gate:

> He sits in the enclosure of the gate
> At the feet of the nobles who are on the threshing-floor.
> He judges the case of the widow
> Adjudicates the cause of the fatherless.
> On lifting his eyes, he sees
> By the thousand acres
> Myriad of hectares;
> He espies the going of Kothar,
> Espies the course of Hasis.
> Behold he brings a bow;
> Lo he fetches an arc.
> Thereupon Daniel, man of Rapa—
> Straightway the Hero, man of Hrnmy—
> Shouts aloud to his wife:
> ' Hear, Lady Danatai!
> Prepare a sheep from the flock
> For the soul of Kothar-and-Hasis
> For the appetite of the Skilled of Handicraft.
> Give the gods food and drink;

> *Serve and honour them: the lords of Ḥkpt*
> *The gods of all thereof.'*

Like so many divine names, Kothar-and-Hasis are two originally different names fused into practically one. Kothar and Hasis can never part ways, going simultaneously to different places or doing different things simultaneously. Such double names shed light on " Yahweh-Elohim " (made by fusing the name of the particular God " Yahweh " with the general name for Deity " Elohim ") and shows that the combination has nothing to do with the blending of literary sources.

Daniel, like all the heroes of the heroic tradition, is a king. It is the duty of kings to protect the helpless: notably the widow and fatherless. The terminology used in our text is close to that often appearing in the Old Testament.

The gift of the bow by a god to the hero is quite common in epic saga. More than one archer (e.g., Pandarus[1]) got his bow from a god. Indic epic confronts us with the same feature. Genesis 21 may contain a toned-down account of a similar tale. Ishmael was to become a great bowman (v. 20), anticipated by the circumstance that his mother Hagar was seated a bowshot away (v. 16), as God blessed his destiny. The actual mention of a divinely-given bow is suppressed from the Bible, for possibly two reasons: to avoid a pagan motif, and to trim down the stature of Ishmael vis-à-vis[2] Isaac. The most famous case of divinely fashioned and given weapons, remains the armour of Achilles made by Hephaistos and fetched by Thetis.

When Aqhat is grown to manhood, he becomes a mighty

---

[1] Iliad 2: 827.

[2] Unless we are to attribute the omission to the almost unbelievable conciseness of which the Hebrew (and Egyptian) prose authors were capable. It is, for example, tantalising to read in a single verse about Shamgar who slew 600 Philistines with an oxgoad. Such a hero merits a story at least as long as the Samson Cycle, if not as long as the Iliad.

Egyptian figure: a bearer of funerary gifts (pp. 102, 107, 108)

Panel from the royal bedstead at Ugarit: two young
princes suckled by a goddess (pp. 146, 198)

hunter, thanks to his wondrous bow. His prowess comes to the attention of Anath, goddess of battle and the chase, who covets his weapon:

> [*She raises her voice*] *and shouts:*
> ' *Hear,* [*O Aqhat the Hero!*
> S]*eek silver and I'll give it to you*
>   [*Gold, and I'll bes*]*tow it on you.*
> *But give* [*me your*] *bow*
>   *Let the Progenitress of* Nations [*ta*]*ke your* [*ar*]*c.*'
> *And Aqhat the Hero replies:*
> ' *I promise sinews of Lebanon*
>   *I promise tendons from buffaloes*
>   *I promise horns of wild goats*
>   *Strings from the sinews of a bull*
>   *I promise reeds from the majestic marsh.*
> *Give* (*them*) *to Kothar-and-Hasis*
> *So that he may make a bow for you*
>   *E'en an arc for the Progenitress of* Nations.'
> *And the Virgin Anath answered:*
> ' *Ask life, O Aqhat the Hero—*
> *Ask life, and I shall give it to you*
>   *Immortality, and I'll bestow it on you.*
> *I shall make you count years with Baal;*
>   *With the sons of El you shall count months.*
> *For as Baal gives life,*
>   *Serving* (*the elixir of*) *life*
>   *Serving and quaffing,*
>   *The Good One singing and chanting over him.* . . .
> *So I shall give life to Aqhat the Hero.*'

As we note, Anath first offers him wealth if he will part with his bow. But Aqhat insists on keeping it, offering instead to provide the materials for a composite bow which she may give to Kothar-

and-Hasis for fashioning into the finished product. The composite bow, made from ibex horns and buffalo sinews, is a detailed complex that unmistakably joins the cultures of the Semitic and Aegean spheres around the East Mediterranean. The epithet of Anath, *yabamat* of nations (?), is not completely clear. The reflex of *yabamat* in Hebrew designates a widow who is made the wife of her dead husband's next of kin to bear progeny for perpetuating the deceased's name. " Widowed-sister-in-law " is rather clumsy in translation: " progenitress " is perhaps more suitable.[1]

It is a stylistic feature of the literature that there should be build-up and climax. Here Anath first offers Aqhat wealth, and when he will not sell his bow for gold and silver, she offers him immortality. For a man to get immortality would be remarkable enough; for him to refuse it is still more worthy of saga. Just as Odysseus refuses the immortality offered by the nymph Calypso (Odyssey 5: 209), Aqhat turns down Anath's offer of immortality:

> *And Aqhat the Hero replied:*
> *' Do not beguile me, O Virgin!*
> *For to a hero your lies are snares.*
> *What does man get as (his) latter end?*
> *What does man get as (his) destiny?*
> *Whiteness is poured on the head*
> *Hoariness, on top of my pate,*
> *And I'll die the death of everyone*
> *Yea I shall surely die.'*

[1] Anath's epithet (written *ybmt limm* in Ugaritic) may possibly turn out to mean " progenitress of heroes " (rather than " of nations "). In any case, two men mentioned in Ugaritic administrative texts, as well as Shamgar in the Book of Judges, are called " sons of Anath." Perhaps men (especially foundlings) who aspired to heroic roles, tended to claim Anath as their mother, in ancient Canaan.

Aqhat thus distrusts the goddess and tells her so bluntly, adding
that he knows that grey hair and death are allotted to him. He
then proceeds to taunt her with her femininity, reminding her
that bows and the hunt are for males, somewhat as Telemachus
orders his mother to return to feminine interests and to leave
bowmanship to the men.

Anath begs Aqhat in vain to relent and then lets him know
that she will punish him for his sin and *hybris*. For permission
to do so, she goes to El, whose consent must be obtained for
every significant divine action. The kindly El is loath to
authorise Anath's revenge, but she extorts his consent by threats
of violence:

> *I'll make [your grey hair] flow [with blood]*
> *[The grey of] your [beard] with gore.*
> *[Then you can ask] Aqhat to save you*
> *Yea [Daniel's] son to rescue you*
> *From the hands of the Virgin Anath.*

The venerable Head of the Pantheon felt constrained to yield to
his impetuous daughter, much as Anu yielded under threats of
violence to his daughter Ishtar who was bent on punishing
Gilgamesh with death for insulting her.

Anath thereupon laid her plan to slay Aqhat as he lunched out
of doors during the chase:

> *As Aqhat sat down to eat*
> *E'en Daniel's son to dine,*
> *Over him eagles were flying;*
> *A flock of birds was soaring.*
> *Among the eagles flies Anath.*
> *Over Aqhat she set him (the assassin);*
> *He strikes him twice on the head*
> *Thrice over the ear;*

He sheds his blood like a libator
Like a slaughterer into his trough.
His soul went out like wind,
His spirit like a gust—
Like smoke from his nose.

So perished Aqhat through the machinations of the goddess.
While the text that follows is fragmentary, the words that are
preserved tell us that it was the bow, not Aqhat's life, that Anath
wanted. Anath indeed weeps, and the leitmotif of his resurrection is sounded.

Daniel is then depicted as defending the widow and fatherless
in the gate, when signs of drought are detected. Moreover, the
eagles begin hovering over Daniel's house. All the portents
indicated that Aqhat had been slain, and sympathetically the earth
was deprived of life-giving moisture. Puah wept and cut
Daniel's garment, initiating the mourning of the family.

Daniel then utters an imprecation, cursing the locality where
Aqhat was slain with seven years of drought:

> *Seven years may Baal afflict thee*
> *E'en eight the Rider of Clouds:*
> *Without dew, without rain*
> *Without the surging of the deeps*
> *Without the goodness of Baal's voice.*

This passage is significant in several ways. First, it fits in with the
widespread idea that the slaying of a hero brings drought and
famine on the scene of the tragedy. We have noted the same
theme in the Gilgamesh Epic. It also occurs in the Bible where
David is represented as cursing Gilboa in much the same wording,
because it was there that Saul and his sons were slain:

> *O mountains in Gilboa*
> *Let there be no dew nor rain upon you.* (2 Samuel 1: 21)

The attitude and utterance of David, far from being inventions of the poet who composed the Book of Jashar which the Bible excerpts here, are plainly reflexes of the same tradition that gave rise to the Ugaritic Epic of Aqhat.

Daniel, who had to perform a number of deeds, including the retrieving of his son's remains for burial, ordered his model daughter Puah to saddle his donkey for him:

> *Puah, who fetches water on her shoulders,*
> *Gets dew on the barley*
> *(And) knows the course of the stars,*
> *While weeping, she saddles an ass*
> *While weeping, hitches a donkey*
> *While weeping, lifts her father*
> *Sets him on the back of the ass*
> *On the beauty of the donkey's back.*

The beast for riding was still the donkey. The horse was as yet limited to drawing the chariot. Puah not only prepares her father's mount and helps him on, but she possesses highly prized virtues; she secures water and good crops for the household, and is also psychic: gifted (like Miriam or Helen) with prophetic insight.

While Daniel is out among the languishing crops, a pair of messengers give him the bad news that his son had perished. He is told that some eagle in a flock of eagles had devoured Aqhat, but he does not know which one specifically. Sighting the flock,

> *He lifts his voice and shouts:*
> ' *May Baal break the wings of the eagles*
> *May Baal break their pinions*
> *Let them fall at my feet*
> *I shall split open their insides and look.*

If there is fat, if there is bone
  I shall weep and bury him;
I shall put (his remains) in the tomb of the gods of the earth.'
From his mouth the word had not yet gone forth
  Nor from his lips, his utterance
When Baal broke the wings of the eagles;
  Baal broke their pinions;
They fell at his feet.
He splits their insides and looks:
There is no fat, there is no bone.
He lifts his voice and shouts:
' May Baal mend the wings of the eagles;
  May Baal mend their pinions.
Eagles, flee and fly!'

Note that Daniel does not achieve his goal by what we would call practical procedure, but by " the creative word." He utters the word, and its fulfilment is immediate. This is the same concept that appears repeatedly in the Bible, starting with Genesis 1. God does not perform the results of the six days of creation by physical labour, but by fiat. He says " Let there be such-and-such," and such-and-such comes into existence. God, of course, has the power without need for any outside agent. Daniel, on the other hand, must invoke Baal to act.

Daniel wants to inter Aqhat in the right tomb: one for slain heroes who become gods of the earth. The word " gods " is similarly used for departed spirits including that of the heroic figure Samuel, brought up by the Witch of Endor.

When Daniel sees that he has not downed the right bird, he mends the eagles by the " creative word," again invoking Baal.

The poet likes build-up and suspense. Accordingly, Daniel sights Hrgb, the father of the eagles, and brings him down and opens him but still finds no trace of the Hero's remains. Then

Hrgb is mended and released. All this is in the same phraseology. Finally, the whole episode is repeated for the third and climactic time, with Ṣml, the mother of the eagles. This time Daniel has the guilty bird, for on splitting her open:

> *There is fat, there is bone.*
> *So he takes Aqhat out of her;*

. . . .

> *He weeps and buries (him).*

. . . .

> *He lifts his voice and shouts:*
> ' *May Baal break the wings of the eagles;*
>   *May Baal break their pinions*
> *If they fly over the grave of my son,*
>   *If they disturb him from his sleep.*'

Daniel then performs a triple magical act to execrate the locality where the murder of his son had been perpetrated, and returns to his house, where he maintains a state of mourning for seven years:

> *The weeping women came into his palace*
>   *The wailing women, into his court . . .*
> *He wept for Aqhat the Hero*
>   *The man of Rapa shed tears for Daniel's child.*
> *From days to months*
>   *From months to years*
>   *Until the seventh year*
> *He wept for Aqhat the Hero,*
>   *Shed tears for Daniel's child.*

After seven years Daniel, Man of Rapa, said
   The Hero, Man of Hrnmy, declared
He lifted his voice and shouted:
'*Depart, O weeping women, from my palace*
   Wailing women, from my court!'

The emphasis on weeping women to wail for the dead is wide-spread. It is represented in some of the finest scenes of Egyptian painting. It is common in Hebrew (e.g., 2 Samuel 1: 24), Greek (e.g., Iliad 24: 166), and other literatures discussed in this book.

After the period of mourning (one of epic length!), sacrifices are made and Puah makes ready to depart on the mission of avenging her brother. She asks Daniel to bless her efforts:

Will you not bless me so that I may go blessed
   Yea fortify me so that I may go fortified?
That I may smite the smiter of my brother
   Destroy the destroyer of my mother's child?

Daniel bestows his paternal blessing on Puah, who now makes herself ceremonially fit *as a male hero* by washing, rouging herself, donning a male hero's garb and sheathing a sword.[1] Reddening the body was, as we have already noted, men's way of being ceremonially and militarily ready for action. Women used yellow paint; men, reddish brown.

Over her masculine attire, Puah wears a woman's dress, apparently with intent to deceive the murderer and gain access to his presence; and conceals her sword, somewhat as the Hebrew hero Ehud concealed his to gain entrance to his victim's court (Judges 3: 16). Puah is admitted to Yatpan's pres-

---

[1] According to Deuteronomy 22: 5, transvestism is an abomination. The strong Hebrew antipathy may be due to reaction against Canaanite usage as reflected in Ugaritic literature.

ence; he welcomes her with mixed wine and (unwittingly?) boasts:

> *The hand that slew the hero Aqhat*
> *Will slay thousands of the Lady's foes.*

For a second time, they quaff the mingled wine, and our tablet comes to an end. That Puah avenges her brother by slaying Yatpan in the immediately ensuing section that should follow, is a foregone conclusion. That Aqhat was brought back to life is equally clear from Ezekiel 14: 16, where Daniel is listed among those who survived with sons and daughters.

Texts 121-124 may have some connection with the Aqhat story. In any case, Daniel, Man of Rapa, appears in them (121: II: 7-8). These texts have to do with deities of the Rapa category (i.e., shades of the dead) who come invited to a feast, arriving in horse-drawn chariots. Daniel's epithet " Man of Rapa " connects him with the Rephaim, who are attested as shades of the dead in Phoenician and Hebrew literature, too.

> *They mount their chariots and they come*
> > *They go a day and a second*
> > > *After sunrise [on the third]*
> *The Rapa'ûma* (=Heb. *Rephaim*) *arrive on the threshing floors of*
> *(Daniel's) plantation.*

The Shade-gods of Baal and the warriors of both Baal and Anath attend the feast, at which oxen and sheep are slaughtered; even fatlings and yearling calves. And the wine flows freely. For a week, the Rapa'ûma are wined and dined in the banquet hall. On the seventh day, Aliyan Baal enters the scene, probably to bestow the blessing that will bring Aqhat back to life and restore fertility to the stricken land. The function of the banquet seems parallel to the one that initiates the restoration of health and fertility in the Kret Epic.[1]

The remaining literary texts from Ugarit are religious and mythological, rather than legendary. In the myths, there are no names of human heroes. We are dealing now with the gods. Yet the purpose of the myths is human enough; it is to satisfy our earthly needs. The myths explain nature so as to satisfy man's craving for the answers to the universe, and to guarantee the regularity of the processes that result in fertility: fertility of mankind, animals and plants. The content of the myths is conveyed through narrative full of action; the ancients were not interested in abstractions. Their thinking was concrete and their gods are portrayed as engaging in lively and significant action. For example, when Baal (the god of fertility and life) and Mot (the god of sterility and death) fight furiously, the action is not only interesting *per se*, but it is significant in that the outcome determines whether the land will be fertile or sterile for a prolonged period.

Fertility is the main concern of the Ugaritic myths. The fertility that the ancients aspired to was within the framework of nature; they wanted each manifestation of fertility in its due season. They wanted nothing (not even blessings such as rain and crops) out of season. What they dreaded was the failure of rain and crops in season. They desired the harvest of barley, wheat, tree fruits, olives and grapes, each at its normal time. Fertility of the soil is an around-the-year affair without any necessary sterile season in Canaan. Only the component segments of Canaanite fertility (i.e., the successive harvests) are seasonal. Nor is precipitation as a whole seasonal in a good year; for when the

[1] With a few changes, the remainder of this chapter is reprinted by permission of Doubleday & Company, Inc., from my contribution in *Mythologie of the Ancient World*, edited by S. N. Kramer, Anchor Books, 1961. Copyright © 1961 by Doubleday & Company, Inc.

winter rain ends, the summer dew begins. Rain is seasonal, and so is the dew. But since, as the text tells us, Baal grants both rain and dew, he functions as the water-giving god during all twelve months of the year.[1] Dew (as the ancients knew) is necessary for the ripening of agricultural products during the summer, such as grapes (which are harvested down to the end of the rainless summer). Accordingly, the great mass of scholarly writing on Baal, who is supposed to die for the rainless summer and return to life for the rainy winter, misses the point of ancient Near East religion as well as of Near East climate. The ancients wanted the regularity of the normal year; with everything, including the rain and dew, in its proper season. They dreaded rainless winters, dewless summers and locust years. A succession of dry or locust years was the terrible scourge that they wanted to avert at all costs. We shall see that the theme of the dying and reviving gods is not seasonal but " sabbatical," having to do with seven-year cycles of fertility and sterility.[2]

The fertility cult was not limited to Baal and his female counterpart Anath. It is true that our longest texts concerning the fertility myths are Baalistic, but it is also a fact that text #52, which deals specifically with this problem, never so much as mentions Baal. In that text, El is the prime mover. The prominence of Baal and Anath in the fertility myths is simply a corollary of their general prominence as young, active and appealing gods. Younger gods tend to be more popular than their elders. Zeus displaced his father Cronus, who had previously displaced his own father, Uranus. In Iran, Ahuramazda, with

---

[1] For documentation, see my *Ugaritic Literature* (Rome, 1949), pp. 3-5; *Ugaritic Manual*, pp. 269-270; *World of the Old Testament*, pp. 98-99. Additional evidence from Ishtar's Descent and the Statue of Idri-mi has been cited in Chapter III.

[2] In other cases too (notably Osiris) there was only one resurrection. The aim of the Osiris cult was to triumph over the one death we must experience, and to live on eternally like Osiris who *once and for all* came back to life.

the passing of time, yielded the limelight to Mithra and
Anahita. Accordingly, the quantitative prominence of Baal
and Anath vis-à-vis El in the fertility myths is simply an
aspect of their quantitative prominence vis-à-vis the older El in
general.

Text #52 opens with the invocation: "Let me proclaim the
Good and Gracious Gods," the heptad of fertility deities who are
to be sired by El for the purpose of establishing seven-year
cycles of abundance. The seven-motif, as we shall see, permeates
the text. The tablet is divided into sections by horizontal lines
drawn by the scribe. The text is in dramatic form, with stage
directions, giving the locale and *dramatis personae* for various
scenes. The origins of drama are religious and text #52 is a
landmark in the prehistory of classical drama.

The prologue mentions the presence of the dignitaries of the
community: civilian and military, ecclesiastical and lay, from the
king and queen down. The note of abundance is sounded in
line 6:

> *Eat of every food*
> *Drink of the liquor of every wine!*

The second section tells of the compound personage "Death-
and-Evil" who holds two sceptres: in one hand, the staff of
bereavement; in the other, the staff of widowhood. They hack
him down like a vine in the field. Thus section #2 is, so to
speak, the reverse side of the coin: in #1 (the prologue), abundance is hailed; in #2, privation is banished.

Section #3 states that something is to be recited, or performed
seven times in keeping with the pervading heptad theme.

Section #4 opens by stating the locale:

> *The field is the field of the gods*
> *The field of Asherah and the Girl.*

The Elysian Fields of Ugarit are thus defined as the field of Asherah (consort of El) and the Girl (apparently Anath). There the " Lads " do something over a fire seven times. What they do is the subject of a considerable body of scholarly literature. The text states

> *They co[ok a ki]d in milk*
> *A* young goat *in butter.*

" Milk " and " butter " are certain and parallel each other perfectly. What is in brackets is broken away and restored. " Cook " is only half there, and most of " kid " is missing. Moreover, " *young goat* " is a *hapax legomenon*, with a conjectural translation that cannot be used to bolster the restoration of " kid." The restored passage has been used to establish the Canaanite custom of seething a kid in its mother's milk, against which the Biblical prohibition " Thou shalt not seethe a kid in its mother's milk," may have been directed. This prohibition has given rise to the Rabbinical insistence that milk and meat must not be eaten together. Since the separation of milk and meat is the cornerstone of Jewish ritual diet, the subject is of wide interest. The above restoration of the Ugaritic passage is possible, but it is so full of hypothetical factors that we will do well to move on without further ado.

The final line of section #4 parallels what we have just quoted, but " fire," written *'iššatu* (which is Semitic) the first time, is now paralleled by the Indo-European *agni* " fire," cognate with Latin *ignis*. The Ugaritic form beginning with *a-* is, however, closer to Sanskrit Agni (familiar to westerners as the Indian god of fire). This Indo-European word is a concrete reminder that Canaan was already influenced by Indo-Europeans prior to the Amarna Age. This is abundantly borne out by vocabulary, proper names, literature and institutions as well as the mythology.

With section #5, we read that Rahmai " Lassie " (=Anath) goes and girds (=grapples with) a goodly hero. Anath's engaging in combat is in keeping with her bellicose character of slayer of dragons, game and men.

Section #6 gives the scene as the Dwellings of the Gods, and specifies another sevenfold ritual.

Section #7 is an expression of zeal for the divine names of some deities called " The Sons of Sharruma," who apparently must be invoked to assure the success of the main section (#10) towards which the first nine sections are the build-up.

Section #8 is the invocation to the Good and Gracious Gods who will be born and nursed at the breasts of Asherah. Dignitaries are on hand, bringing good sacrifices to the feast.

Section #9 brings the scene back to the Elysian Fields:

> *The field of the gods*
> *The field of Asherah and Rahmai*

and all is ready for the main scene.

Section #10 opens at the seashore where two women are to be created over a fire. El is the aged god, and it is a question whether he will remain impotent, so that the women will function as his daughters and remain childless; or whether he will rise to virility for the occasion so that the women may serve as his wives and bear offspring. The myth and the drama whereby it was re-enacted, are full of suspense; for El's impotence would mean the onslaught of lean years, whereas his virility would herald the inauguration of a cycle of plentiful years.

El fashions the two women and puts them in his house. His staff (symbolising his penis) is lowered, but he shoots heavenward, bagging a bird, which is plucked, cleaned and roasted over the fire. His prowess with the bow inspires hope for his virility. He then tries to copulate with the two women, whereupon the text brings us to a crisis of suspense, for

> *If the women cry ' O husband, husband!*
> *Your rod is lowered*
>   *The staff of your hand has fallen '*
> *While the bird roasts over the fire*
>   *Yea broils over the coals,*
> *Then the women are the wives of El*
>   *The wives of El and his forever.*
> *But if the women cry ' O father, father!*
> *Your rod is lowered*
>   *The staff of your hand has fallen '*
> *While the bird roasts over the fire*
>   *Yea broils over the coals,*
> *The girls are the daughters of El*
>   *The daughters of El and his forever.*

Marriage and adoption could be on more, or on less, permanent bases. A marriage contract could permit a short-term union, or call for a permanent and indissoluble marriage. The same variation could hold for daughtership (called *mârtûtu* in Babylonian),[1] a legal state into which a girl could be adopted. The permanence of whatever relationship emerges between El and the two women is in keeping with the seriousness of the drama; on it depends the long-range fertility of the land. What the women say will determine the future, whether for good or for evil. To the relief and joy of the populace, the women exclaim:

> *' O husband, husband!*
> *Your rod is lowered*
>   *The staff of your hand is fallen '*
> *While the bird roasts over the fire*
>   *Yea broils over the coals.*

[1] e.g., in the Nuzu contracts of the Amarna Age. Such social institutions were not limited to isolated communities but were likely to be spread over a wide area within the Amarna Order.

So the two women are the wives of El
El's wives and his forever.

This guarantees a favourable outcome, but not without further suspense, for, as we shall now note, the first children to be born of the union are not the Heptad but a pair of celestial deities:

He bends, their lips he kisses
Lo their lips are sweet, sweet as pomegranates.
From kissing, there is conception
From embracing, impregnation.
They go into labour and bear Dawn[1] and Dusk.

Whatever importance Dawn and Dusk may have in the fertility cult, they are not the primary gods of fertility whose functioning is the goal of the text.

The birth of children was announced by messenger to the fathers who left obstetrics in the feminine hands of the midwives and parturient women.

Word was brought to El
' El's wives have borne.'

But El knows the results without having to be told the details, for he first asks and then answers his own rhetorical question:

What have they borne?
My children, Dawn and Dusk.

Thereafter, he joins his wives in conjugal love again. Then he returns to his own abode till the women go into labour and bear

---

[1] Šaḥar (" Dawn " or " Morning Star ") is also connected with the rains of fertility in Hosea 6: 3. The imagery of text ♯52, wherein El impregnates two human wives, reverberates in the Hebrew prophets; cf. Ezekiel 23 (N.B. v. 4) and Hosea *passim* (e.g., 1: 2 followed by 3: 1). Hosea connects this theme with agricultural fertility; for depending on the relationship of the women to Him, God either gives or withholds food and drink (Hosea 2: 10-11).

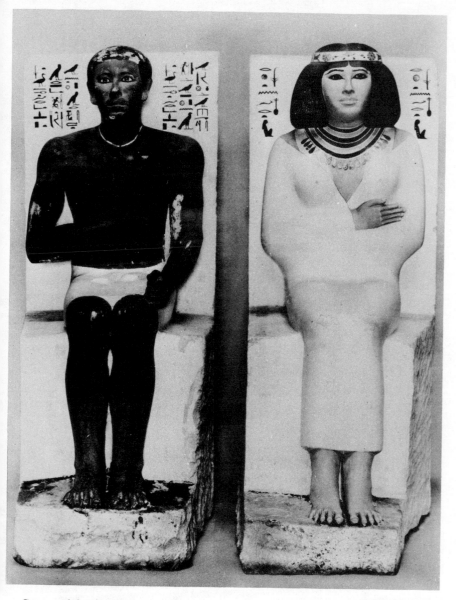

Ceremonial paint: Rahotep is painted reddish-brown, while his wife Nofret is yellow (pp. 136, 168, 231)

An Egyptian painting, from the Papyrus of Ani, of women wailing for the dead (p. 168)

him another brood. Word is brought to him and this time the babes are the Good and Gracious Gods of fertility who suckle the Lady's breasts, thereby imbibing the nourishment that provides them with the power for their important role. The newborn gods are voracious giants, with

> *A lip to earth, a lip to heaven*
> *So that there enter their mouth*
> *The fowl of heaven*
> *   And fish from the sea.*

El then addresses his seven sons and directs them to the wilderness:

> *There you shall sojourn among the stones and trees*
> *Seven full years*
> *   E'en eight circling (years)*
> *Till you Good Gods walk the field*
> *   E'en tread the corners of the wilderness.*

Long years of retirement to the wilds among the stones and trees is typical of Indic epic, where beloved heroes do this (often for expiation) pending a happy return to civilisation. The seven (" e'en eight ") years of sojourn in the wilderness mean that a bad sabbatical cycle has taken place and, by the process of alternation, a good sabbatical cycle is about to begin. It is, therefore, likely that text #52 is connected with a ritual to end a succession of lean years and inaugurate a cycle of fat years.

We now approach the happy ending. The seven lean years are over and the Good Gods are ready to enter the Sown, where the Guardian who is to let them in is stationed.

> *They met the Guardian of the Sown*
> *   And shouted to the Guardian of the Sown:*
> *' O Guardian, Guardian, open!'*
> *And he opened an aperture for them so that they entered.*

They then ask for the entertainment due to strangers:

> *If [there is] bread, give that we may eat*
> *If there is [wine], give that we may drink.*

The Guardian answered that there were both food and drink and the text ends on the affirmation of plenty.

Text #52 thus reflects a religious ritual for initiating a seven-year period of plenty. The form is dramatic and was doubtless acted out. Our text is the libretto with stage directions. The authority that is invoked to produce the results is a myth: the story of how El procreated the Heptad who preside over the plenteous sabbatical cycle, and how they auspiciously entered the arable terrain bringing their blessings to it. The myth is the precedent to be invoked for re-establishing *in time* the *primeval* event. We thus have the myth, the verbal utterance and the act: the complete formula for agricultural prosperity (without any trace of the Baal cult).

Quantitatively, the Baal and Anath texts form the bulk of the fertility myths from Ugarit, in keeping with the popularity of those younger gods in the religion of Canaan. About a dozen tablets deal with Baal and Anath myths, but there is no proof that they were intended to constitute a single composition. When we group them as parts of " The Baal and Anath Cycle," we do so as a matter of practical expedience. We must discuss them in some order, and we try to arrange them in the most meaningful sequence. And yet, no sequence can claim to be the one and only sequence that a Ugaritic priest would have prescribed.

One of the main themes in the mythology is kingship among the gods. Just as Zeus wrested the kingship of the gods from Cronus, and the latter from Uranus, Baal wrested the kingship from the sea-god Yamm. Text #137 tells how the pantheon was assembled under the presidency of El, when Yamm sent his

messengers with the insolent request that Baal be surrendered to
him in bondage:

> *So says Yamm your lord*
> > *Your master, Judge River:*
> ' *O gods, give up him whom you harbour*
> > *Him whom the multitudes harbour;*
> *Give up Baal and his partisans*
> > *Dagon's Son, that I may inherit his gold.'*

The gods were seated for banqueting when Baal spied the
messengers coming. The gods, anticipating the unpleasant
message, bent their heads in sadness, but Baal, showing the
courage befitting the king-to-be, took his stand by El.

> *As soon as the gods saw them,*
> > *Yea saw the messengers of Yamm*
> > > *The emissaries of Judge River,*
> *The gods lowered their heads on top of their knees*
> *E'en on the thrones of their lordships.*

Baal rebuked them:

> ' *Why have you lowered, O gods,*
> *Your heads on top of your knees*
> > *E'en on the thrones of your lordships?*
> *Let the gods twain read the tablets*
> > *E'en the messengers of Yamm*
> > > *The emissaries of Judge River.*
> *Lift, O gods, your heads*
> *From on top of your knees*
> > *From the thrones of your lordships*
> *And I shall answer Yamm's messengers*
> > *The emissaries of Judge River.'*

Baal's leadership commands the respect of the gods who react by obeying him:

> *The gods lift their heads*
> *From on top of their knees*
> *From the thrones of their lordships.*

The messengers twain arrive and fail to pay obeisance to the head of the pantheon:

> *At the feet of El they do not fall*
> *Nor prostrate themselves in the gathered assemblage.*

Baal is already meditating violent revenge in his heart. He has a sharpened sword with flashing blade. Messengers (as in the Homeric world) had a kind of diplomatic immunity, so that no matter how great the provocation, Baal had no right to vent the violence of his feelings on them. The scene we are about to witness is a forerunner of an episode in the Iliad (1: 188-222), where Achilles is about to slay Agamemnon because of Agamemnon's insolent demands, but two goddesses restrain him. Just as Achilles yields for the time being, so too does Baal. In fact, El abjectly surrenders him:

> *The Bull, his father, El, replies:*
> ' *Baal is your slave, O Yamm,*
> *Baal is your slave [forev]er*
> *Dagon's Son, your bondsman.*
> *He will bring your tribute like the gods*
> *[Yea] bring your offerings like the sons of holiness.*'

Thus betrayed by the cowardice of the venerable but senile Father of the Gods, Baal flies into a rage and

> *[Seiz]es [a knife] in his hand*
> *A butcher knife in his right*
> *To slay the messengers ...*

Whereupon

> *[Ana]th grabs [his right hand]*
> *Yea Astarte grabs his left*

and they tell him that he must not slay the emissaries of Yamm. The text breaks off after a few fragmentary lines. It is possible that the goddesses told Baal to bide his time and things would turn out in his favour, even as Hera and Athena advised Achilles, who, in obedience to them, refrained from slaying Agamemnon.

Baal's opportunity came. Text #68 tells how he vanquished Yamm and from him seized the kingship. The divine craftsman, Kothar-and-Hasis, fashioned two clubs and gave them to Baal for conquering Yamm. The need for two clubs is a corollary of the ancient psychology that required climactic action: the first club would strike a preliminary blow; the second would deal the final and crushing blow. Kothar-and-Hasis predicts to Baal the victorious outcome of the battle:

> *Am I not telling you, O Prince Baal*
> *Yea declaring, O Rider of Clouds?*
> *Lo your enemies, O Baal,*
> *Lo your enemies shall you smite*
> *Lo you shall destroy your foes!*
> *You shall take your eternal kingship*
> *Your everlasting sovereignty!*

Then the divine craftsman gives the clubs their appropriate names:

> *Kothar brings down two clubs and proclaims their names:*
> *' Your name is Driver.*
> *Driver, drive Yamm—*
> *Drive Yamm from his throne,*
> *River from the seat of his sovereignty!*

> *You shall swoop from the hand of Baal*
> *Like a falcon from his fingers!*
> *Strike the shoulders of Prince Yamm*
> *Between the hands of Judge River!* '

Note that the imagery is in terms of falconry. The clubs will fly from the hand of Baal and strike his enemy Yamm, just as a falcon swoops from the hunter's hand to catch the prey. The expression "between the hands" means "on the back" in Hebrew as well as in Ugaritic. The "creative word" of Kothar-and-Hasis is immediately translated into action:

> *The club swoops from the hand of Baal*
> *Like a falcon from his fingers.*
> *It strikes the shoulders of Prince Yamm*
> *Between the hands of Judge River.*

But Yamm is not felled by the blow and still remains in the fray. So Kothar-and-Hasis names the next club "Expeller" and commands it to fly from the hand of Baal and deal Yamm the knock-out blow on the head:

> *So the club swoops from the hand of Baal*
> *Like a falcon from his fingers.*
> *It strikes the head of Prince Yamm*
> *Between the eyes of Judge River.*
> *Yamm sprawls and falls to earth . . .*

Baal thus conquered Yamm and wrested from him the kingship of the gods.

Victory, however, often leaves a host of new problems in its wake for the victor. On this occasion, immediately after the victory, Astarte rebukes Baal for slaying Yamm. Baal is now king but his future is fraught with vicissitudes as the mythology before us will bring out.

Text #75 tells of Baal's encounter with ravenous monsters in the wilderness. The weird creatures (part bovine, part anthropomorphic) are reminiscent of the Aegean Minotaur on the one hand, and of the Mesopotamian Bull of Heaven on the other:

> *On them are horns like bulls*
> *And humps like buffaloes*
> *And on them is the face of Baal.*

The text is fragmentary with many of the line-ends missing. That the sabbatical cycle of fertility is an underlying motif is, however, clear from passages like the following:

> *Seven years the god is full* / . . .
> *Even eight circling (years), till* . . .

Then Baal perished, and the years of sterility came on, for we read:

> *Thus Baal fell* . . . . . . *like a bull*
> *Yea Hadd collapsed* . . . .

Baal had many ups and downs, slain for many a cycle of sterility and privation, and risen for many a cycle of fertility and plenty. The multiplicity of his ups and downs is required by nature itself in the Near East. Canaan is characterised by a succession of seasons that normally produce a fertile year. With some luck, a number of such fertile years follow one after the other to form a fertile cycle. But unfortunately, rain does not always materialise in the rainy season; nor is there always sufficient dew in the summer. Moreover, locusts may plague the land and devour the crops. A series of bad years is the major natural catastrophe against which the fertility cult was directed. The meteorological history of Canaan, where Baal was pitted against Mot in the minds of the people, required the concept that the conflict between the two gods took place repeatedly. In the frame of reference of Canaanite religious psychology, each of the two gods was both vanquished and triumphant many a time in the course of any century.

One of the larger subdivisions of the Baal and Anath Cycle is called the " Anath " text, which opens with a banquet scene of the gods. Baal is honoured on the occasion with roasted meat cut with a keen blade from the breast of a fatling. Also

> *A cup is placed in his hand*
> *An amphora in both hands.*

Asherah, consort of El and mother of " the seventy gods," graces the occasion. Wine flows in profusion:

> *They take a thousand pitchers of wine*
> *Ten thousand they mix of its mixture.*

Like the Greeks in Homer, the Canaanites often cut their wine, and enhanced the pleasures of roast meat and mixed wine with music and song:

> *(A lad) began to sing and chant*
> *With cymbals, a goodly song;*
> *The lad good of voice chanted.*

Thereafter

> *Baal went up into the heights of Saphon*
> *Baal viewed his girls*
> *He eyed Pidrai, Girl of Light,*
> *Also Tallai, Girl of Rain,*

. . . .

The daughters of Baal, as we know from several Ugaritic passages, are three in number: Pidrai, Tallai and Arsai. They are appropriately nature goddesses: Pidrai symbolising light; Tallai, rain and dew; Arsai, earth. Some scholars insist that they are not the daughters but the consorts of Baal. The texts call them Baal's *banât-*, which means primarily " daughters " and second-arily " girls." Since the triad of Baal's daughters is reflected in the triad of Allah's daughters according to the pre-Islamic Arabs,[1] there is some outside confirmation that the three goddesses are daughters of Baal. This does not rule out their serving as his consorts as well, because the ambivalence of relationships in an ancient pantheon may be remote from the familiar patterns of human society.

Col. II begins with a reference to the scent of game, around the double doors of Anath's house. This is appropriate because she is a goddess of the hunt and of battle. Suddenly troops confront her:

> *And lo Anath fights violently*
> *She slays the sons of the two cities*
> *She fights the people of the seashore*
> *Annihilates mankind of the sunrise.*

The reference to the people of the west (seashore) and east (sun-rise) is a common idiom called a " merism " or combination of antonyms to indicate totality (like our English " they came great and small " which means " everybody came "). Accordingly, Anath is said to be slaying " everyone." The scene we are about to witness is a parallel to the Egyptian (rather than Mesopotamian) story of the near-destruction of mankind. The Mesopotamians (followed by the Hebrews) conceived of the near-destruction of mankind at the hands of the god(s) in terms of a deluge. But the Egyptians had a myth about a brutal goddess, Sekhmet, who went berserk and would have exterminated the human race had she not

---

[1] See my " The Daughters of Baal and Allah," *Moslem World* 33, 1943 pp. 50-51.

been stopped before it was too late. Ugaritic mythology, confronting us with a variant of this tradition, tells of how the violent Anath slew men and exulted as their cut-off heads and hands flew through the air:

> *Under her (flew) heads like vultures;*
> *Over her (flew) hands like locusts.*

Again, note the merism: " under " and " over " indicate " everywhere " about her. The ancient Near Easterners used to cut off heads and hands to count and gloat over their victims slain in battle. Heads and hands are therefore symbols of victory, figuring in the art as well as texts of the Near East. Our present text is paralleled by Syrian seal cylinders of the Amarna Age, showing the victorious goddess with heads and hands filling the atmosphere.

Sekhmet of Egypt was stopped by flooding the area with beer dyed blood-red with ochre. The bloodthirsty Sekhmet, mistaking the reddened beer for blood, drank her fill and was put to sleep by the beer. Anath, somewhat similarly, is depicted as wading in the blood of her human victims:

> *She plunges knee-deep in the blood of heroes*
> *Neck-high in the gore of troops.*

She battles on with club and bow until she reaches her palace. At this point, we are confronted with a typical feature of the literature. All the fighting so far is merely the first round. Another scene, paralleling this one, will come later and tell of the climax (i.e., final victory). So our text states that on this first round " she was not sated." She thereupon renews the battle, adding new tactics:

> *She fights violently—*
> *Slays the sons of the two cities.*

> *She hurls chairs at the soldiers,*
> *Hurling tables at the armies,*
> *Footstools at the troops.*

Brawl tactics, specifically the throwing of furniture, are famous from Odysseus' battle against the suitors in his halls at Ithaca. In Psalm 23, " Thou preparest a table for me in the presence of mine enemies," may mean that God provides His own with ammunition.

With her tactics in the second round, Anath scores the victory and is overjoyed at the massacre she has wrought:

> *Much she fights, and looks;*
> *Slays, and views.*
> *Anath swells her liver with laughter;*
> *Her heart is filled with joy,*
> *For in the hand of Anath is victory.*
> *For she plunged knee-deep in the blood of soldiers*
> *Neck-high in the gore of troops.*
> *Until she is sated*
> *She fights in the house—*
> *Battles between the tables.*

The parallel with the Odyssey is many-sided. Anath is depicted returning from the hunt, trying to enter her own palace which is occupied by intruders. Her first battle, out of doors, does not end with her in full possession of her premises. But the second battle, concluded indoors, leads to her repossessing her palace. Both the tactics of furniture-throwing and the massacre of the intruders to repossess one's own palace, remind us of Odysseus' victory in his halls. After her victory, Anath first

> *Washes her hands in the blood of soldiers*
> *Her fingers in the gore of troops.*

187

But the blessings of peace follow the ravages of war:

> *She draws water and washes:*
> *Dew of heaven*
>   *Fat of earth*
>   *Rain of the Rider of Clouds.*

All of the myths we are discussing lead up to the theme of nature functioning with regularity and benevolence to bless mankind with fertility. The formula " dew of heaven and fat of earth " recurs in the blessings of Isaac (Genesis 27: 28, 39). " Rider of Clouds " refers to Baal in Ugaritic, but to Yahweh in Psalm 68: 4.

The acts of Anath bring on the corresponding functions of nature:

> *Dew! The heavens pour it forth.*
> *[Rain!] The stars pour it forth.*

The text goes on to tell of the abundance of game, too.

Baal next dispatches his messengers to Anath, telling her to lay aside warfare and establish peace, promising her to reveal the secret of nature if she will come to his mountain abode:

> *The message of Aliyan Baal*
>   *The word of Aliy the Mighty:*
> *'(Bury) enmity in the earth of battles*
>   *Put mandrakes in the dust*
>   *Pour (a) peace (offering) into the midst of the earth,*
>   Conciliation *into the midst of the fields*

. . . .

> *To me let your feet race*
>   *To me let your legs hasten,*
> *For I have a word to tell you*
>   *An utterance, to declare unto you:*

The word of the tree and the whisper of the stone
  The sound of the heavens to the earth
    Of the Deeps to the stars.
I understand lightning which the heavens do not know
  The word which men do not know
    Nor the multitudes of the earth understand.
Come and I shall reveal it
In the midst of the mountain of me, God of Saphon
  In the sanctuary, in the mountain of mine inheritance
    In the Good Place, on the Hill of Power.'

When Anath beholds the Messengers coming, she is stricken by misgivings that some ill may have befallen Baal. Before they have time to deliver their joyous message, Anath

> *Lifts her voice and shouts:*
> *'Why have Gupan and Ugar come?*
> *What foe has risen against Baal*
>   *Or enemy against the Rider of Clouds?'*

Anath then recounts her past victories over Baal's enemies. Those battles symbolise the triumph of the forces of good (or life) over the forces of evil (or death).

> *Have I not crushed Yamm, El's Darling,*
>   *Nor annihilated the great god River?*
> *Have I not muzzled the dragon*
>   *Nor crushed the crooked serpent*
>   *Mighty monster of the seven heads?*
> *I have crushed Mot, darling of the earth gods;*
>
> . . . .
>
> *I have destroyed the house of El-Zebub;*

189

*I have battled and gained possession of the gold of those
who (once) drove Baal from the heights of
Saphon . . .*

The sea gods figure prominently among the foes of Baal, lord of
the earth and fertility. The dragon (*tannín*) is well known from
Scripture. The crooked serpent is none other than Leviathan,
who is actually named as such in other Ugaritic texts that we shall
presently examine. His seven heads give the number of the heads
that God crushed according to Psalm 74: 14 ("Thou hast
crushed the heads of Leviathan"). In Revelation 12: 3 ff., the
seven-headed monster of evil that emerges from the sea is a
reflex of the old Leviathan myth symbolising the triumph of
Good over Evil. Later still, in the Aramaic incantation bowls
(from about A.D. 500 in Babylonia), magicians invoked the
precedent of God's conquest of Leviathan, to dispel the forces of
evil from the homes of their clients. All this has a bearing on the
New Testament and various forms of Jewish dualism (N.B. the
Qumran Scrolls), whereby the forces of good (or light or God)
are pitted against the forces of evil (or darkness or Satan). This is
frequently attributed to borrowing from Zoroastrianism. But,
as we now see, the myth of the dualistic battle was deeply
entrenched in Canaan from pre-Hebraic times. The myth of the
conflict was absorbed by the Hebrews along with the language,
literature and lore of Canaan from the very start of Hebrew
history in Canaan. We know the parallel (and related) myth of
the Greeks, about the seven- (or nine-) headed Hydra slain by
Heracles. The earliest attestation of the myth is a seal cylinder
from Mesopotamia of the third millennium B.C. (Dynasty of
Akkad) showing heroes vanquishing the seven-headed monster.
Accordingly, all the available evidence points to the spread of
this dualistic myth from the Semitic to the Iranian sphere; not
vice versa. That Iranian back-influence may have heightened the

already existing dualistic tendencies in the Semitic world is quite likely, starting with the Achaemenian Conquest and continuing into Roman times, but that is very different from attributing the origin of Christian dualistic tendencies to non-Jewish sources.

Mot (" Death ") is the most prominent adversary of Baal. He appears often enough in Hebrew poetry and his cult is reflected in the early Hebrew name Az-mawet (" Mot-is-Strong "). Appeasing the forces of evil, as well as adoring the forces of good, is familiar in many religions (cf. the cults of the lethal Nergal in Mesopotamia, and of the evil Seth in Egypt).

El-Zebub, as we have noted above, is already an evil deity. He reverberates as Baal-Zebub,[1] the prince of the demons in the New Testament.[2]

The gold guarded by dragons on mountains is a common motif in Indo-European epic.

Anath ends her address to Gupan and Ugar by concluding her tale of conquests over Baal's foes, who had once

> Driven him from the seat of his kingship
> From the dais, from the throne of his sovereignty

and she asks

> What enemy has arisen against Baal
> Or foe against the Rider of Clouds?

The messengers allay her fears:

> No enemy has arisen against Baal
> Nor foe against the Rider of Clouds.

Then they deliver their message and invitation, repeating the very words put into their mouths by Baal, as quoted above.

---

[1] In 2 Kings 1: 2-3, 6, 16, Baal-Zebub is a pagan god of Ekron consulted by the Israelite King Ahaziah.

[2] i.e., Beelzebub (variant: Beelzebul) in Mark 3: 22.

The secret that Baal offers to reveal to Anath is the word of nature. The passage describing it is one of the finest in Ugaritic anticipating the Scriptural formulation of the same idea: " The heavens declare the glory of God, yea the firmament tells of His handiwork. Day utters word to day; and night imparts know-ledge to night. There is neither utterance nor words whose sound is unheard. Throughout all the land their sound goes forth; at the end of the world are their words " (Psalm 19: 1-4). In Canaan, whether at Ugarit or in Israel, the poets heard the voice of nature; heavens and earth talked to them, revealing the glorious mystery of the god(s) and creation. For those ancients, nature was animate; with the segments thereof conversing in words that the initiated could understand.

Anath accepts the invitation, and instead of wasting time sending further messages back and forth, she decides to race ahead of Gupan and Ugar.

> *Then she sets face towards Baal*
> *On the heights of Saphon*
> *By the thousand acres*
> *Yea myriad hectares.*

This formula expresses the speed at which gods travel. Some-what prosaically, we could render it " by leaps and bounds."

Baal entertains Anath, upon her arrival, with roasted ox and fatling. She draws water and washes with

> *Dew of heaven, fat of earth*
> *Dew that the heavens pour*
> *Rain that the stars pour*

and game abounds because of her felicity; for she is the Lady of fertility and of the hunt.

Baal's invitation is not without ulterior motive. In exchange for his secret, he wants Anath to intercede on his behalf to get a palace. Diplomacy in divine circles is as devious as among men. Baal's tactics were to get Anath to appeal to Asherah to ask El, the head of the pantheon, to authorise Kothar-and-Hasis to construct a palace for Baal. Baal was the only important god without a palace of his own. His newly won kingship required his possessing one. His plea included the statement that just about all the gods had palaces:

> *There is the dwelling of El, the shelter of his sons*
> *The dwelling of Lady Asherah of the Sea*
> *The dwelling of Pidrai, Girl of Light,*
> *The shelter of Tallai, Girl of Rain,*
> *The dwelling of Arsai, Girl of Yᶜbdr*
> *The dwelling of the famed brides.*

Anath assures Baal that she will, if necessary, compel El to grant the request, by dire threats of violence.

> *And the Virgin Anath declared:*
> ' *The Bull, El, my father, will yield*
> *He will yield for my sake and his own*
> *[For I shall] trample him like a sheep on the ground*
> *Make his grey hair [flow] with blood*
> *The grey of his beard [with gore]*
> *Unless he grants Baal a house like the gods*
> *[Yea a cour]t like the sons of Asherah!* '

Anath then departs for the abode of El where the two cosmic rivers, the sources of the Two Deeps, have their origin. There she threatens her aged sire with physical violence.[1] El, afraid of his brutal daughter, has hidden in the innermost chamber: the eighth chamber within a chamber.

---

[1] Compare Ishtar, who by threatening to upset the order of things through violence, extorts from her father Anu permission to kill the human object of her hatred.

> *El answers from seven chambers*
> *Out of eight compartments:*
> ' *I know you to be impetuous, O my daughter,*
> *For there is no restraint among goddesses.*
> *What do you desire, O Virgin Anath?* '

Now that El has been cowed into granting whatever she wants, Anath can afford to be filial and give up her crude tactics:

> *And the Virgin Anath replied:*
> ' *Your word, O El, is wise*
> *Your wisdom, unto eternity*
> *Lucky life is your word.*
> *Our king is Aliyan Baal*
> *Our judge, above whom there is none.*

Anath's appeal was carefully planned. Asherah and her brood were already there to add their voices to Anath's in getting El's authorisation for building Baal's palace:

> *There shout Asherah and her sons*
> *The Goddess and the band of her kin:*
> ' *Baal has no house like the gods*
> *Nor a court like the sons of Asherah.'*

Vociferously, they remind El that practically every god, except Baal who is now king, has a palace. El has no choice but to authorise the construction.

Asherah's messengers, Holy and Blessed, are dispatched to Caphtor, where Kothar-and-Hasis has his atelier. They are to convey to the divine craftsman El's orders to erect the palace.

Text #51 takes up the story. Like Hephaistos busy at his forge when Thetis comes to request armour for Achilles, so too Kothar-and-Hasis is described at work making fine objects in his atelier:

> The skilled one went up to the bellows.
> In the hands of Hasis were the tongs.
> He pours silver
>> Casts gold
> He pours silver by the thousands (of shekels)
>> Gold he pours by the myriads.

The text then enumerates the handsome creations he is making: a table, a footstool, shoes, a bowl, etc.—all fit for the gods.

The construction of Baal's mythical house is a forerunner of the erection of Yahweh's historical First Temple in Jerusalem. The two accounts are organically related because of common background and attitudes. In both cases the god's interests had grown to a point where he could not condignly go on any more without a house. The Bible tells that it was no longer fitting that Israel's king should dwell in a cedar palace while God still lived in a tent (The Tabernacle). Times had changed; Israel had arrived; with the added stature of Israel among the nations, the cultic requirements for Israel's God rose. We have seen how Baal's rise to kingship required the building of a palace for him. The biblical and Ugaritic accounts of the building materials (cedars of Lebanon covered with metal) link the mythical house of Baal and the historic house of Yahweh.

The definitive authorisation is sent through Anath to Baal with instructions to invite certain creatures (their identity is not yet clear, for we cannot translate their names) whereupon nature itself will fetch the building materials for him. Anath, overjoyed, darts through space to the heights of Saphon to tell the good news to Baal:

> Be informed, O Baal!
> I bring your tidings.
> A house will be built for you like your brethren
>> Even a court, like your kin.

> *Invite . . . . . . into your house*
> *. . . . . . in the midst of your palace*
> *So that the mountains will bring you much silver*
> *The hills, the choicest of gold*
> *And build a house of silver and gold*
> *A house of lapis gems.*

The combination of silver, gold and lapis-lazuli is familiar from Egyptian and Sumerian mythological texts, too. It is a reflection of actual art that gloried in the colour scheme produced by the three materials.

Baal now summoned the divine builder.

> *After Kothar-and-Hasis arrived*
> *He set an ox before him*
> *A fatling in the midst of his presence.*
> *A throne was set so that he might be seated*
> *At the right hand of Aliyan Baal*
> *Until he had eaten and drunk.*

After wining and dining the guest, Baal got down to business and instructed Kothar-and-Hasis to build the palace promptly

> *in the midst of the heights of Saphon.*
> *The house shall comprise a thousand acres*
> *The palace, ten thousand hectares.*

But a major disagreement arose between Baal and Kothar-and-Hasis as to whether the palace should have a window. A new type of building was coming into vogue: " the window house " (called *bît-ḫillâni* in Babylonian). The divine architect recommended this new type of building with a window; Baal, however, stubbornly objected to windows. Finally, the architect prevailed, with the consequence that Baal's adversary Mot entered Baal's palace through the window. Mot's (i.e., Death's) entrance

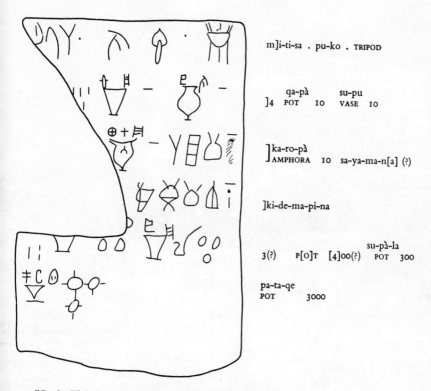

m]i-ti-sa . pu-ko . TRIPOD

    qa-pà   su-pu
]4 POT 10   VASE 10

]ka-ro-pà
AMPHORA 10 sa-ya-ma-n[a] (?)

]ki-de-ma-pi-na

                    su-pà-la
3(?)   P[O]T [4]oo(?) POT 300

pa-ta-qe
POT   3000

Hagia Triada Tablet 31 with transliteration (pp. 210, 211)

The ruins of the palace at Hagia Triada in Southern Crete (pp. 206 ff.)

through windows is a theme reflected in Jeremiah 9: 21. The dialogue between Baal and Kothar follows:

> *And Kothar-and-Hasis declared:*
> *' Hear, O Aliyan Baal,*
> *Perceive, O Rider of Clouds!*
> *Shall I not put a window in the house*
> *A casement in the midst of the palace? '*
> *And Aliyan Baal replied:*
> *' Do not put a window in the house*
> *A casement in the midst of the palace! '*
> *And Kothar-and-Hasis replied:*
> *' You will come around, Baal, to my word.'*

Kothar then repeated his advice, but Baal would not be budged, and added that he had three girls (Pidrai, Tallai and Arsai), whom he presumably did not want to expose through windows to any outsider.

From the majestic trees of Lebanon, and the choicest cedars of Antilebanon, the palace was erected. Then a mighty conflagration (which we are to compare with the " fire of Hephaistos") is applied to the house for a week, at the end of which the palace emerged resplendent with gold and silver. This may reflect a process of melting and applying precious metal to sheathe the wood and bricks, giving the illusion of a house built of solid gold and silver. When the process was completed

> *Aliyan Baal rejoiced:*
> *' I have built my house of silver*
> *Yea made my palace of gold.'*

Thereupon Baal made a great feast to commemorate the event, slaughtering bulls, sheep and goats, fatlings and yearling calves to regale his guests.

197

> *He invited his brethren into his house*
> *His kin into his palace.*
> *He invited the seventy sons of Asherah.*

He also invited specialised deities: personified animals and objects, some of which are paralleled in other literatures of the East Mediterranean. Homer tells of animated tripods that come to, and go from, the banquets of the gods, automatically. This parallels the deified pithoi in the following passage. In Hittite ritual, thrones can be personified quite as in the following:

> *(Baal) caused the ram gods to drink wine;*
> *Caused the ewe goddesses to drink wine.*
> *He caused the bull gods to drink wine;*
> *Caused the cow goddesses to drink wine.*
> *He caused the chair gods to drink wine;*
> *Caused the throne goddesses to drink wine.*
> *He caused the pithos gods to drink wine;*
> *Caused the jar goddesses to drink wine.*

Note how each category comes in parallel pairs, male and female giving poetic form to what would otherwise be a prosaic list. The text adds that the wining and dining continued

> *Till the gods had eaten and drunk*
> *And the twain who suck the breast had quaffed.*

The twain may be the two deified kings. As in Homer, the kings at Ugarit were accorded divine status.[1] Note that dyarchy probably existed at Ugarit, somewhat as at Sparta. The institution at both sites would appear to be the legacy of a common Aegean heritage. On a carved panel on the royal bedstead from Ugarit, two princes (whose duality suggests dyarchy) are depicted sucking the breasts of a goddess, thereby imbibing the milk that

[1] Cf. the divinity of King Kret, discussed above.

198

imparts divinity to them. The kings of Ugarit, therefore, have a place in the pantheon. It is part and parcel of the epic that kings should move in divine as well as in human circles; cf. Homer, the Gilgamesh Epic, and the Patriarchal Narratives in Genesis.

After the banquet, Baal sallied forth and captured ninety cities. His conquests inspired him with so much confidence that he felt secure enough to have a window installed in his house.

> *And Aliyan Baal declared:*
> ' *I'll install (it), Kothar son of Yamm,*
>   *Yea Kothar, son of the Assemblage.*
> *Let a window be opened in the house*
>   *A casement in the midst of the palace.*'

Thus did Baal come around to following Kothar's advice.

> *Kothar-and-Hasis laughed.*
> *He lifted his voice and shouted:*
> ' *Did I not tell you, O Aliyan Baal,*
>   *You would come around, Baal, to my word?* '
> *He opens a window in the house*
>   *A casement in the midst of the palace.*

All this is connected with the functioning of Baal as the storm god, because a rain and thunder storm ensue. Perhaps it is somehow connected with the " windows " of heaven, mentioned in Genesis 7: 11 as the source of rain.

At this seemingly happy juncture, trouble looms ominously for Baal. His foes seize the forest and mountainsides, and his arch-enemy Mot resolves on wresting the kingship for himself, saying:

> *I alone am he who will rule over the gods*
>   *Even command gods and men*
>   *Dominate the clans of the earth.*

Baal is obliged to communicate with Mot in the underworld, but warns his messengers, Gupan and Ugar, to beware of Mot lest he swallow them alive:

> *Do not draw near to the god Mot*
> > *Lest he make you like a lamb in his mouth*
> > *Yea like a kid in his gullet.*

The negotiations end in the confrontation of Baal and Mot in the underworld as we read in text #67. Mot's summoning of Baal is connected with Baal's conquest of the seven-headed Leviathan. Perhaps Mot felt sympathy for the forces of evil, since he was after all destructive like them. On being summoned, Baal is terrified of Mot and all nature becomes, as a result, unproductive:

> *Aliyan Baal feared him*
> > *The Rider of Clouds dreaded him.*
> *Word went back to the god Mot,*
> > *Was relayed back to the Hero, El's beloved:*
> *' The message of Aliyan Baal*
> > *The reply of Aliy, the Warrior:*
> *" Hail, O god Mot!*
> *I am your slave, e'en yours forever." '*
> *The two (messenger)gods departed*
> > *Nor did they sit.*
> *Then they set face towards the god Mot*
> > *In the midst of his city Hamrai.*
> *Lo the throne on which he sits*
> > *Is the land of his inheritance.*
> *The twain lift their voices and shout:*
> *' The message of Aliyan Baal*
> > *The reply of Aliy, the Warrior:*
> *" Hail, O deity Mot!*

I am your slave, e'en yours forever." '
The deity Mot rejoiced.

The capitulation of Baal is complete, since he becomes by his own declaration the slave of Mot in perpetuity. In the Old Testament there are two kinds of slave: the native (Hebrew) slave who has the right to go free in the seventh (or sabbatical) year; and the eternal slave, who never becomes free of his master.

Baal's capitulation meant his descent to Mot and to death. But before doing so, Baal copulated with a heifer who bore him a tauromorphic son. Then we find Baal fallen dead on the earth. When a pair of messengers bear the sad tidings to the head of the pantheon (El, or Latpan),

> *Thereupon Latpan god of mercy*
> *Goes down from his throne*
> *Sits on the footstool*
> *And from the footstool sits on the earth.*
> *He pours the ashes of mourning on his head*
> *Yea the dust of scattering on his pate.*

El also dons a special garb for mourning and lacerates himself, wandering in grief through mountains and forest. Anath too wanders in grief until she comes upon the corpse of Baal lying on the earth. With the help of the sun goddess, Shapsh, Anath removes the corpse to the heights of Saphon for burial with numerous sacrifices in his honour.

Anath then proceeds (in text #49) to the abode of El and Asherah, and

> *She raises her voice and shouts:*
> *' Let Asherah and her sons rejoice*
> *E'en the goddess and the band of her kin*
> *For Aliyan Baal is dead*
> *The prince, Lord of Earth, has perished.'*

It will be noted that this mythology is cosmic, not local. Baal is the Lord of the entire Earth; not the Baal of Ugarit, Byblos, Tyre or Sidon. El and Asherah are the chief god and goddess of the whole pantheon. Baal and Anath are the universal gods of fertility. And so forth.

The news that Baal is dead meant that another god would have to be appointed king in his stead. El and Asherah finally decide on their son Athtar the Terrible as king to replace Baal:

> *Thereupon Athtar the Terrible*
> *Goes up into the heights of Saphon*
> *Yea sits on the throne of Aliyan Baal.*
> *His feet do not reach the footstool,*
> *His head does not reach its top.*
> *So Athtar the Terrible says:*
> *' I cannot be king in the heights of Saphon.'*
> *Athtar the Terrible goes down*
> *Goes down from the throne of Aliyan Baal*
> *To be king over all the grand earth.*

Though Athtar became king of the earth, he was unequal to the magnitude of Baal's kingship in Saphon, as the inadequacy of his physical stature indicated.

Meanwhile Anath nursed her desire for vengeance on Baal's slayer. Eventually she asks Mot for her brother Baal, and Mot admits his guilt, whereupon

> *She seizes the god Mot;*
> *With a sword she cleaves him;*
> *With a fan she winnows him;*
> *With fire she burns him;*
> *In the millstones she grinds him;*
> *In the field she plants him.*

Mot is thus destroyed, but his being planted in the ground is somehow connected with the future growth of the soil. Perhaps the fact that he had swallowed Baal explains why Mot's body can give rise to life.

The planting of Mot is the prelude to the resurrection of Baal. El himself anticipates the joyous moment, but even the chief of the pantheon depends on dreams for information. When El dreams of nature functioning with abundance, he will know that Baal has come back to life:

> *In a dream of Latpan god of mercy*
> > *In a vision of the Creator of Creatures*
> *The heavens rain oil;*
> > *The wadies flow with honey.*
> *Latpan, god of mercy, rejoices.*
> > *His feet on the footstool he sets;*
> > > *He cracks a smile and laughs;*
> *He raises his voice and shouts:*
> *'Let me sit and rest*
> > *So that my soul may repose in my breast*
> *Because Aliyan Baal is alive—*
> > *Because the Prince, Lord of Earth, exists.'*

Shapsh, the sun goddess who sees all, is dispatched to find Baal. When she finds him, he is battling once more with Mot. Baal had attacked Mot, knocked him to the ground, and forced him from the throne of his kingship for seven years. And now, in the seventh year, Mot accuses Baal of having subjected him to seven years of annihilation. Mot's words refer to what Anath had done to him, in avenging Baal:

> *On account of you, O Baal, I have seen shame;*
> > *On account of you I have seen scattering by the sword;*

On account of you I have seen burning by fire;
On account of you I have seen grinding in the millstones.

. . . .

Soon Mot and Baal are again locked in mortal combat:

They tangle like hippopotamuses;
　Mot is strong, Baal is strong.
They gore like buffaloes;
　Mot is strong, Baal is strong.
They bite like serpents;
　Mot is strong, Baal is strong.
They kick like racers;
　Mot is down, Baal is down.

As the fight is thus fought to a draw, Shapsh arrives and intimidates Mot with the threat of El's punishment on Baal's behalf:

' *Hear, O god Mot!*
How can you fight with Aliyan Baal?
How will the Bull, El, your father, not hear you?
Will he not remove the supports of your seat
　Nor upset the throne of your kingship
　　And break the sceptre of your rule? '
The god Mot was afraid
　The Hero, beloved of El, was scared.

There are other Baal and Anath fragments. As long as nature continues to function and to malfunction, the conflict of Baal and Mot continues. The aim of the cult was always to secure the victory of Baal over Mot, to usher in a seven-year cycle of plenty, so that the populace might enjoy the blessings of abundance.

As we have already noted, the fertility cult transcended Baalism. Text #77 is lunar, dealing with the marriage of

Details from the Standard of Ur, showing typical occupations of peace and war (p. 276)

Stela of Hammurapi's law-code (pp. 35-37, 279)

Yarih ("Moon"), with the Mesopotamian lunar goddess Nikkal (from Sumerian Nin-gal). The wedding is to result in fertility symbolised as the child that the bride will bear to the groom. The text is divided by a scribal line into two sections. The first part is essentially of masculine interest, and deals with the groom's courtship and payment of the marriage price. The second part has to do with the ladies and the bride's dowry. We may close our discussion of Ugaritic mythology with Yarih's proposal of marriage:

> *I shall pay her bride price to her father:*
> *A thousand (shekels) of silver*
>   *E'en ten thousand of gold.*
> *I shall send jewels of lapis-lazuli.*
> *I shall make her field into vineyards*
>   *The field of her love into orchards.*

The handsome price is, of course, beyond the range of normal human ability to pay, but the term *muhr* " bride price " is taken from real life. Moreover, his promise to make her fertile, reflects the real attitude towards marriage, whose purpose was human fertility. A husband was like a farmer who cultivates the soil so that it yields a harvest. A woman is like a field, who needs the seed and cultivation of a husband, if she is to be fertile. Our text is, therefore, a *hieròs gámos*: a wedding of the gods, whose fertility brings on terrestrial abundance for mankind.

The mythology of Canaan is important in more ways than one. Its chief significance lies in its effect on ancient Israel. Both where the Old Testament incorporates it, and where the Old Testament reacts against it, Canaanite mythology continues to exert its impact upon us through the Bible. The epics of Ugarit are, as we have seen, of central significance for the history of literature, for they link the early literatures of Greece and Israel.

VI

The Minoan Tablets from Crete

From about 2000 B.C. the Aegean had a script of its own, inspired by the Mesopotamian and Egyptian systems of writing familiar in the East Mediterranean since fairly early in the third millennium. The process whereby those ancient systems evoked the invention of the Cretan Hieroglyphs, is " stimulus diffusion," not outright borrowing. The Minoans got the idea of writing from their predecessors; they did not slavishly copy the Mesopotamian or Egyptian system. In fact, Minoan writing marks a great step forward by way of simplification. The older scripts were highly complex with signs corresponding to all kinds of syllables: closed syllables and even polysyllabic words. The Minoan system has only open syllables. It marks the transition from the older cumbersome systems to the alphabet.

To be sure, the Minoan system did not sweep away all the clutter of its antecedents. Like the earlier scripts, it continued to use logograms (word-signs) for numerals and various commodities. Sometimes it combines a pictograph of an object with the word for the object spelled out syllabically. This results in a quasi-bilingual which provided a check on the decipherment of Linear B and the starting point for the decipherment of the tablets from HT (Hagia Triada), near the south shore of central Crete.

There is a continuity of Minoan writing, starting with the

Cretan Hieroglyphs, continuing through the various forms of so-called Linear A and Linear B, and the Cypro-Minoan, down to the Cypriote texts that continue until late in the third century B.C. Both Linear B and the late Cypriote texts are in Greek. Some of the signs are identical (in both form and sound) in both sets of these Greek texts despite the lapse of time and difference in locale.

The late Cypriote inscriptions are sometimes written in duplicate: one version in alphabetic Greek, and the other in syllabic Greek. In the nineteenth century, the British scholar, George Smith, broke into the Cypriote syllabary, thus beginning the decipherment of the Minoan system.

The largest corpus of texts in the Minoan system is called Linear B. It consists of about 4000 tablets found at Knossos on Crete and at a number of sites on the Greek mainland: notably Pylos and Mycenae. Linear B starts towards the close of the fifteenth century and lasts into the twelfth century B.C. In 1952, an English amateur named Michael Ventris succeeded in assigning enough correct values to the Linear B syllabary to establish the basis for reading the texts. His solution was based on the premise that the language was Greek. Many scholars began to work without delay on the Linear B tablets within the framework of Ventris's decipherment and the status of the new field after the first three years of activity is given in *Documents in Mycenaean Greek* (Cambridge U. Press, 1956) by M. Ventris and J. Chadwick. Though the texts are all economic and administrative, they throw the recorded history of the Greek language back to about 1400 B.C., long before the traditional date of the Trojan War. The ascendancy of the Greeks in the Peloponnesus and on Crete (at least at Knossos) is now established for the second half of the second millennium B.C. But the book of Ventris and Chadwick marks something else of importance; it has shattered the artificial barriers between the " Orient " and Greece that had hitherto

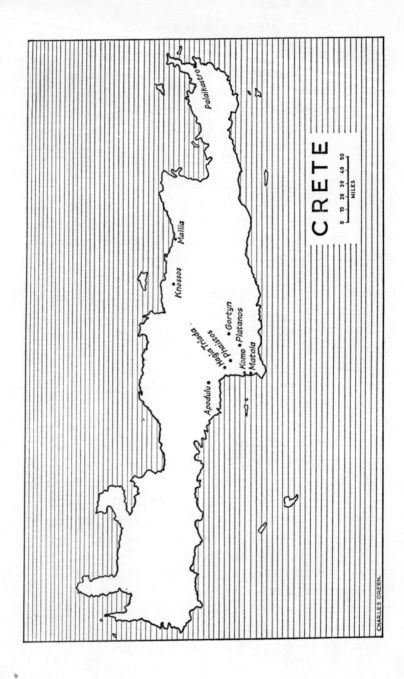

CRETE

0 10 20 30 40 50
MILES

Palaikastro

Mallia

Knossos

Hagia Triada
Phaistos
Gortyn
Komo • Platanos
Matala

Apodulu

CHARLES GREEN.

dominated the philological tradition. That book draws heavily on cuneiform and Egyptian evidence, for the administrative and economic system of the Minoan/Mycenaean sphere has affinities with other East Mediterranean lands, in which the most important single cultural component was Mesopotamian.

The rapidity with which the interpretation of the Linear B tablets has developed is due to their Greek character. The field of Aegean studies is in the hands of classicists, who welcomed, and were qualified to work on, the new branch of Hellenic philology. Even before the decipherment of Linear B, it was plain to see that the languages of the Minoan tablets from other sites on Crete were not in any way similar to the B language. This could only mean that a different group of specialists would have to take over the task of decipherment and interpretation.

The only group of " A " texts comprehensive enough for initial study is the H T corpus of about 150 tablets. They are also administrative and economic; their script is not identical with, but quite similar to that of the B tablets. Most of the signs and their phonetic values are the same in both systems. Accordingly, the solution of the HT problem became possible as soon as Ventris deciphered the B tablets, provided that the HT language belongs to an already known linguistic group. The problem would in any case be full of hurdles because of the fewness of the HT texts and their limited repertoire. Yet the fact that we know the pronunciation of a number of words whose meanings are fixed by context guarantees the possibility of decipherment if the language is one that is well known from other sources.[1]

We do not yet know the language(s) for which the Cretan Hieroglyphs were originally designed. But we do know that Crete was polyglot and that the Minoan system of writing was used on Crete for more than one language. On the north side

[1] Our methodology is inherent in this sentence. We are on sure ground only when both the reading and the meaning are certain.

(Knossos) and the south side (HT) of Central Crete, at about 1400 B.C., the Minoan system of writing was adapted to two different languages. The one at Knossos was Greek; the one at H T was probably Semitic as we shall now demonstrate.

The district of Crete that includes HT is the Messara. Prior to the Amarna Age, Babylonian influence penetrated the district, for, as we have observed in Chapter 11, Babylonian importations of the Hammurapi Age have been excavated at Platanos, in the Messara. Komo is their probable port of entry. HT is not far off; and the Harvester Vase found at HT portrays a crowd led by a leader whose fringed garb has Mesopotamian features. Accordingly, not only does the period of the HT tablets (*ca.* 1400, and so in the Amarna Age) favour the use of Semitic, but specifically the Messara is known to have undergone Babylonian influence prior to the writing of the H T tablets.[1]

In December of 1956, I received my copy of *Documents in Mycenaean Greek*. Two texts discussed therein were of particular interest to me. One was a Pylos tablet that had confirmed Ventris's decipherment. On it were depicted various vessels including tripods as well as vases with three, four or no handles. The syllables accompanying the vessel-pictograms spell out the correct Greek designations according to values established by Ventris, who had not seen this Pylos tablet until after he had achieved his decipherment. The other tablet that attracted my attention was HT #31, on which were written vessel pictographs, each with a word inscribed syllabically over it. Inasmuch as the

---

[1] The HT tablets are said to come from a L(ate) M(inoan) Ia context (see W. C. Brice, *Inscriptions with Minoan Linear Script of Class A*, Society of Antiquaries, London, 1961, p. xi). LM Ia has been dated about 1580-1510 B.C. However, Minoan chronology will probably have to be lowered since it is linked with Near East chronology that is being reduced for all periods prior to the Amarna Age. Moreover, the HT signs are often more developed than the corresponding B forms, suggesting our late date of around 1400 B.C. for the HT tablets.

Pylos tablet, whose Greek interpretation is beyond question, established the Aegean usage of recording vessel-inventories by pictographs plus syllabic entries *in the language of the* B *tablets, it is* reasonable to suppose that HT #31 is a comparable inventory of vessel-pictographs accompanied by the words for the vessels *in the language of the* HT *tablets.* The names of three vessels on HT #31 looked Semitic to me immediately; one of the cups was labelled *su-pu,* another *su-pà-la,* while a handled vase was labelled *ka-ro-pà.* These three vessel-names appear in both West and East Semitic; *su-pu* looks like Ugaritic *sp,* Hebrew *sapp-* or *sipp-,* and Akkadian *sapp-; su-pà-la* looks like Ugaritic *spl,* Hebrew *sipl-* or Akkadian *sapl-; ka-ro-pà* looks more like Akkadian *karp-* than the Ugaritic variant *krpn.* I prepared a brief article on these three readings plus a very few other possible Semitic words in HT and sent it by airmail towards the close of December, 1956, to my friend, the late Dr. O. G. S. Crawford, for publication in his journal, *Antiquity.*

Crawford replied promptly and told me he had reason to think that I was on the verge of a major discovery. He told me to continue my study of the Linear A tablets and that he would print the results in the 1957 volume of *Antiquity.* His letters to me included the rhetorical question, " What could the Minoan language be except Semitic? " I was not willing to go quite that far, but I knew enough of history to realise that the Semitic languages were widely used internationally around the East Mediterranean during the period in question. So I spent the rest of the winter and spring of 1957 poring over the photographs of the HT corpus. My only companion in the task was Joan, my wife, who shared my work, hopes and frustrations in a labour that would otherwise have been lonely. I was not yet in communication with other Minoan scholars; nor did the studies of other scholars such as Furumark, Meriggi and Goold-Pope reach me until different months of 1958. Perhaps it was for the best, for though more knowledge of their valuable work might have kept me from making certain errors in detail, I had the advantage of coming to the subject without too many of the prejudices and false assumptions that were current in various forms.

My first HT publications were articles that appeared in September and December, 1957, in *Antiquity*. The first article proposed that the HT language was Semitic; the second, that it possessed some East Semitic features.

The word for " a kind of wheat," whose reading appears four times and is uncontested and whose meaning is fixed by the WHEAT determinative, is *ku-ni-su*: a well-known Akkadian word for " emmer-wheat " in the form attested many times in the Nuzu tablets.[1]

At this point we must pause to explain the situation to the reader who is either not conversant with ancient scripts and languages, or who has not been confronted with the general problems of cryptanalysis. The HT tablets are lists, inventories and allocations of goods. Much of the limited material consists of proper names, logographically written numerals, and commodity logograms and determinatives, which tell us nothing of the language of the texts. To clarify this with a simple analogy: a phrase like " one hundred pounds " is obviously English; but " 100 lb." (in which the numeral and noun are logographic) might appear in a text written in other languages as well. Our present corpus of HT texts confronts us with only a few dozen

---

[1] The identification of *ku-ni-su* with Akkadian *kunišu* is of importance because it has been well received by even the most cautious and reluctant scholars such as Chadwick and Peruzzi. Cf. J. Chadwick, " Minoan Linear A: A Provisional Balance Sheet," *Antiquity* 33, 1959, pp. 269-278 (see p. 277); and E. Peruzzi, " Recent Interpretations of Minoan (Linear A)," *Word* 15, 1959, pp. 313-324 (see p. 318). The first to accept my Semitic identification of HT was Maurice Pope of South Africa. Professor Pope has since made valuable contributions of his own. Incidentally, it was A. Furumark who first correctly defined *ku-ni-su*, and Pope who following my line of thought, first proposed its Akkadian identification.

regular words such as common nouns, adjectives and verbs. An isolated word for a pot might be a loanword; but several words for various pots, "wheat" and the conjunction "and"—all in Semitic—are not likely to be loanwords. To state the matter quite simply: a language of the East Mediterranean during the Amarna Age, in which *u* is "and" and *ku-ni-su* is "wheat" is just as likely Semitic as that language of the Nuclear Age is English in which *a-n-d* is the conjunction, and *w-h-e-a-t* is a grain.

The Semitic of the Amarna Age as used by foreigners is not classical but provincial and full of foreign elements. The HT tablets are no exception. In addition to the native Cretan elements, we find Hurrian and West Semitic names. The Hurrians were ubiquitous in the Amarna Order. They are found all over Western Asia and Egypt; they formed a large segment of the Ugaritic and Alalakh populations; they predominated in Nuzu. The HT name *da-ku-se-ni*[1] is apparently the Hurrian name Daku-šenni (var. Tagu-šenni). It is striking that *ku-ni-su* (with *-i-*) is limited so far to Nuzu (*kunîšu*) and HT (elsewhere it is *kunâšu*). Accordingly, HT and Nuzu share a feature of the northern provincial Akkadian found in conjunction with Hurrian personal names.

The West Semitic elements are more numerous than the Hurrian. The name or title *da-we-da*[2] is apparently West Semitic *dawîd-* meaning "chief," whence the name "David" is derived. *Da-ku-na*[3] is "Dagon," a western deity worshipped by the Philistines, and honoured with a temple at Ugarit. *Ku-pà-nu*[4] is the same as Ugaritic Gupan: a name borne by a deity in the religious texts and by men in the administrative tablets from Ugarit. *Ku-pà-na-tu*[5] also appears as a name in HT, and is the

[1] HT 103: 2, 4; 104: 1-2.
[2] HT 10: a: 4; 85: a: 2; 93: a: 7; 122: a: 7.
[3] HT 103: 4.
[4] HT 1: a: 3; 3: 7; 49: 5-6; 117: a: 3; 122: a: 6, 7.
[5] HT 47: a: 1-2; 119: 3.

perfect Semitic feminine of Gupan- (with the suffix *-atu*). *Ku-pà-na-tu-na*,[1] inscribed on a stone vessel from Apodulu (just west of the Messara) may well consist of *Gupan* plus the combination of suffixes that appears in Hebrew as *-ātôn* (as in *'ᵃqallātôn*: an epithet of Leviathan).

The content of the HT tablets is far less important than the probability that they are Semitic. It is the identification of their language that is significant. We now see that the Mycenaean Greeks did not have to borrow the literature and other aspects of Near Eastern civilisation from abroad; instead they found it already entrenched on Aegean soil much as the earliest Hebrews found it already entrenched on Palestinian soil. The Amarna Age is like the Hellenistic Age, albeit in reverse. Both ages saw the East Mediterranean united by a common culture in all of the area. In the Amarna Age, the common denominator was Semitic; in the Hellenistic Age, it was Greek. Just as the Christian and Roman West grew out of the Hellenistic synthesis, early Israel and Mycenaean Greece sprang from the Amarna synthesis. It is within this framework that we are to evaluate the tablets in Minoan script from HT. They confirm the evidence of the Babylonian seal cylinders found on Crete.[2]

---

[1] Reproduced in A. Furumark, " Linear A und die altkretische Sprache ' (mimeographed for private circulation), Berlin, 1956, plate 21.

[2] Cf. S. Davis, " New Light on Linear A," *Greece & Rome* 6, 1959, pp. 20-30, who aptly states: "... Linear A ... will throw a great deal of light on pre-Greek civilisation in the Aegean area, and so help to a better understanding of early Greek civilisation itself. It is worthwhile to stress the fact that the Oriental background of classical studies is being felt more and more to-day among scholars. The interwoven nature of Mediterranean civilisation needs to be more fully appreciated " (p. 30).

POSTSCRIPT (5 FEBRUARY 1962)

After these pages were in proof, I received the new edition of the Minoan texts by Brice (*op. cit.*) with improved photographs and hand copies. Hitherto I had not been able to do much with the Linear A dedications inscribed on cultic objects at a number of sites in eastern and central Crete. On a libation table from Palaikastro (text I, 3), Brice's keen eye discerned a group of four signs that I recognized at once as *ki-re-ya-tu*, the West Semitic word (*qiryat—*) for "city." The text begins with *le ya-sa-* [   ] which in West Semitic means "To Y." Y. is taken by all Minoan scholars to be the deity whose name (*Ya-sa-sa-ra-mu*) occurs on six other cult objects from different Minoan sites. The text ends with *ki-te-te-bi . ki-re-ya-tu=*West Semitic *kî têṭeb qiryatu* "that the city may do well." In other words, the table was dedicated to the deity so that the city might thrive. This is the first Semitic interpretation of a passage with sentence structure controllable by inflectional and syntactical features. I accordingly re-examined all the Linear A texts and found that a libation table from Knossos (text I, 8) opens with the word *ta-nu-a-ti=* Phoenician *ṭanû'at* "it was set up (as a votive offering)." The Dictaean libation table (text I, 1) opens with *ta-na-i——*, which looks like an active form of the same Phoenician root *ṭn'* "to set up (as a votive offering)." A libation bowl from Apodulu (text I, 14) opens with *ya-ta-no-?* *u-ya-* [   ] which may correspond to Phoenician *ytn wyṭn'* "he gave and set up (as a votive offering)." Part of a large jar from Knossos is incised with a graffito (text II, 3) including the two syllable word *ya-ne*: the correct way for West Semitic *yayn-* "wine" to be written in Minoan script.

This development raises the study of Minoan Linear A to a

new level. It confirms the correctness of the Semitic vocabulary such as *u* (28: a: 1; 117: a: 1; I, 4) "and," *ku-lo* (often in HT) "all," *a-ga-nu* (text II, 2) "bowl" etc., in addition to other Semitic words mentioned above in this chapter.

We can now approach the West Semitic names in the HT documents more comprehensively. Once we compare HT *ki-re-tá* and *ki-re-ta-na* with Ugaritic *krt* and *krtn*, we see that the names used in Crete and Canaan share the feature of adding the suffix *-ân* to personal names. HT *ka-du-ma-ne* (29: 6)= Ugaritic *qdmn*, now appears as the name familiar from "Cadm-us" (the Phoenician who traditionally introduced the alphabet to Greece) plus *-ân*; HT *mi-na-ne* (28: 1: 1-2; 117 : a: 1-2)= Alalakh *mi-na-an*= Ugaritic *mnn*, is "Min-os" plus *-ân*; and HT *da-na-ne* (126: a: 1) = Ugaritic *da-na-nu* and *dnn*, is Hebrew "Dan" plus *-ân*.

What emerges is the fact that Crete and Canaan in the second millennium B.C. form a single cultural entity, writing essentially the same language and using many of the same personal names.

Herodotus (1: 105; 2: 44; 4: 147 ff.; 6: 47, etc.) knew about the early Phoenician penetration of what is now Greek territory. But many modern scholars still choose to discount his testimony and instead follow current schools of thought.

It turns out that the Greeks learned both of their systems of writing from the Phoenicians; first the Minoan syllabary, and then the alphabet.

The Phoenicians were influential throughout the East Mediterranean early in the second millennium B.C. They were gradually displaced by Indo-European invaders in all areas north of the Syro-Lebanese coast. When the Mycenaean newcomers replaced West Semitic Linear A at Knossos with Linear B Greek around 1400 B.C., the shift in the balance of power was already under way. But in Cilicia, Phoenician continued to be written (alongside Hieroglyphic Hittite) until late in the eighth century B.C. On Cyprus (and to a lesser extent even in Attica), Phoenicians continued to write their own language until well in the Hellenistic Age.

We do not know precisely what the biblical author had in mind when he ascribed to Noah the prophecy that the sons of Japheth "will dwell in the tents of Shem" (Genesis 9: 27). But no interpretation is at present more likely than that it refers to the Indo-European displacement of the West Semites, first traceable epigraphically when Greek Linear B supplanted Phoenician Linear A at Knossos.

VII

Further Observations on Homer

The first five chapters have stated the problem and set forth enough of the comparative evidence to demonstrate the thesis of this book. It is desirable, however, to add some general and detailed observations, on Homer in this chapter, and on the Bible in the next chapter. To the specialist many of the following remarks, based as they are on the plain meaning of the text, may seem naïve. No break-through in any field is likely to be achieved without directness and simplicity verging on naïveté.

The Linear B tablets reflect the administrative side of the Mycenaean World. Homeric epic deals with the aristocracy and its idealised past. Our Homeric text has been edited by subsequent generations, but wherever we can control it, it appears to reflect the Heroic Age more accurately than do the emendations. The authenticity of the text is due to two successive factors. The earlier factor is that in the formative period of Greek epic (15th-10th centuries, B.C.), when the compositions that set the pattern for the Iliad and Odyssey were already in circulation, Mycenaean civilisation was still flourishing. Accordingly, the Homeric picture of Mycenaean life, institutions, artifacts and beliefs is basically correct. The second factor is that the milieu of the epic had become so familiar and revered, that no one could take serious liberties with it during the period of the composition and redaction of Homeric epic (9th-6th centuries). Fifth-century authors, such as Herodotus and Thucydides, speak of Homeric epic as the outstanding classical and virtually canonical text of antiquity. This can only mean that by the 5th century, not only the composition but also the primary transmission and editing had taken place. The authorised Vulgate Text of Homer that we now use is essentially the same as the texts read by Herodotus and Thucydides. There were, of course, variants; but they did not affect the general sense. The major differences between different schools of Homeric manuscripts in the fifth century must have been comparable to the differences that exist between the Jewish and Samaritan Pentateuchs; most of them are ortho-graphic and linguistic trivia plus a few tendentious variants of partisan significance but not affecting the composition as a whole nor even any major portion thereof.

In later times, say, during the Ptolemaic Period, the various texts of Homer differed among each other in a way comparable with the Old Testament manuscripts found at Qumran.[1]

Archaeological discovery repeatedly vindicates the text against the hypotheses of the critics, so that Homeric epic emerges more and more as a trustworthy mirror of the times and spirit of the Mycenaean Age.

The key to understanding Mycenaean Civilisation is its position in the international framework of the East Mediter-ranean during the second half of the second millennium. Mycen-aean Greece lay on the northwest fringe of the Amarna Order. The most fundamental thread in the fabric of that Order was Mesopotamian, but after the Age of Hammurapi (ca. 18th century B.C.), Mesopotamia had no more striking power or vigour to reach anywhere near the Aegean directly. Mesopo-

---

[1] Textual uniformity is imposed on earlier diversity. All this means is that until the text has won its canonical status, variants are tolerated. But once the text is revered as canonical, there arises the urge to establish the one and only right text. This is what happened with Homeric Epic among the Greeks, and the Old Testament among the Hebrews, and with many other sacred texts among other nations.

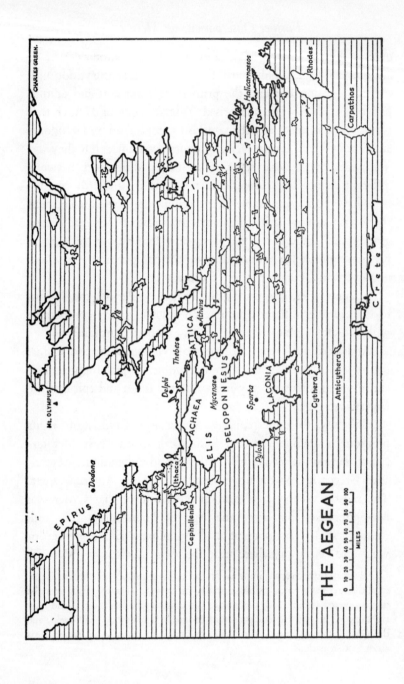

CHARLES GREEN.

THE AEGEAN

0 10 20 30 40 50 60 70 80 90 100
MILES

Rhodes

Carpathos

Halicarnassos

Crete

Mt. OLYMPUS ▲

EPIRUS

Dodona

Cephallenia

Ithaca

Delphi

Thebes

ATTICA

Athens

ACHAEA

Mycenae

ELIS

PELOPONNESUS

Pylos

Sparta

LACONIA

Cythera

Anticythera

tamian influence had, however, been so built into Hurrian, Hittite, Phoenician and other East Mediterranean cultures, that through them it persisted in the Levant.[1] Homeric tradition does not mention Mesopotamia, Babylonia or Assyria, but instead Egypt, Phoenicia, Syria, various Anatolian countries, Cyprus, etc., via which Mesopotamian culture lived on in the West.

The Homeric tradition has its own way of telling us that Minoan/Mycenaean civilisation was intertwined with the culture of the Semitic Phoenicians. Iliad 14: 321-322 makes Phoenix (named after the ancestor of the Phoenicians) the maternal grandfather of Minos. This is the ancient way of indicating affinities between the Phoenicians and Minoans. Archaeology bears out early cultural connections between the two.

Homeric Epic often mentions Egypt. Thus the Odyssey 4: 229-232 describes Egypt as a land abounding in both curative and poisonous drugs, where everybody is a physician. This poetic statement is reducible to a prose truth. No nation of remote antiquity has a more illustrious medical history than Egypt.[2] The medical papyri are landmarks in the history of diagnostics, medicine and surgery. As we have seen in Chapter IV, Greek epic absorbed much from Egyptian literature.

None of the component groups in the East Mediterranean complex was homogeneous. Egyptians from the Delta could not understand the speech of Egyptians from Elephantine. Some Hebrews were herding flocks in the hills while others were engaged in navigation. The Greeks harboured differences as

---

[1] During the seventeenth and early sixteenth centuries B.C., the Hyksos Empire facilitated the channels of intercommunication in the Levant. After the expulsion of the Hyksos from Egypt around 1570 B.C., the Egyptian Empire (which reached its maximum size under Thothmes III during the first half of the fifteenth century) played this role to a considerable extent.

[2] See R. O. Steuer and J. B. de C. M. Saunders, *Ancient Egyptian and Cnidian Medicine: The Relationship of their Aetiological Concepts of Disease,* Univ. of Cal. Press, Berkeley and Los Angeles, 1959.

great as the contrast between the Athenians and Spartans of classical times. The Trojan allies were composed of many nations speaking various languages (Iliad 4: 438).

Each component group within the international East Mediterranean synthesis had its own individuality as well as its common ground with the other nations in the synthesis. The Hebrews and Mycenaean Greeks were certainly different from each other, but no more so than either was from other nations in the synthesis. The Mycenaeans differed from the Hebrews less than either did from the Upper Egyptians. The latter were subject to a narrow parochialism, whereas the Greeks and Hebrews were more cosmopolitan, consciously sharing the same "Levantine" internationalism.

Both the Iliad and the Odyssey have antecedents in the East Mediterranean. The Iliad, insofar as it is the story of the recapture of Helen, is anticipated in the Ugaritic Epic of Kret. Kret's fair wife, Hurrai, is being withheld from him at Udum. Kret corresponds to Menelaus, Hurrai to Helen, and Udum to Troy. Hurrai is called the fairest in the harem of the first born of King Pebel, who rules Udum. Accordingly, Pebel corresponds to Priam, and his firstborn to Paris. The Helen of Troy theme runs through the Patriarchal Narratives, too, as we have seen. The Wrath of Achilles over a woman appears unmistakably, though with inartistic brevity, in the Samson Story. Samson's wife is given to another man, whereupon he flies into a rage that does not subside until many Philistines perish. The Philistine milieu of the Samson Story is significant, for the Philistines are of Aegean origin.[1]

---

[1] Note that the date (roughly 1100 B.C.) as well as the Aegean milieu are right for both the Hebrew and Greek narratives. We are only interested in the transmission of culture through people, in specific time and place. The comparison of phenomena from the ends of the earth, and from one extremity of historic time to the other, lies completely beyond the character and scope of this book.

The plot of the Odyssey has more detailed antecedents than the Iliad in the literatures of the ancient Near East. To recapitulate: the plot, insofar as it is the episodic wanderings of a hero that end in coming home, has marked similarities to the Gilgamesh Epic. Both texts start out with descriptions of the hero who travelled far and wide, gaining great experience. Nor is the resemblance limited to such generalities. The two epics share detailed episodes. Just as Gilgamesh interviews Enkidu in Hades, so does Odysseus interview Achilles in Hades; and as Gilgamesh turns down the goddess Ishtar's proposal of marriage, so too Odysseus turns down the goddess Calypso's proposal of marriage. Yet it is a mistake to derive the plot of the Odyssey too narrowly from the Gilgamesh Epic. The Odyssey makes frequent mention of Egypt, so that it need not surprise us to find rudiments of the plot of the Odyssey in Egyptian literature. In Middle Egyptian literature, two compositions shed light on the Odyssey. One is the Romance of Sinuhe, which tells of a courtier who wandered throughout Palestine and Syria as an exile, but at last after many adventures was able to return home. The other is the tale of the Shipwrecked Sailor, who after being washed ashore on a magic isle, got back to Egypt laden with gifts. The episode of the land of the Phaeacians in the Odyssey unmistakably harks back to the Isle of the Shipwrecked Sailor. Note, too, that the Shipwrecked Sailor, like the Odyssey, has a nautical setting (unlike Gilgamesh and Sinuhe). In Late Egyptian literature (during the height of the Mycenaean Age), the scene shifts to the Mediterranean with the Misadventures of Wenamon. Wenamon sets out on an official mission which leads him through a series of escapades on various coastal points and islands, ere he returns home safely. This type of story was naturally popular among the various peoples who embarked on nautical enterprises on the Mediterranean. Note that in all these stories (Gilgamesh as well as the Egyptian tales), appears the theme of the *nóstos* "homecoming."

Stories spread throughout the Levant via various categories of mobile social strata. Sailors were then, as always, good carriers of stories. Merchants engaged in foreign trade were just as likely to entertain each other (and their customers) with stories as travelling salesmen do to-day. Military stories circulated largely through mercenaries; and Aegean troops often served as mercenaries. We must attribute the transmission of written literatures in large measure to the scribal schools such as the one at Tell el Amarna where Egyptian lads were trained in Akkadian by copying and studying literary texts of the Babylonians. As we have noted, fragments of the Gilgamesh Epic have been found in Palestine and Anatolia; and it is not impossible that fragments of it will some day be found in Crete in the vicinity of Hagia Triada or at least somewhere in the Messara. Literature was spread orally by another mobile stratum of society: the guild of minstrels.

The minstrel was welcome wherever he might travel. No festive board was complete without his song. The minstrel, if truly inspired, whether by the Muse or Apollo, was believed capable of retelling actual happenings as if he had been there or heard the tale. Thus in Odyssey 8: 487-520, at Odysseus' request, Demodocus sings of the Trojan Horse and the sack of Troy just as accurately as though he had been there. The minstrel is thus inspired by a god (Odyssey 8: 499) and is described as "divine" (Odyssey 16: 252). The poet of the Iliad calls on the Muses to tell him who the Danaans and their lords were, because otherwise we mortals hear only rumours and know nothing (Iliad 2: 484-6). Epic poetry is divinely inspired (Iliad 1: 1) and as such is just as true as oracles, and for the same reason. It is no accident that oracles (such as those at Delphi) were enunciated in the same dactylic hexameter as the epic. Both were regarded as the word of god, and therefore merited the same mode of expression.[1] The guild minstrels, because of their divine inspiration, were held in honour and reverence wherever they went (Odyssey 8: 477-481).[2] Their profession required of them not only the repetition of an ancient repertoire, but also the addition of new ones, because their clientele was fond of the latest songs (Odyssey 1: 351-2).

Music was an art fostered by the mightiest of heroes. Achilles is represented as entertaining himself with his lyre (Iliad 9: 185-6). We compare David, the warrior skilled in poetry, singing and musical instruments. David is represented as employed as musician and singer in Saul's court. When he is exiled to the court of Achish, the Philistine King of Gath, we must imagine him singing his Judean repertoire in Philistine Gath, and enriching his own store by exposure to the Gathite minstrels. Psalm 8, attributed to David, is to be sung to the accompaniment of the "Gathite" instrument (verse 1); but cf. also Psalm 81: 1; 84: 1.

The texts of the Iliad and Odyssey inform us that the tales of those epics were circulating in amorphous bulk from which the poet had to select his material. The poet could have started the Iliad much earlier in the story, but he consciously decides to begin with the strife that broke out between Achilles and Agamemnon (Iliad 1: 6). Similarly Odyssey 1: 10 requests of the goddess: "Tell us, O goddess, daughter of Zeus, of these things, beginning at any point whatever." The Odyssey thus opens at the point chosen by the inspired poet. It could have started at some earlier stage of the story, had the poet so wished. There was thus an accumulation of literary narrative circulating among the bards. The creative poet, in fashioning a poem like

[1] The " Word of Yahweh " (i.e., oracles) enunciated by the Prophets is normally in poetry for the same reason.

[2] By the same token, the Prophets of Israel were sacrosanct and enjoyed general immunity.

the Iliad or Odyssey, could select his subject matter, reshape it and while working within the matrix of the tradition and its already existing materials, produce a masterpiece that remains forever fresh.

The older biblical compositions (such as the Pentateuch and the historical books called the Former Prophets) shows the same general development. Earlier works are often cited, such as the Book[1] of the History of Man (Genesis 5: 1), the Book of the Wars of Yahweh (Numbers 21: 14), the Book of Jashar (Joshua 10: 14; 2 Samuel 1: 18), etc. The canonical Book of Judges is composed of Cycles mostly concerning the individual Judges. The composition as a whole is given unity by leading up to the demonstration that national life under the Judges was chaotic and a more stable form of kingship was necessary.

The Iliad and Odyssey have more dramatic unity than the early Hebrew compositions, but nonetheless incorporate older cycles, too. The stories of Bellerophon, Phoenix, Meleager, Niobe and Oedipus are examples of pre-Homeric compositions extracted and incorporated quite effectively into Homeric epic.

The perfection of Homer and Bible, each in its own way, is the culmination of long literary development around the East Mediterranean. The outmoded assumption that each was a wondrous revelation among primitive people never made sense *a priori*. The pre-Homeric and pre-Mosaic literatures of Mesopotamia, Egypt and Ugarit show us, in large measure, the common origins of our earliest Greek and Hebrew classics.

The complexity of the variant traditions current prior to the composition of our Greek and Hebrew classics made it hard to avoid discrepancies. For example, Pylaemenes, leader of the

---

[1] " Book " (*sêfer*) can only refer to a written document. Other sources in the Bible may be oral, when not qualified by *sêfer* or by some other word that implies writing.

Paphlagonians, is slain in Iliad 5: 576, but in 13: 658 (cf. 13: 643), he is still alive. Similarly, Samuel's death appears twice, in 1 Samuel 25: 1 and again in 28: 3. Such editorial unevennesses do not bother the reader until he is taught to pay attention to them instead of to the story.

The problem before us at present is one of taking Homeric epic on its own terms against the background of collateral material from the ancient Near East. Failure to do so takes Greek Epic out of its historic development and places it in an artificial position. A distinguished Homeric scholar has singled out the scene where Achilles draws his sword to slay the inviolate Agamemnon but is restrained by two goddesses, as exemplifying the innovations of the poet of the Iliad.[1] However, as we have seen above, this scene is anticipated at Ugarit, where two goddesses restrain Baal from using his sword against the inviolate messengers who bring an insulting message. Accordingly, this scene is no innovation in the Iliad; it is part of the ancient repertoire, probably already old when it was used in the Baal and Anath Cycle at Ugarit of the Amarna Age. The glory of the epic is not in innovation of subject matter but in forging old materials into a majestic whole where even the traditional clichés cast a magic spell, and often give the illusion of having been coined for the passsage that we happen to be reading.

To cite one more example from recent literature: Cedric H. Whitman (*Homer and the Heroic Tradition*, Harvard U. Press, Cambridge, 1958, p. 157) contrasts the materialistic attitude of Agamemnon with the spirituality of Achilles, because Agamemnon offers amends of cities, bronze, gold, tripods, women and an advantageous marriage, whereas Achilles at first refuses them and is disinterested when they are finally delivered. Actually, this is all a reflex of an integral part of East Mediterranean epic, fully attested in the Bible and in the Ugaritic Epic of Kret. Kret

[1] H. T. Wade-Gery, *The Poet of the Iliad*, Cambridge, 1952, pp. 32 ff.

wants Hurrai, just as Achilles wants Briseis. Kret turns down Pebel's offer of gold, silver, horses, chariots and other valuable gifts, and instead insists on the girl. As far as we can tell, Kret (unlike Achilles) remains uninterested in the material things and takes only his beloved Hurrai. If we begin to moralise about the superiority of Achilles' love and spirituality, the Ugaritic text places us in an uncomfortable position. The hero of the earlier Ugaritic epic would then appear to be more spiritual than Achilles of the later Greek epic, in that Achilles finally accepts, while Kret refuses the material things to the end. Obviously, the unfavourable comparison is unnecessary.[1] More important is our realisation that both the Ugaritic and Homeric variations stem from the same basic tradition. Uncompromising love for a particular woman (in spite of bribes) is part of the repertoire of the royal epic appearing in the Near East in the wake of the Indo-European migrations.

Scholars are bothered by the statement in Odyssey 19: 179 that Minos, when nine years old, ruled Knossos. Ancient kings had to deal directly with the gods. Such important dealings called for maturity on the part of the king. Minos, however, is a very special king. He was the son of Zeus and received the law from Zeus. The wonderful role of Minos is enhanced by the fact that at the tender age of nine he was able to exercise his role of divine king. Hebraic tradition goes still further. Our text (1 Samuel 13: 1) tells us that Saul began to reign when he was only one year old! The commentators are, of course, at a loss to understand this oddity and generally emend the text by adding

[1] Actually such gratuitous comparisons would put Abraham on the lowest rung of the moral ladder because Genesis 20: 14, 16 tells us that he accepted cattle, slaves and silver from Abimelech, when the latter released Sarah from his harem to Abraham. More constructive is our simple recognition of the fact that in the Helen of Troy motif, material amends are offered to the wronged husband in Ugaritic and Hebrew, as well as in the Greek variants of the same tradition.

a numeral (such as " 20 ").[1] But the precociousness of both Saul and Minos confirms both traditions.

Folkways taken from real life are often common to Homer and Semitic Asia. When Nestor meets Agamemnon wandering about at night, he asks whether he is looking for one of his mules or comrades (Iliad 10: 84). That a noble might be searching for animals is paralleled by Saul's wandering in quest of lost asses (1 Samuel 9: 3ff.).[2]

In Odyssey 24: 214-320, Odysseus makes trial of his old father, Laertes. Note especially line 240 where Odysseus engages in mockery at his aged father's expense. Only in Odyssey 24: 318-9 does Odysseus feel pangs of compassion inducing him to stop making sport of Laertes and tell him the truth. The motif of keeping innocent or loved ones guessing and worried before telling them the happy truth appears in the Middle Egyptian tale of the Eloquent Peasant and in the Biblical Story of Joseph.

Instructions to spare a lady's feelings lest sad news cause her to suffer from excess of weeping is part of the repertoire. Kret tells his son Ilhu not to tell Octavia that he (Kret) is seriously sick because she is so sensitive (Ugarit #125: 31-35). Similarly Telemachus orders Eurycleia not to tell Penelope of his departure for eleven or twelve days lest she mar her fair flesh with weeping (Odyssey 2: 376).

When Zeus' son Sarpedon meets his fate, Zeus expresses grief for his dead son by causing blood to rain (Iliad 16: 459-461). In Egypt, the function of rain is replaced by the Nile which fructifies

---

[1] M. Noth, whose reluctance to emend is admirable, states that the biblical writer probably omitted the numeral because " he had no evidence " (*History of Israel*, p. 177, n. 1). Here, as so often, the correct understanding emerges once we put the text into its Mediterranean framework. The reader should note that the statement of Saul's precociousness is derived from an epic source out of keeping with the more realistic data in the biblical narrative.

[2] That Saul was a noble from birth is clear from 1 Samuel 9: 1, where his father is called a member of the nobility (*gibbôr ḥáyil*).

the soil. Accordingly, the biblical Plague of Blood (Exodus 7: 19-25) is the Egyptian equivalent of the bloody rainfall in the Iliad. We have native Egyptian utterances of this mode of expressing bane: e.g., " forsooth, the river is blood " (which is a pessimistic description of Egypt).[1]

Another of the Plagues of Egypt is paralleled in Homer. The Achaeans fighting about the corpse of Patroclus (Iliad 17: 366-9) are enveloped by darkness although all the others are fighting in broad daylight (: 370-3). It will be remembered that the darkness of Egypt was also selective. Egypt was enveloped in darkness except for the Hebrew habitations which were full of light (Exodus 10: 21-23).

In a crisis, it is always annoying in real life when someone wastes precious time by reminiscing. And yet long reminiscing in a crisis is a device of the epic to enhance the suspense. Nestor's lengthy reminiscing in Iliad 11: 655-761 reminds us of Utnapishtim's reminiscing about the flood in Gilgamesh Epic tablet 11. In both cases, the poets bring the monologue to bear on the main problem quite effectively.

Eyebrows are called " blue " (literally " of *kúanos* ") in passages like Iliad 1: 528; 17: 209, etc. In the Ugaritic Epic of Kret the heroine, Hurrai, is said to have brows of lapis-lazuli. Also in the Egyptian text of the Shipwrecked Sailor, the serpent has brows (and beard) of lapis-lazuli. The sculptors of the ancient Near East frequently inlaid the eyebrows of their statues with lapis-lazuli. Whether *kúanos* is lapis-lazuli[2] or a paste imitation thereof, the Homeric idiom is in keeping with a well-known Near East feature attested in both art and texts.

All over the ancient East, as we have observed, red (actually reddish brown) is the colour appropriate for men, and yellow, for

---

[1] A. Gardiner, *Egyptian Grammar*, 3rd ed., Oxford, 1959, p. 93.

[2] *Uqnû* in Akkadian; spelled *iqnu* (possibly pronounced *iqna'u*) in Ugaritic. Greek *kúan-os* may stem from the same origin.

women. The frequency of red ochre and yellow ochre in excavated towns, suggests that men and women painted themselves
with the appropriate colour of ochre. On the paintings of Egypt
and Crete, red men and yellow women are quite familiar. The
warriors on Etruscan paintings are red. Kret rouged himself to
become ceremonially fit. And two of the most heroic men of the
Old Testament, Esau and David, are described as naturally red:
showing that they were born to be heroes. The colour *xanthós* as
applied to heroes like Achilles probably means reddish brown
(rather than "fair" or "blond") because it is also applied to
horses where it seems to designate "sorrel." By the same token,
leuk-ólenos (lit. "white-armed") applied to goddesses and
women, may actually refer to the yellow colour of ceremonially
painted ladies. Plutarch (*Ancient Customs of the Spartans*, #24, in
vol. III of the Loeb edition of the *Moralia*, p. 439) states that the
Spartans wore red garments because red is the manly colour,
and also has the merit of frightening the inexperienced foe and of
not revealing blood from a wound.

The best example of a major episode in Greek epic with close
affinities to a known Oriental source, as a whole and in detail, is
the story of Odysseus in the land of the Phaeacians. A great
wave of Poseidon shattered the raft of Odysseus,who saved himself by bestriding one of the planks (Odyssey 5: 365-371). The
Egyptian sailor similarly saved himself by clinging to a board
when waves broke the ship. The Phaeacians were not ordinary
folk; Odyssey 6: 201-205 tells of their wondrous nature and of
how dear they were to the immortals and of how they dwelt
farthest from mankind. The Isle of the Egyptian text is also a
wondrous spot inhabited by a giant talking serpent. Alcinous
asks Odysseus to recount the glories of the Phaeacians after
returning home to wife and children (Odyssey 8: 241-245). The
serpent asks the Egyptian sailor to remember him when he returns to Egypt; he also predicts that the sailor will be rejoined to

his wife and children. The reader of the Odyssey can never check on the veracity of the tale, because a big mountain has been flung about the city of the Phaeacians cutting it off from the rest of the world (Odyssey 13: 152, 177). Neither can the reader check on the Isle of the Shipwrecked Sailor because it, too, disappeared after the Sailor left it. Both Odysseus and the Egyptian Sailor sailed homeward laden with gifts from their hosts.

A widespread principle had it that the gods were immortal and omniscient. This principle is stated in Genesis 3: 22 where God tells the other deities that man, who has usurped the divine prerogative of universal knowledge, must not be allowed to grasp immortality as well: " Behold the man has become like one of us, knowing good and evil; and now (beware) lest he stretch forth his hand and take also of the tree of life so that he eat and live forever." In Homer, the gods in theory know everything (Odyssey 4: 379; Iliad 2: 485), but yet they can be kept in ignorance and be deceived by each other. Not even Zeus is immune to being deceived in his ignorance by his wife Hera. Also in Egyptian and Mesopotamian mythology, the gods are often the victims of ignorance and deception. Moreover, gods can even die, despite the doctrine of divine immortality. Iliad 5: 388 relates that Ares, bound by men, would have perished, if a woman had not apprised Hermes who saved him. Individual gods die under extenuating circumstances in the ancient Near East mythologies, too. The god Kingu is put to death in the Babylonian Creation Epic. Cf. also Sophocles (Antigone: 199-200), who speaks of a wretch who would burn his father's city and gods, inferring that men can annihilate deities by destroying their images.

One of the most intimate bonds between religion among the Greeks and among the peoples of Western Asia is the prominence of mountains as the abode of the gods. Olympus is for the Greeks what Saphon is for the Canaanites: the sacred mountain abode of the pantheon. Actually, the sacred mountain is not fixed in any of the widespread traditions. The Mountain of God can be Sinai, Jerusalem, Gerizim (or Ebal), Carmel, etc., depending on the time, place and milieu in the Bible. To the peninsular Greeks, Zeus was the god of Olympus (though it is well to remember that the Greek world had many different Mount Olympuses); to the Cretans, he was the god of Cretan Ida; to the Trojans, he was the god of Trojan Ida (Iliad 24: 290-291). All over the Greek World (e.g., Greece, the Islands, the Troad, or Ionia), one pantheon was worshipped, but there were different cultic centres of a local character. The identity of the sacred mountain could vary from cult to cult, locally. This was also true of Canaan where Baal was worshipped as the Baal of the particular community, or of the nearby mountain shrine. The ancients recognised the universality of Zeus or Baal; but their cultic practices were often geared to the Zeus or Baal of their own locality. The Prophet Jeremiah clearly recognised the same discrepancy in Yahwism; he sanctioned only universal Yahwism but condemned regional Yahwism whereby each town had its own god.[1] But the simple devotee was not troubled by such theological inconsistencies. The same localism confronts us in Mesopotamia, so much so that the Assyrian kings often list Ishtar of Nineveh and Ishtar of Erbil as two distinct goddesses.

Zeus is the " father of men and gods " (Iliad 1: 544, etc.).[2] At Ugarit, El is not only the father of the " seventy gods " but he is also " the father of mankind." In the main Hebrew tradition, with its monotheistic orientation, there are no other divinities for God to be father of, but God's fatherhood of mankind is a basic theme (Deuteronomy 32: 6).

Despite the polytheism of the East Mediterranean nations,

---

[1] Jeremiah 2: 28; 11: 13.

[2] Epictetus (*Discourses* I, iii, 1) states the doctrine that God (*ho theós*) is the father of men and of gods (*tôn theôn*). He equates Zeus with God (v. 2).

monotheistic trends were always present even in such crass poly-
theisms such as we find in Homer and in Egyptian literature.
For *theós* can mean " God " (with a capital G) in Homer,[1] like
p³ nṯr in Egyptian. Herodotus (3: 40) relates that Amasis told
Polycrates that *tò theîon* " The Deity " (i.e., God) is jealous. This
is not only of interest for the monotheism that one can find in
ancient Greece and Egypt, but for jealousy as an attribute of God.
The jealousy of God is one of the frequent attributes of God in the
Bible; e.g., in the Ten Commandments: " Ye shall not worship
them (i.e., other gods) because I, Yahweh, your God, am a jealous
God " (Exodus 20: 5).

Gods travel at high speeds that were then technically beyond
the reach of men. For example, Hera travels with the speed of
thoughts or wishes (Iliad 15: 80-83). In the Ugaritic poems, the
gods travel " by the thousand acres, yea myriad of hectares."
While modern usage would not sanction the use of areas instead of
distances for measuring speed, the Ugaritic idiom colourfully
depicts the high speed at which the gods travel.

It was not seemly for men to meet with gods face to face.
Jacob victoriously wrestled with a deity and then declared " I
have seen God face to face but my soul has been saved " (Genesis
32: 31). This clearly implies that seeing God face to face would
ordinarily mean death for a mortal man, but the heroic figure of
Jacob is " greater than lifesize." When Gideon beheld an angel of
Yahweh face to face, he was dismayed, but " Yahweh said unto
him: ' Peace to you! Do not fear! You shall not die! ' "
(Judges 6: 22-23). According to the tradition in Deuteronomy
34: 10, Moses was the only Prophet who knew God " face to
face." Against this background, we may turn to Odyssey 6: 329
where Pallas Athena did not appear to Odysseus " face to face "
because she feared Poseidon.

When the characters of epic and heroic saga are on significant

---

[1] Iliad 21: 103 (cf. Odyssey 14: 444).

missions, they are led divinely. Odyssey 21: 196, 201 states that Odysseus might return to Ithaca only under the guidance of a *theós* (: 196) or a *daímōn* (: 201). Similarly, Bellerophon reached Lycia under the blameless convoy of the gods (Iliad 6: 171). Note Exodus 23: 20, " Behold I am sending my angel before you, to guard you on the road and to bring you to the place that I have prepared "; and Numbers 20: 16, " We cried out to Yahweh and he heard our voice. So he sent an angel and brought us out from Egypt."

Gods in the guise of strangers might visit cities in order to observe whether men were violent or upright (Odyssey 17: 483-7). Hebrew tradition embodies the same idea; cf. Genesis 18: 20 ff. which tells of the divine visit to Sodom and Gomorrah to investigate whether the sinfulness of those cities was as bad as reports indicated. (This incidentally illustrates that the gods were not always omniscient but might have, quite like men, to examine situations personally, in order to verify reports.)

It is a mistake to think that tales of gods among men are necessarily fiction or hallucination. There are still societies to-day in which strangers who behave in certain ways are considered divine. When strangers seem divine, they instil a fear that evokes offerings.[1] Odyssey 16: 181-5 tells that Telemachus made offerings to Odysseus who seemed divine. In Judges 13, a man (v. 11) told a barren woman that she would conceive and bear a son who would save his people (vv. 2-5). Small wonder that the woman attributed to him the likeness of an angel (v. 6). The woman's husband, Manoah, felt impelled to prepare a kid for the angel of Yahweh (v. 15), plus a further offering (v. 19). Lest we conclude that the angel is less than divinity, note the words of Manoah in v. 22: " We shall surely die for we have seen God."

The attributes of individual gods in any pantheon are often paralleled in another pantheon. Poseidon is credited with con-

---

[1] Cf. Acts 14: 8-18 (N.B. vv. 11-13, 18).

structing the walls of Troy (Iliad 21: 446-7) much as the seven wise mythical beings who built the walls of Erech.[1] Poseidon is also singled out as the one god who felt no pity for Odysseus (Odyssey 1: 20); cf. Enlil who alone of the gods resented the saving of Utnapishtim from the Flood (Gilgamesh 11). Poseidon hated Odysseus for blinding Poseidon's son Polyphemus. Poseidon, however, does not slay Odysseus but makes him a wanderer far from home (Odyssey 1: 74-75): a fate worse than death not only according to Homer, but also according to many other traditions from the ancient Near East, including Egypt and Israel.

The river in the land of the Phaeacians is personified as both a god and a king in the Odyssey (5: 445-450). In Hammurapi's Code the River in which the ordeals are given is personified as a god. At Ugarit, Yamm " Sea " (=Nahr " River ") is personified as both a god and a ruler. " Sea " and " River " are personified fairly often in Old Testament poetry, too. A comparison of Jonah 2: 3 (" Nahr encompasses me ") with v. 5 (" Tehom encompasses me ") shows that " Nahr " (" River ") is a name of the sea-god. It is interesting also to compare Jonah 1 in which The Sea is treated as the Sea god; N.B., v. 15 " And they lifted Jonah and cast him to The Sea; and The Sea desisted from his wrath."[2]

Hephaistos is of particular interest because his counterpart at Ugarit (i.e., Kothar-and-Hasis) comes from Caphtor, even as Hephaistos has connections with Cretan Ida. A striking resemblance in detail is the association of both gods with fire. In Homer, fire can be called " the flame of Hephaistos." The special character of this fire is best brought out in Iliad 21: 331-376 where it is

[1] Stated twice in the Gilgamesh Epic; early in tablet 1, and late in tablet 11. The latter passage has been translated above, in Chapter 111.

[2] Note that the theme of wrath and its subsidence after dire consequences is not limited to the human sphere (as in the Wrath of Achilles paralleled by the Wrath of Samson); it extends to the divine sphere too. More important than the " Wrath of Yamm (the Sea) " is the Wrath of God: a major motif that merits a new analysis. We shall return to this topic later on in this Chapter.

Hephaistos who is charged with neutralising the eddying Xanthus River by fire. At Ugarit, the palace of Baal is completed after a week of Kothar-and-Hasis' special conflagration. Cf. the constructive wondrous fire in Exodus 32: 24.

That both Hephaistos and Kothar-and-Hasis are described as making fine weapons, jewellery and furnishings, is not surprising but required by their role in the pantheon. It may be worth noting, however, that both are also the architects and builders of the gods' palaces. Thus Iliad 20: 10-12 tells that Hephaistos made Zeus' house on Olympus with polished colonnades. One of the major scenes in Ugaritic mythology is the planning and erection of Baal's palace on Saphon, by Kothar-and-Hasis, with cedar columns covered with metal.

The harpies of Homer are the spirits of the storm that can snatch people away without leaving any tidings behind them (Odyssey 1: 241). We may perhaps compare the climactic disaster that befell Job's family in Job 1: 19; " And behold a great wind came from across the wilderness, striking the four corners of the house, and it fell upon the youths and they died. And I alone escaped to bear you tidings." The difference between no one to bear tidings, and only one escapee to bear the tale, is not an insuperable barrier between the role of the Homeric spirits of the storm and the calamitous great wind of the Hebrews.

Throughout the ancient Near East, as we have previously observed, two divine names are often fused into a single name. Amon-Re is a case in point. Yahweh-Elohim is the most important Hebrew example. Ugarit is full of examples, sometimes asyndetically (e.g., Qadish-Amrar), more frequently with the conjunction (e.g., Qadish-and-Amrar, Kothar-and-Hasis, etc.). In Homer, we may note Death-and-Fate (N.B. the sg. verb in Iliad 3: 101). Strength-and-Force occurs in Hesiod (Theogony: 385) and recurs as one of the *dramatis personae* in Prometheus Bound. Other examples are Fear-and-Panic (Theogony: 934) and Sleep-and-Death (Theogony: 758) although they are each described as terrible gods (in the pl.). Such combinations in Ugaritic are sometimes treated as grammatically singular, and sometimes dual. Herodotus (8: 111) tells of the satirical invention of the divine Persuasion-and-Necessity by Themistocles who wanted to extort money from the Andrians, who countered with a refusal because of their divine Poverty-and-Impotence.

Homeric gods (like the heroes who believed in them) often ride in horse-drawn chariots. (Horse-drawn chariotry, it will be remembered, was introduced by the Indo-European conquerors who penetrated the Near East after 2000 B.C.) The Ugaritic gods, however, regularly ride on donkey back with one exception: the Rephaim (or shades of the dead), who ride on horse-drawn chariots. The afterlife was for the aristocracy, even as the only earthly society worth describing in the epic was the heroic aristocracy.[1] Accordingly, since the divine shades of the dead were the departed heroes, it was natural that they should carry on in their " Valhalla " with horse-drawn chariots.

There is a feature of the Homeric concept of the gods that apparently is Indo-European and never penetrated the Semitic sphere. Homer not infrequently gives the equivalent of men's terminology in the language of the gods. For example, the river that men call " Scamander" is called " Xanthus " by the gods (Iliad 20: 73-74). The notion of a language of the gods appears in Sanskrit, Greek, Old Norse and Hittite literatures.[2] It is unattested in Egyptian and Semitic texts because the Egyptians never doubted that the gods spoke Egyptian and at least some of the Semites (certainly the Hebrews who never doubted that God

---

[1] The only inhabitants of Hades mentioned in the Odyssey are aristocrats. Common people had no more standing in the next world than in this one.

[2] For sample passages, see J. Friedrich, " Göttersprache und Menschensprache im hetitischen Schrifttum," *Sprachgeschichte und Wortbedeutung* (*Festschrift Albert Debrunner*), 1954, pp. 135-9.

and the angels spoke Hebrew) could not imagine the gods speaking any but their own dialect.

Homeric kingship differs from the later concepts that have come down to us, wherein royalty is sharply distinguished from, and vastly superior to, the nobility. In Homer we cannot speak of great kings, but only of kinglets. Priam is King, not of some vast realm, but only of the Troad. Moreover, his son Alexander (or Paris) is called a *basileús* " king " (Iliad 4: 96) even though it was not he but his father who was the supreme ruler of Troy. Any member of the heroic nobility—especially if he had some troops under his command—could be called " king." Antinous is also called *basileús* " king " (Odyssey 24: 179); he aspired to the kingship of Ithaca through the hand of Penelope in marriage, though he perished before that was to be. Yet he merited the title of " king " because he belonged to the aristocracy eligible for kingship.

Since the kings were the ruling class, a king derived much of his power within his class, from the size of the troops at his command. Achilles was *basileús* of the Myrmidons (Iliad 16: 211). Agamemnon, however, is superior to Achilles because he was king over a greater number of men (Iliad 1: 281). Agamemnon, with his hundred ships, commanded the largest and best contingent among the Achaeans (Iliad 2: 577-8) and therefore was made head of the Achaean coalition. When we read in Genesis 14 that Abraham, who had a private army of 318 men, headed a coalition that included three Amorite chieftains (Eshkol, Aner and Mamre by name), we may assume that Abraham's contingent was the largest of the four. Actually, a coalition of 1000 men looms large when compared with the numbers of troops mentioned in the Amarna Letters.

While the land of the Phaeacians lies somewhat beyond the realities of this world, the social institutions of the islanders fit more or less into actual sociology. Alcinous, the supreme king of the land, is represented as presiding over twelve subordinate kings. The twelve look very much like chiefs of an amphictyony, with a superior authority (Alcinous) placed over them. When Alcinous decides to bestow gifts on Odysseus, he orders the twelve *basilêes* " kings " to bring the gifts (Odyssey 8: 387-395).

The right for a king to rule could be terminated by the frailties of old age. Old Laertes had once been the ruler (*wánax*) of the Cephallenians (Odyssey 24: 378) and permanently enjoyed the title of " shepherd of the people " (Odyssey 24: 368). Yet when he was smitten by grievous old age, his son Odysseus took over the rule of Ithaca. The Odyssey portrays Odysseus as king while Laertes is still alive. Moreover, Laertes does not live in Odysseus' palace. The displacing of a decrepit king by his son appears in the Legend of Kret and in the history of Israel, where the most noteworthy example is Solomon's accession to the throne while the senile David is still alive.

It was not always certain that a father would be succeeded by his son. Odyssey 1: 394-404 informs us that there were many " kings " in Ithaca that might succeed Odysseus, but in any case Telemachus insisted that he at least retain possession of his house and slaves that Odysseus had won for him. Similarly, though David wrested the kingship from the House of Saul, he felt constrained to give Saul's estate to Saul's heir (2 Samuel 9: 7).

If a ruling king and his heir were both dead, the kingly set would be expected to dispose of the estate in accordance with custom. Odyssey 2: 331-336 states that in case of Telemachus' death, the kingly suitors would divide Telemachus' possessions and award his house to Penelope and her husband-to-be.

The king had the right not only to bestow gifts but to take them back if he so decided (Iliad 1: 299). At Ugarit, we meet with royal grants bestowed, or transferred to a new favourite, as the crown might wish.[1] When Job (1: 21) states " Yahweh has

---

[1] Published by J. Nougayrol, *Palais royal d'Ugarit* III, Paris, 1955, pp. 47 ff.

given and (now) Yahweh has taken away," he is attributing to God the right that kings enjoyed. In fact, the theocratic ideas of Israel had it that God as the supreme and everlasting king had the right to bestow and transfer human kingship. Thus the Prophet Samuel tells King Saul: "Yahweh has torn away the kingship of Israel from you to-day, and given it to another better than you" (1 Samuel 15: 28). That human kings in Israel had the right to transfer the grants they had made is clear from 2 Samuel 16: 4 where David gives what he had bestowed upon Mephibosheth[1] to Ziba.

Rank meant much within the aristocratic order. At the banquets each man got a portion commensurate with his station. The expression *daìs eíse* "equal feast" (Odyssey 8: 98; 11: 185; etc.) means in fact "proportionate feast," for the guests were not equal. At the feast during which Samuel wanted to indicate Saul's role-to-be, Samuel directed the cook to give to Saul "the thigh and the (fat) that was on it" (1 Samuel 9: 24). This was "reserved" for Saul "for the occasion," showing condign honour for the future king at the *proportionate* feast. See Iliad 1: 460-1 for the thighs wrapped with fat and raw flesh as the preferred portion at the proportionate feast (Iliad 1: 468).

The warriors who constituted the aristocracy were awarded land grants to recompense them for their share in conquering the country. Both in Greece and in Israel, the theory of society was basically the same. The conquerors were the fighting and ruling stratum; the conquered natives were degraded to the labouring class. In Sparta the latter were called the Helots. In Israel the Canaanites were the "hewers of wood[2] and the drawers of water." Between military campaigns, the aristocracy enjoyed the advantages of a landed gentry. Boaz, in the Book of Ruth

---

[1] Who in real life was called Meribbaal (1 Chronicles 8: 34).
[2] More accurately, "gatherers of firewood."

(2: 1), is called a *gibbôr ḥáyil*,[1] " a war lord " (i.e., a member of the heroic aristocracy), but since the story unfolds during a peaceful interlude, he is depicted as administering his extensive farm. Odysseus during the fray could fight bravely and well, but he boasts also of his agricultural as well as military skill (Odyssey 18: 365-386); N.B., Odyssey 18: 371-5 for Odysseus' ability to plough with oxen. This side of the heroes' life also appears in the Hebrew narratives. King Saul (like King Odysseus) is depicted as ploughing his field with oxen in 1 Samuel 11: 5. Earlier still, in the Patriarchal Age, Isaac is depicted as an able farmer, eminently successful in agriculture (Genesis 26: 12).

The fitness (physical and moral) and deportment of kings were serious matters, for they were believed to bring on a corresponding state of land and people. Odyssey 19: 109-14 states that a faultless king who fears the gods and rules his mighty men justly, brings on fertility of earth, trees, cattle and sea. This concept is not limited to the epic; it pervaded thought in the East Mediterranean and adjacent areas throughout antiquity. Sophocles (Oedipus Tyrannus: 25-28) tells of the blight on Theban grain, cattle and women in travail, because of the King's sin. 2 Samuel 21: 1-2 tells of three years of famine that befell Israel in David's reign because of wrong perpetrated against the Gibeonites by his predecessor, King Saul; nor would the famine have ceased, had not amends been made by David to the offended Gibeonites. When David ill-advisedly conducted a census in Israel, his offence could only bring on a famine, or military defeat, or pestilence (2 Samuel 24).

---

[1] The feminine is *'éšet ḥáyil* " Lady." Neither this social class nor the terminology to designate it was limited to Israel. Thus Ruth the Moabitess is an *'éšet ḥáyil* (Ruth 3: 11). Note that the model *'éšet ḥáyil* described in Proverbs 31: 10 ff. is the wife of a member of the ruling class who sits in the gate with the elders of the land (v. 23). Like Penelope, she excels in fine handiwork, prudence and industry. The common translation " virtuous woman " misses the point.

There was more than one pattern of kingship among the allies of Agamemnon and Priam. Iliad 12: 310-328 tells that the Lycians were ruled by two kings simultaneously: Sarpedon and Glaucus. Excelling among the foremost Lycians on the battle-field, they were honoured as gods and enjoyed special seats, banquets with fat sheep and full cups, and extensive orchards and wheat fields. Their simultaneous kingship shows that dyarchy obtained among the Lycians. In later times, the Spartans kept up dyarchy with two simultaneously reigning Heraclid lines. The Midianites are led by two chieftains (*śârîm*), Oreb and Zeeb, in Judges 7: 25. In Judges 8, the Midianites are led by two kings (*m^elākîm*): Zebah and Zalmunna (note v. 12).

The divine appointment of kings is widespread. Divine favour could change from dynasty to dynasty, or from one branch of a ruling house to another. The Iliad reflects rivalry between the Priam and Anchises branches of the same family for the kingship of Troy. Aeneas, son of Anchises, harbours a grievance against Priam who did not honour him although he (Aeneas) was a brave warrior (Iliad 13: 460-1). Achilles hints at Aeneas' aspirations to rule Troy in Iliad 20: 178-186; and Poseidon foretells that Aeneas shall be king among the Trojans, as will his son's sons yet to be born (Iliad 20: 306-8). In the period of the Judges, Hebrew rulership constantly changed from tribe to tribe and from one person to another. With Saul, the beginnings of stability appear but not sufficiently to assure the kingship of his line over all Israel. The Hebraic theory was that the spirit of God departed from Saul to David.

Some divine ancestry was necessary for anyone who claimed membership in the Mycenaean aristocracy. This is repeatedly borne out in Homeric epic, but it is also reflected in parts of the Old Testament that have survived monotheistic purification. Genesis 6: 4 plainly reports the divine paternity of the ancient heroes: " The deities came in unto the daughters of men, who bore them (sons). The latter are the heroes who of old were men of fame."

There are many varieties in the types of divine descent. For example, the unwed girl (*parthénios*) Polymele, daughter of Phylas, bore Eudorus to the god Hermes. The girl's claim was accepted and the incident considered honourable, for not only did Phylas nurse and cherish Eudorus as his own son, but after Eudorus was born, the hero Echecles married her after giving countless gifts of courtship (Iliad 16: 179-192).

More often, the mother was married. Polydora bore Menesthius to the river-god Spercheius, but in name she bore him to Borus, son of Perieres, who openly married her (Iliad 16: 173-178). This is significant as the key to the ancient theory of heroic genealogy, for it reflects paternity at two levels: human and divine. A man's inheritance comes from his human father, but his qualitative superiority among mortals comes from his divine father. When Odysseus is called Zeus-born (*diogenés*; e.g., Odyssey 23: 306) this does not mean that the poet has forgotten, even for a moment, that he is the son of the human Laertes. In Iliad 10: 144, he is called *diogenès laertiádē* " Zeus-born son of Laertes." Zeus is often described as impregnating noble ladies, not so much to gratify his lust for women, but because divine parentage was a necessity among the claims of the aristocracy. Odysseus is a superman because he is *diogenés*; but he is king of Ithaca because of his human father Laertes. Jesus is divine because of his heavenly Father; but he derives his kingship of the Jews from the mortal Joseph, who was heir to the throne (Matthew 1). While normative Judaism has tried to strip the Old Testament of this phenomenon, vestiges have nonetheless remained in the text. Isaac is the heir of his human father Abraham, but the aged Sarah was caused to conceive by God: " And Yahweh visited (*pāqad*) Sarah as He had said; and Yahweh did unto Sarah as He had spoken. And Sarah conceived and bore to Abraham a son

244

for his old age, at the time that God had promised him " (Genesis
21: 1-2). The verb *pāqad* is used for a husband visiting his wife
for coitus in Judges 15: 1.

If only one hero were the son of Zeus, or El, we might have
grounds for expecting the great god to spare him; but if the entire
heroic aristocracy is of divine descent, Zeus (or El) cannot save
his human son without upsetting the order of things. Zeus is in
fact pained that his son Sarpedon is to die, but Hera reminds Zeus
that many sons of gods are fighting around Troy, and that if
Zeus spares his son, other gods will do the same for their sons, so
that the earthly system would cease (Iliad 16: 445-449). Kret,
though the son of El, is also menaced by death like all other
mortals.

The terminology of Homer doubtless has refinements that
merit attention. Laomedon begot Hicetaon, scion (*ózos*) of
Ares (Iliad 20: 238). Idomeneus claims to be *Zēnòs gónos* (Iliad
13: 449) " son of Zeus " and then goes on to explain that Zeus
begot Minos, Minos begot Deucalion, and Deucalion begot
Idomeneus (: 450-3), showing that *gónos* " son " can be used
loosely for any descendant, such as a grandson or great-grand son.[1]

Hector, the son of Priam, boasts of being the son or lad (*páïs*)
of mighty Zeus in Iliad 13: 54.[2]

When Achilles boasts of a superior ancestry in Iliad 21: 189,
it is interesting to note that he does not base his claims on his
divine mother Thetis, but on the fact that his grandfather Aeacus
was sired by Zeus. This is what makes Achilles better than

---

[1] Achilles is often called the " Aiakid " (Iliad 16: 165) usually translated
as the " Son of Aeacus ", although Achilles was the son of Peleus, who in turn
was also the Aiakid " Son of Aeacus " (Iliad 16: 15). Thus the patronymic in
-*id* can refer to the grandfather as well as father, even as Hebrew *ben*.

[2] Jesus is called the *páïs* of God in Acts 3: 13, 26; 4: 27, 30; cf. David's
title in 4: 25; and Kret's title *ǵlm il* " Lad of El." The Septuagint of Genesis
18: 17 has God referring to Abraham as his *páïs*.

Asteropaeus, whose grandfather was only Axius the river-god (Iliad 21: 157-160, 190-1).

The divine maternity of Achilles is neatly paralleled by Shamgar's. Just as Achilles is son of the goddess Thetis, Shamgar is the son of the Canaanite goddess Anath (Judges 3: 31; 5: 6). Anath is singularly appropriate because she is a bloodthirsty slayer of men in the Ugaritic myths: a worthy mother of Shamgar who slew six hundred Philistines with an oxgoad.

Divine mothers seem to worry about their human sons, just like our mortal mothers. Thetis regrets her son's destiny (Iliad 1: 414 ff.) even as the goddess Ninsun regrets the dangerous activities of her mortal son Gilgamesh.

There are other examples of divine maternity (e.g., Aeneas borne by Aphrodite to Anchises) but it was far more common for the heroes to be born of human mothers to male gods. Nobody can be sure of his father, as Odyssey 1: 214-223 tells us. Even the gods are not sure of their paternity. The goddess Eidothea cautiously says of Proteus: " He, they say, is the father who begot me " (Odyssey 4: 387). Similarly, Telemachus says with all due reservation of Odysseus: " My mother says that I am his child; but I do not know, because no one has by himself ever known his own parentage " (Odyssey 1: 215-6).

How can one be sure of his father in a world where the gods impregnate the daughters of men? This sort of thing went on not only in Greece, but, as we have seen, in heroic Israel as well (Genesis 6: 1-4). This notion is not only important for the study of early pagan antiquity, but for late antiquity as well, when paganism was displaced by Judaism, Christianity and Islam. When a new religion supplants an old religion, the gods of the old often survive as the demons of the new. Beelzebub was a great god in pagan antiquity, but he appears in the New Testament as King of the Demons. In Mandeanism (which is post-Christian as well as post-Jewish), the *elâh(în)* (which refers to the God of the

Jews, Christian and Muslims) are debased to the status of
" demons." There is a large corpus of magical texts from
Babylonia of the Sassanian Era, designed to exorcise demons.[1]
In these texts, which are mostly Jewish and Christian, the Indo-
Iranian deities called *daiva* appear as demons. But the interesting
thing is not merely the terminology; the demons of these texts
are constantly appearing to women in the forms of their husbands,
and impregnating them. As a result, the names of the clients are
always matronymic because no one could be sure of his paternity.
Whether the Jews and Christians of Mesopotamia picked up
such ideas from the Greeks or Iranians is not very important, for
both the Greeks and Iranians had such notions. Greek paganism
is reflected in the texts (e.g., Hermes is a kindly spirit helping
men even as he does in the Greek tradition since Homer); but
the Iranian element is even stronger to judge from the terminology
and onomasticon. This topic is of enormous importance because
demonology preoccupied the West from the dawn of Christianity
to virtually modern times. It was the spread of Judeo-Christian
religion that debased the pagan gods into demons.

Among the fanciful notions of ancestry was the claim of
descent from some famous tree or rock (Odyssey 19: 163).
Such ideas are not playful inventions of Homer. Jeremiah (2: 27)
tells of people who " say to the tree ' You are my father ' and to
the stone ' You have borne me '."[2]

Eponymous ancestors are exceedingly common. Dardanus
founded Dardania[3] (Iliad 20: 215-216). Similarly Ilos gave his

[1] The subject is treated in Chapter XII of my *Adventures in the Neares
East*, Phoenix House, London, 1957.

[2] See also *Ugaritic Manual*, p. 231, #20.

[3] i.e., from the ancients' point of view. For the modern scholar, the
eponymous ancestor is usually a later invention. For example the Twelve
Tribes of Israel are represented as, and bear the names of, the Twelve Sons of
Israel. This kind of reconstruction was used to establish solidarity among tribal
confederacies. Its efficacy is clear when we consider that Jews of different

name to Ilios, and Tros to Troy (Iliad 15: 215; 20: 230-2). The Children of Israel are named after their ancestor Israel, and each of the Twelve Tribes bears the name of one of Israel's sons. Zephaniah 2: 5-6, as we have seen, singles out Kret as the eponymous ancestor of the Cretans.

Expressions like " Sons of the Achaeans " are typologically the same as the Hebrew " Sons of Israel " or " Sons of Judah " and seem to stem from related social systems. While individuals are often called " Son of So-and-So " (without their own personal name), sometimes they are called " Father of So-and-So "; e.g., Odysseus refers to himself as " Father of Telemachus " (Iliad 4: 354) exactly in the familiar Semitic style (e.g., Arabic *Abû-Fulân* " Father of So-and-So ").

Codified law was not the norm in the Homeric milieu. The idea of codes was probably familiar in learned circles ever since the establishment of Mesopotamian commercial colonies in Asia Minor and elsewhere around the East Mediterranean. But even in Mesopotamia itself, the law courts did not cite the codes in handing down decisions, but rather functioned in accordance with custom and accepted opinion. Assyriologists read thousands of court proceedings and contracts without a single reference to any code. The kind of law that is reflected in Homeric epic is called *thémistes* (Odyssey 16: 403) or the sum total of oracles by which the gods regulate human society. This is much the same as the Hebrew concept of Torah which we translate The Law (meaning the Pentateuch). Very little of the Torah is law in the strict legal sense. The spirit of Torah is rather the oracles that

---

culture and different race feel related to each other because of the tradition that they stem genealogically from Abraham, Isaac and Jacob. In such matters it is not the historicity, but the psychological acceptance of the claim that is important. 1 Maccabees 12: 21 has both the Spartan and Judean allies descended from Abraham. Such notions helped cement friendship and facilitate co-operation.

"Yahweh spoke unto Moses" (Numbers 1: 1, 48; 2: 1; 3: 5, 11, 14 et passim). The primary form of such oracles is not written but oral. The Greek dramatists still preserve the old view that the immutable, unwritten laws of the gods take precedence over man-made enactments (Antigone: 454-455). Even Rabbinic Judaism that places so much emphasis on the Written Law puts in theory the Oral Law on an equal footing with the Written Law, deriving both from the same Revelation on Sinai.

The Greeks, like the other people of the Near East, resorted to ordeals when there was no other basis for judgment in court. Antigone: 264-5 mention the ordeal by fire to prove one's innocence. Isaiah 66: 16 mentions Yahweh's judging by fire; cf. 43: 2 which refers to both common media of ordeals: by fire and water.

All societies have their own traditions regarding how close kinship can be between two people contemplating marriage. Alcinous wed Arete, the daughter of his brother Rhexenor (Odyssey 7: 61-66). It is interesting to compare Hebrew law which apparently permits a man to marry his niece (but definitely not a woman to marry her nephew[1]).

When Nausicaa wants Odysseus to marry her, she plainly assumes that he will be willing to remain with her people (Odyssey 6: 244-5). Sinuhe stayed with his wife's people until he returned to Egypt when he left her (and their children) behind for all time. This is what Assyriologists called *erêbu*-marriage. The Middle Assyrian Laws have provisions, as well as the terminology, for this kind of marriage. Genesis has this institution in mind in stating that "man shall leave his father and mother and cleave unto his wife" (Genesis 2: 24). Jacob's marriage to Rachel and Leah involved his remaining with their family, because Genesis 31 portrays his departure with his wives and

---

[1] Leviticus 20: 19-20.

children, from Laban's house, as an illegal escape. Samson's marriage was also of the *erêbu* type, for whatever life he and his wife had together was at her father's house (Judges 15: 1). Moses also had contracted an *erêbu*-marriage with Zipporah, for they continued to live with her father, Jethro. From the Homeric, Egyptian and Biblical examples, it appears that *erêbu*-marriage was especially common when the man married a foreign woman in her homeland. But Genesis 2: 24 and the Assyrian Code suggest that *erêbu*-marriage could take place otherwise, too.

The relations between Penelope and the suitors is one of the most interesting areas of sociological investigation in Homeric epic. It is assumed that Penelope cannot remarry if Odysseus is still alive. The situation is that covered by Hammurapi's Code ##133-135, stipulating that if a man is captured, his wife cannot leave his house to wed another man, unless the husband has not left her provided for. Odysseus has left his wife well provided for. However, other considerations complicate the picture. He had been gone so long that he could reasonably be presumed to have died, and his widow's marriage to any Ithacan nobleman would elevate the latter to serve as Odysseus' successor. Furthermore, the entertainment of the suitors was wasting the estate of Odysseus that Telemachus was entitled to inherit. In Hammurapi's Code, the ultimate concern in family life is with the next generation and with the inheritance rights necessary for its welfare. For practical reasons, Telemachus would like his mother to leave (Odyssey 19: 533), and her parents also want her to remarry (Odyssey 19: 157-161). Telemachus is now a man able to run his own household without his mother to guide him (*ibid.*). However, he is ashamed to drive her out against her will (Odyssey 20: 343-344), though he is ready to give lavish gifts if his mother will remarry willingly (Odyssey 20: 342). All these aspects of the situation should be compared with ancient Near East law and custom. Driving out one's mother from the deceased father's house was so common that cuneiform lawcodes and marriage contracts took steps to forbid it, unless the widow wanted to remarry or had acted reprehensibly and deserved to be driven out by her sons. Hammurapi's Code forbids a widow to remarry if the remarriage might be detrimental to her children. Telemachus' majority, however, makes it right for her to leave; the more so because her remaining at home is eating her son's substance. As in cuneiform law, Penelope has the usufruct, but not the inheritance rights, of her husband's estate. Her remarriage would moreover terminate her connection with Odysseus' estate, in keeping with the laws and customs of the entire ancient Near East.

Penelope's behaviour while waiting for her husband to return or in any case putting off remarriage to anyone else, is admirable *vis-à-vis* Odysseus. However, the text informs us that her attitude was impractical towards her son and parents who are more than willing to have her remarry.

When captive women were the favourites of their captors, they could be classed as wives rather than concubines. Briseis is thus mentioned as the wife of Achilles in Iliad 9: 336 and 19: 297-8. The beautiful Sarai was taken into Pharaoh's harem as a wife (Genesis 12: 19).

When a married woman is seized by another for himself, the latter brings trouble upon himself. And when he is a king, he causes misfortune to his subjects as well. Helen is a bane to the Trojan community into which she is taken (Iliad 3: 159-160). When Sarah is taken by Pharaoh, Pharaoh and his household become the targets of Yahweh's plagues (Genesis 12: 17); and when Abimelech takes her, he and all his harem are smitten with sterility (Genesis 20: 17-18).

Odyssey 19: 399-404 relates that Eurycleia laid the baby Odysseus on the knees of his maternal grandfather, Autolycus, so that the latter might name him. We are to compare the birth of Joseph's great-grandsons on his knees in Genesis 50: 23. The difference between the maid's placing the child on the ancestor's knees, and the ancestor's receiving the child directly from the mother's womb at birth, is not essential but incidental. We might also note that Autolycus named the child " Odysseus " (Odyssey 19: 409), meaning " the victim of enmity "; such etymologising of personal names is exceedingly common in the Bible.

Machaon, the faultless physician, is called " the son of Asclepius " (Iliad 4: 193-4) or *Asklēpiádē* (: 204) the " Asclepiad " or " scion of Asclepius." Members of any particular guild were envisaged as a peculiar species of the human race descended from a common ancestor. Thus all the physicians claimed descent from Asclepius, even as Genesis 4: 20-22 tells us that Jabal was the ancestor of all the tent-dwelling owners of cattle, that Jubal was the ancestor of all the musicians, and that Tubal-Cain was the ancestor of all copper and iron smiths. Actually this is akin to the Platonic World of Ideas whereby all things are but re-flections of perfect prototypes. The perfect physician is Asclepius; all the others are but copies of him. The Sumerians attributed all the professions, arts and crafts to divine prototypes: which anti-cipates somewhat more closely the Platonic formulation. (This illustrates the Near East background of elements in classical Greek philosophy. It would be a mistake to conclude from a book like the present one, that it was only in the realm of literature that the earlier Near East made an impact on Greece. We are not imply-ing that the Sumerians produced philosophers like Socrates, Plato and Aristotle. In fact, a comparison of the Iliad or Odyssey with the Gilgamesh Epic or Ugaritic Epics shows that the Sumer-ians and Semites never produced a Homer either. All we are saying is that the Greeks did not produce perfection from a vacuum; and that instead, archaeological discovery shows us the heritage with which they worked and on which they built.

This holds for Greek science and philosophy as well as Greek script and literature.)

The guilds were closed corporations, into which the members were born. The only exception was through adoption. Nuzu tablet N: vi: 572 records an adoption in which the adoptive father was to teach his adopted son his trade.[1] The lawcode of Hammurapi (#188) (cf. the Hittite Code #200B) regulates such adoptions. It was a criminal offence for a person to learn a trade through adoption and then try to escape from the duties of son-ship according to Hammurapi's Code.

Guild members, being considered different from the rest of the population, often lived apart. Gilgamesh Epic 11: 35 mentions the *âl um-ma-ni* " city of the craftsmen." The Hebrews had Levitical cities (Leviticus 25: 32) where the Levites owned their inalienable estates. The Mesopotamians established commercial colonies where their *tamkârū* had their homes and head-quarters.

Throughout the epic, there is emphasis on the social prestige of the actors. As we have repeatedly noted, there are no villains among the main personages. Even the leaders of the wooers are described laudably as " Antinous and godlike Eurymachus, the leaders of the wooers, who in quality (*aretē*) were far the best " (Odyssey 4: 628-9). The men who are described are the pick, not the common run; e.g., *Ithákēs exaíretoi* (Odyssey 4: 643) " chosen youths of Ithaca " as distinct from hirelings or slaves, and synonymous with the aristocratic *koûroi* in l. 652 (cf. also : 666). This feature of " picked men " is highlighted in Egypt and Israel as we shall point out later.

In discussions, youth was expected to defer to age. When Diomedes offers counsel to his elders, he prefaces his remarks with a request that his elders be not angry at him, the youngest in their

[1] E. R. Lacheman, *Miscellaneous Texts (Publications of the Baghdad School* vi), 1939, pl. 522.

midst, for speaking (Iliad 14: 111-112). This all-too-natural feature of actual life concerns us only insofar as it was accepted as part of the epic repertoire that reverberates in Hebrew drama. Elihu prefaces his address to his elders thus: " I am younger in days, whereas you are old. Therefore I deferred and was afraid to declare my view to you " (Job 32: 6-7).

Hospitality was the cornerstone of virtue. The epic includes not only the great virtue in protecting the stranger, but the little formalities observed when welcoming a guest. The preparation and offering of refreshments are featured in Homeric, Ugaritic and biblical literatures. It is also characteristic of the Greek and Ugaritic texts to have the host ask the guest why he had come. Thus Iliad 15: 90-91 has Themis, after welcoming Hera with a cup, ask her: " Hera, why have you come? You are as one distraught. Surely your husband, the Son of Cronus, has scared you." Iliad 1: 202 has Achilles receive Athena with the question: " Why have you come again, O child of Aegis-bearing Zeus? "[1]

Not only the host, but the guest had responsibilities. Telemachus tells the wooers that if they fight, they will bring shame on their feast (Odyssey 16: 293-4). Both the Ugaritic texts and the biblical Book of Proverbs express revulsion at strife during banquets.[2] Another offence of guests at the banquet was lewdness with the women in the halls. Baal of Ugarit loathes the abuse of handmaids during feasts even as Odysseus had a grievance against the wooers for dallying with his slave girls. Plutarch (Life of Theseus 30: 3) mentions the insolence of the centaurs, who were guests, with the women of their hosts.

Nothing was worse than to wander homelessly over the face of the earth. Poseidon punished Odysseus not with death, but by

[1] Asking why the visitor has come is typical of Ugaritic literature. In such commonplace matters, it is not the thing itself that counts, but rather its inclusion in the epic repertoire. So much of the highly selective repertoire consists of such banalities that we cannot pass over them in silence.

[2] Ugaritic text 51: III: 17-22; Proverbs 17: 1.

forcing him to wander far from home for many years (Odyssey 1: 74-75). As we saw in Chapter 1, even murderers wandering to escape retribution were the objects of pity. Murder was bad enough, but the attitude towards the murderer was more kindly than ours to-day. Some of the greatest heroes were murderers and atoned for their crimes with exile. Patroclus as a small youth had slain Amphidamus' son in anger over the dice. Menoetius therefore brought his son Patroclus to Peleus (Iliad 23: 85-90), who protected him in his house where he became the bosom friend of Achilles. In Hebrew tradition, too, the greatest of heroes, Moses, was a murderer. He slew an Egyptian in wrath and paid for his crime by flight and many years of exile.

Regicide (or more exactly slaying one of the kingly class) was a particularly grave crime, precisely because of the respected position of the aristocracy. Amphinomus advises against slaying Telemachus because " it is a dread thing to slay one of kingly stock " except if the gods counsel it (Odyssey 16: 401-403). David's reluctance to slay his enemy Saul, and Saul's family, stems from the abhorrence of regicide; for David was not one to shrink from shedding blood under different circumstances.

When a person is murdered, his soul can be put to rest in Hades only after proper amends are made. For example, Achilles sacrificed twelve Trojan nobles to gratify the soul of Patroclus.[1] On the other hand, the blood of Abel cried forth from the earth because Cain had slain him and no amends had been made. The worst kind of death was " dying like a fool " (2 Samuel 3: 33) as Abner died. It may be more or less this kind of death that

---

[1] Iliad 23: 179-182. This is to be compared with David's sacrificing seven princes of Saul's house to appease the offended Gibeonites (2 Samuel 21: 6-9). Human sacrifice was abhorrent to later Hebrews and Greeks alike. But under certain conditions the early Greeks and Hebrews did sacrifice human beings to gratify the living or the dead, or to secure the welfare of the many through the sacrifice of the individual. For the safety and success of their expedition, both Agamemnon and Jephthah sacrificed a daughter.

Telemachus has in mind when he predicts for the wooers death " without atonement " (Odyssey 2: 145) if they persist in their outrageous conduct (which is what actually happens in Book 24).

The religious parallels between Homer and Bible are strong because of the fluidity of cultural interchange in the area. When people of different cultures meet, they often exchange religious ideas with facility whereas it is harder to exchange more complicated scientific and technological ideas. Moreover, all people are interested in religion and morals; but not necessarily in higher mathematics or manufacturing processes. But over and above the religious interchange around the East Mediterranean, the mobility of religious personnel did much to spread religious ideas and cultic practices.[1] The ancients were not as denominationally minded as we in matters of their clergy. They were more concerned with obtaining the services of a *bona fide* professional member of a priestly guild who was qualified to intercede between the mortals and immortals, than with finding a religious leader whose sole qualification was like-mindedness. The Danites made off with the Levite because he was qualified by birth and training, not because he shared a peculiarly Danite theology with his captors.[2] Balak of Moab hired the Aramean Balaam to curse Israel solely because of Balaam's international reputation as an execrator.[3] In the following discussion of religious matters, some of the points are rather general, but others are of specific character where diffusion, not spontaneous parallel development, has been at work.

The idea of a covenant between a man and the god of his father(s) is fully developed in Homeric tradition. Diomedes thus asks Athene to stand by him as she had stood by his father, Tydeus, and that he in return would offer to her a specified sacrifice.[4] The entire Bible—New as well as Old Testament—is

[1] Cf. Chapter II.   [2] Judges 18.
[3] Numbers 22: 6.   [4] Iliad 10: 283-294.

permeated with the idea of the Covenant relationship between God and the descendants of the Fathers. The clearest formulation of worshipping the God of the Fathers is Genesis 31: 53 where Jacob and Laban swear by their respective ancestral gods: namely those of Abraham (Jacob's ancestor) and of Nahor (Laban's ancestor). Moreover, Jacob swears by the God of his father, Isaac.

In the case of Abraham, there can be no god of the father, because his father Terah is the pagan parent of the first true believer according to the tradition. The Covenant between God and Abraham is strictly personal, for the two talk together and God promises protection to Abraham and his seed in exchange for Abraham's devotion. This concept is found outside Scripture. For example, Odysseus in appreciation for past help and future aid, promises to call on Athene as first among the immortals of Olympus (Iliad 10: 462-464). We can see how such devotion was expressed on specific occasions when Odysseus sets aside the spoils taken from the slain Dolon, until they could be prepared as an offering to Athene (Iliad 10: 570-571).

Oaths were taken seriously, often because the deities would avenge false or broken oaths sworn in their names. But some oaths are made by things; e.g., Achilles swears by his sceptre in Iliad 1: 233-244 much as Ishtar swears by her lapis necklace (Gilgamesh 11: 164). " Styx the dread river of oath " (Iliad 2: 755) is to be compared with the deified River in which the ordeal was administered according to Hammurapi's Code. "Judge River," a common epithet of Yamm, the water god in Ugaritic literature, reflects the same general concept.

Homer also refers to oaths by God. " Until God (*hó ke daímōn*) judges between us " (Iliad 7: 377-8, 396-7) is just as monotheistic as " May Yahweh judge between me and you " (Genesis 16: 5; 1 Samuel 24: 12).

Since misery is the divine vengeance on those who take false oaths (Iliad 3: 278-280), and unfulfilled vows could cause pestilence (Iliad 1: 93), small wonder that it occurred to some of the Greeks that sensible people should not make vows at all (Antigone: 388-390). This idea also developed in Israel. Ecclesiastes (5: 5) notes " it is better for you not to vow than to vow and not fulfil " and (9: 2) contrasts the reckless man who takes oaths with the prudent man " who fears oath(s)." In general, he advises us not to be in any hurry to utter words (e.g., to make vows) to God (Ecclesiastes 5: 2), for it will do us no good to say that we acted " in error " when the day of reckoning comes to pay what has been vowed; for that would only bring the wrath of God upon our affairs (5: 6).

The question of whether sin must be intentional is of interest. As we have noted in Ecclesiastes, evil consequences follow unfulfilled vows even when there has been no intentional wrong. In Hebrew law and custom, inadvertent sin (Leviticus 4: 2, 27; Numbers 15: 27) is nonetheless sin, and must be atoned for. In fact, no one is expected to avoid sin completely (1 Kings 8: 46), and it is a function of religion to provide the means of expiation. Heinous sins, like that of Oedipus,[1] were committed by great heroes unwittingly. Tragic errors in Greek epic may be perpetrated by mistake. Agamemnon thought he was acting quite within his rights in wresting Briseis from Achilles, and the latter does not contest the legality of the act. But this touches off the wrath of Achilles, which was again within the hero's rights. Yet the consequences were tragic, regardless of intention.

One way of averting disaster is to purify ourselves of whatever

---

[1] The bold essay of I. Velikovsky (*Oedipus and Akhenaton: Myth and History*, Doubleday, Garden City, N.Y., 1960), deriving the Oedipus legend from Egypt of the Amarna Age requires refinement but is of importance in that it tries to trace a legend embodied in the Odyssey to a specific historic figure: Ikhnaton (ca. 1377-1358 B.C.). Oedipus' confrontation with the Sphinx is one of several familiar details that suggest the transference of the tale from Thebes of Egypt to Thebes of Greece.

ritual defilement may be sullying us. This defilement need have nothing to do with moral wrong. Even so blessed an event as a wife's bearing a child brings on her a defilement that only ritual purification can remedy according to Leviticus 12: 2-8. Ancient Hittites and Orthodox Jews and Muslims are among the many peoples to whom ritual purity is of prime significance. Adherents of religions with codes of ritual purity like to rid themselves of defilement as soon as possible because defilement displeases the god(s) and invites misfortune. Before Odysseus and Diomedes are ceremonially fit to dine and offer libations to Athene, they wash in the sea (Iliad 10: 574-579). Iliad 1: 313-4 tells how Agamemnon's troops cast their defilement into the sea. This custom is, as we have already observed, also reflected in Micah 7: 19 where God is asked to annul our sins by casting them into the depths of the sea.

Prayer is preceded by washing and raising the hands, looking towards heaven and pouring wine from a cup (Iliad 24: 300-307). These elements are also found in Ugaritic ritual (Kret: 62-78), where they precede supplication via sacrifice.

Old Testament sacrifice has close technical analogues with Homeric sacrifice. Iliad 1: 459-463 and 2: 421-431 describe how the animal is slain by having its head drawn back so that its throat can be slit; then it is flayed. Cf. 2 Chronicles 35: 11 for slaughtering (by slitting the throat: which is still obligatory in Judaism and Islam) followed by the flaying. The lads with the five-pronged forks (Iliad 1: 463) are to be compared with the priest bearing the trident at the sacrifices in 1 Samuel 2: 13-15.

Important households had their own altars for cultic practice. The halls of Odysseus (and Laertes) had an altar for Zeus, God of the Court (Odyssey 22: 334). Solomon's Temple (which took considerably less time to build than the Palace) was in fact the royal chapel. Far less important personages among the well-to-do had their own private shrines; e.g., Micah in Judges 17.

Prophets were in demand because through them men knew, from the predicted outcome, what courses of action to choose or to avoid. Yet kings, who can be all too human, often disliked prophets whose oracles were unfavourable. Agamemnon had taken a cordial dislike for Calchas " a prophet of evil " who never had a happy message for him (Iliad 1: 106 ff.). Ahab, feeling the same towards Micaiah son of Imlah, said, " I hate him, because he prophesies not good but evil concerning me " (1 Kings 22: 8).

The traditions about the Prophet Teiresias are of prime interest for their biblical parallels. Odysseus consulted his departed spirit in Hades (Odyssey 10: 490-5; 11: 89-137) much as Saul had the ghost of the Prophet Samuel called up from Sheol (1 Samuel 28: 3-20). The drama preserves other features with Old Testament analogues. Teiresias accuses the king (Sophocles, Oedipus Tyrannus: 350-3) even as Nathan, Micaiah and the literary Hebrew prophets upbraided the kings of Israel and Judah. Like the Hebrew prophets, Teiresias enjoyed prophetic immunity and tells King Oedipus he (the King) cannot hurt him (Oedipus Tyrannus: 447-8). Creon accuses Teiresias of professionalism for private gain (Antigone: 1035 ff., 1055) even as the priest Amaziah levels the same charge against Amos (Amos 7: 12). The mobility of the prophetic guilds explains much of the similarity in the status, activities and attitudes pertaining to the prophets of Israel and Greece.

The backbone of the army—then as now—was the infantry, who suffer much and get little glory. While we read of the individual heroes it is all too easy to forget " the cloud of foot-soldiers " that followed (Iliad 23: 133) the leaders into battle. The Assyrian annals tell of the cloud of dust raised by the infantry, even as Balaam describes the multitude of the Israelite host in terms of the dust they raise (Numbers 23: 10).

Soldiers were not valued equally. " Chosen youths " are

contrasted with "servants" in Odyssey 16: 247-8. In Odyssey 4: 643-4 (cf. : 666) the "chosen youths" of Ithaca are, as we have observed, contrasted with "hirelings and slaves." The latter passage is particularly interesting because the men were chosen for a navigational exploit. In the Egyptian tale of the Sailor, the crew was "the pick of Egypt." A special mission would merit the careful selecting of men; thus Aegisthus "chose out twenty men, the best in the land, and set them to lie in wait" (Odyssey 4: 530-1). Similarly Agamemnon "chooses" twenty rowers for his ship to return the girl to her father Chryses (Iliad 1: 309). So important was the process of selection that the Hebrew word *bāḥûr* "chosen" became the noun designating a desirable youth.[1] Odyssey 24: 107 describes a highly desirable group of able-bodied men as being not only picked, but of like age; such were the wooers: the best men that could be picked in any city (: 108).

The heroic age indulged itself in the conceit that its famed warriors were a match for the gods. The epic envisaged gods as well as men participating in every battle. In this regard the Homeric Epics are in agreement with the ancient Hebrew records such as Exodus 15 and Judges 5. Diomedes wounded and routed Aphrodite on the battlefield and was fit to fight with Zeus (Iliad 5: 318-362, 457). Nor was Diomedes able to defeat only a female immortal, for in Iliad 5: 850-861 he wounds Ares, the god of war. Indeed the Danaans battled against the gods, and the poet gives us a catalogue of the deities bested in battle (Iliad 5: 380 ff.). The biblical analogue is Jacob who tangled with a deity and won; whereupon the vanquished deity renamed him Israel because he strove with gods and prevailed (Genesis 32: 25-31). Odyssey (4: 397) states that "hard is a god for a mortal man to master," but the outstanding heroes were in many cases equal to it. Diomedes chides Aphrodite and tells her to go on

[1] i.e., from the noble warrior class.

beguiling weak women but to keep away from battle (Iliad 5: 348-351), even as Aqhat chides Anath and tells her to engage in feminine pursuits but not to wield weapons.

A Homeric word for a warrior is *epíkouros* " helper " (Iliad 12: 101). The Hebrew *ᶜôzēr* " helper " also designates " warrior " in 1 Chronicles 12: 1 (cf. Ezekiel 32: 21, etc.).

Tactical as well as strategic moves were normally taken only after consulting the gods through oracular priests. The Mari tablets reflect considerable priestly influence on governmental affairs, military and civilian. The Lachish ostraca show that prophets directed their oracular instruction to the military commanders through channels of communication. Sometimes the oracular priest was assigned to the unit as auxiliary commander.[1] Iliad 2: 858 tells us that the Mysians were led by Chromis and Ennomus the augur.

The small Achaean military unit was a squad of ten men (Iliad 2: 126). The decimal system of organisation is exceedingly widespread and ultimately harks back to the habit of counting on the ten fingers. Nonetheless, it may be of interest to note that the ancient Hebrews grouped men in tens, fifties, hundreds, thousands and myriads. This system is still attested in the Qumran Scrolls, and to this day a quorum of men in the Synagogue is ten. Companies of fifty men appear in both the Homeric and biblical texts.

On occasion, rival forces would agree to let individual champions decide the issue. Paris suggests that Hector set him " in the midst " to engage in single combat with Menelaus (Iliad 3: 69), to settle the war. The most familiar biblical parallel is the combat between the champion Goliath and David. The Philistine identity of Goliath ties in with the similarity between

[1] For references see my *Ugaritic Literature*, Rome, 1949, pp. 124 f. Note also Saul's consulting oracles through the priest Ahijah (1 Samuel 14: 2-3, 18 ff.).

his title "the man of the midst "[1] in 1 Samuel 17: 4, 23 and the Homeric "(champion) in the midst ": referring to the fight between the two armies that watched.

David's weapon in slaying the Philistine champion was the sling (1 Samuel 17: 49-50). The use of the sling is attested many times in the Bible; but only once in Homer (Iliad 13: 600). It is a mistake to conclude from a *hapax legomenon* that the item referred to was a rarity, or that the text might be in error. Time after time, the tradition is justified by discovery, even in the case of *hapax legomena*. For example, the only reference to writing in Homer occurs in the Story of Bellerophon where signs are inscribed on a tablet. The thousands of Linear B tablets now unearthed illustrate the literacy of the Mycenaean World, so briefly but correctly indicated by the Homeric text. The same must be said for the unique Homeric reference to the "sling."

A far more important weapon was the bow and arrow. Illustrious bowmen are often described in Homer. Some of them, like Pandarus, received their divinely fashioned bows as gifts from some god; quite like Aqhat, whose bow was made and given by Kothar-and-Hasis. The composite bow[2] made with the bull's sinew (Iliad 4: 122, 151) and horn of the wild ibex (Iliad 4: 105) is essentially the same as the composite bow described in the Ugaritic Legend of Aqhat. The bow was so important that David's training of Judean troops is described in terms of bowmanship (2 Samuel 1: 18) and the weapon used by El, head of the Ugaritic pantheon, is the bow (Ugaritic text 52). Arrows were rendered doubly lethal by poisoning their tips (Odyssey 1: 261-2; Job 6: 4).

The passage, 2 Samuel 1: 18, mentioned above, is interesting in that it refers to training troops for combat. The title to the

---

[1] Hebrew *'iš habbênáyim.*

[2] Cf. W. E. McLeod, "Egyptian Composite Bows in New York," *American Journal of Archaeology* 66, 1962, pp. 13-19.

martial Psalm 60[1] also states the purpose of the document as military training. The verb used is *l-m-d* " to learn," causative " to teach." Not only men, but also horses, had to be schooled for combat. The Babylonian Creation Epic (4: 54) describes war-horses as " knowing, in destruction; schooled (*lmd*) in annihilation," employing the same verb.

We must not underestimate the amount of planning that preceded ancient campaigns. Spies were regularly sent out for securing the intelligence information needed before the assault. The dangerous business of spying had to be well rewarded. Nestor promises that the bold spy will receive a black ewe with a nursing lamb from each commander, and will have a permanent invitation to the feasts and drinking bouts of the kings (Iliad 10: 215-7). Spying is also singled out in the Hebrew tradition; e.g., prior to the Hebrew Conquest of Canaan.[2] Judges 7: 9 ff. relates how Gideon was instructed by a nocturnal vision of Yahweh to penetrate the enemy camp with his attendant at night; much as Agamemnon is impelled to rise at night (Iliad 10: 1 ff.) and have a pair of able men penetrate the enemy's defences during the dark hours for information prior to the assault on the morrow (Iliad 10: 254 ff.).

Surprise tactics were of the greatest importance, and a high premium was set on ingenuity in devising them. Agamemnon, when in bad straits, went to Nestor to contrive some good device for warding off evil (Iliad 10: 17-20). The most famous contrivance for deceiving the foe was the Trojan Horse, filled with warriors under Odysseus as their leader (Odyssey 4: 271-289). We have already noted the Late Egyptian Tale of the Taking of Joppa, which deals with the

---

[1] This Psalm (like 16, and 56 through 59, also) is called a *miktām*. Perhaps the meaning of this problematic term is " a psalm for military training."

[2] Joshua 2: 1 ff.

penetration of that city by men concealed in baskets on donkey-back.[1]

Nor were the ancient expeditions without their supply lines. Iliad 9: 71-72 tells us that the Achaeans received daily supplies from overseas by ship. The concept of an Achaean beach-head living exclusively off the land is inaccurate.

There were many conventions for warfare, practised throughout a wide area. It was conventional to stop hostilities at nightfall. Heralds acting as referees thus call off the fight between Hector and Ajax because nightfall is the sign to end hostilities and it is good for us to obey Night (Iliad 7: 282, 293). Cf. 2 Samuel 2: 24-26 for calling off the battle after sunset.

The repertoire also includes the cessation of hostilities because a goddess tells one or more of the combatants that the continuation of the fight will enrage the head of the pantheon. In Odyssey 24: 541-544, Athene tells Odysseus to stop fighting the Ithacans lest Zeus be angry at him. In Ugaritic mythology, the sun-goddess Shapsh orders Mot to stop fighting with Baal, lest El find out and strip Mot of his authority (49: VI: 22-29).

The brutality of war is universal, but the details of how the brutality is executed and recorded for posterity, differ from culture to culture. Moreover, certain types of brutality are considered right in certain societies. Iliad 6: 55-60 states that Agamemnon "rightly advised" (: 62) Menelaus to slay the captive Adrastus (instead of holding him for ransom) and not spare any Trojan male foetus in the womb. Such ruthless destruction in warfare is more or less the same as the "ban" or "devotion" (called *ḥérem* in Hebrew) of conquered communities such as Jericho and Ai in the Book of Joshua. The obligatory slaying of captured enemy heroes is found, for example, in 1 Samuel 15: 18-33, where Agag, King of the

---

[1] For a Hebrew example of surprise tactics, note Judges 7: 15-22.

Amalekites, is captured and hacked to death. 1 Samuel 15 brings out the prohibition against sparing the conquered people and cattle. In bitter warfare, ransom was ruled out (Judges 5: 19). The Bible parallels the Homeric atrocity of destroying even the unborn foetuses in the passages that tell of ripping open pregnant women (2 Kings 8: 12; 15: 16; Amos 1: 13; Hosea 13: 16) by the conquerors.

All of the ancient warring nations had systems of rewarding the soldiers for brave and successful service on the battlefield. Hammurapi's Code contains provisions for regulating the professional soldier's royal grant consisting of both land and chattels. At Ugarit, we have a number of royal decrees assigning or transferring estates to nobles in exchange for their services to the crown; and military service must have been high on the list. In Israel the whole theory of land ownership was that the conquerors received parcels of the land they conquered, for themselves and their heirs in perpetuity. Homer tells us of land and chattels allocated to warriors for their hard service in battle. Laertes won his farm (Odyssey 24: 207) and Achilles won the girl Briseis (Iliad 2: 690; cf. 1: 162) because they had "toiled much" in battle. A grateful sovereign could also turn over a captured city to a captain who had served him well on the battlefield. Menelaus declares that had Odysseus returned he would have given him a city in Argos (near Menelaus's terrain), from which he would have expelled the inhabitants and whither he would have transplanted Odysseus with the latter's people and possessions (Odyssey 4: 168-182). Turning over a conquered city to a favourite is paralleled (quite historically) in the Bible: Pharaoh conquers the city of Gezer and presents it as a dowry to his son-in-law Solomon.[1] The taking over of a whole city by a new population is mentioned in Judges, when the Danites destroyed Laish, slew the inhabitants, occupied it themselves and

---

[1] 1 Kings 9: 16.

rebuilt the place under the new name of " Dan " (Judges 18: 27-29).

Death is a common topic in Greek Epic. It is treated along much the same lines in the Semitic and Greek sectors of the East Mediterranean. For instance, one of the death penalties was by stoning. This is what " donning a coat of stone " refers to in Iliad 3: 57 (cf. Aeschylus, Agamemnon: 872). The Hebrew references are fairly common: Exodus 17: 4; 19: 13; 21: 28; Deuteronomy 13: 11; 17: 5; 22: 21, 24; Joshua 7: 25; 1 Samuel 30: 6; I Kings 21: 10; etc.).

Death for offending a god is an international motif found in the epic repertoire. The comrades of Odysseus died for devouring the cows of Helios Hyperion (Odyssey 1: 7-9). Onan died because he committed an act that displeased Yahweh (Genesis 38: 10). Enkidu perished because he insulted Ishtar. Aqhat sealed his own fate by insulting Anath.

Death was envisaged as the result of being wounded by a god's shaft. Apollo's arrows killed men, while the arrows of his sister, Artemis, killed women. Iliad 24: 605-6 relates that Apollo slew the six sons, and Artemis the six daughters of Niobe. In Iliad 21: 483-4, Artemis is tauntingly reminded that Zeus had empowered her to slay women. Note also Iliad 19: 59 for women slain by the arrows of Artemis. The arrows of God cause men to die in Hebrew poetry.[1] Note Psalm 64: 7 " God will shoot them suddenly with an arrow "; Zechariah 9: 14 " And Yahweh shall appear against them, and His arrow shall go forth like lightning "; etc. When Job is afflicted with disease and other misfortunes, he complains that the Almighty has transfixed him with poisoned

---

[1] Hebrew monotheism made it technically impossible for a special deity to slay women. In spite of vestiges of the pagan past, monotheism automatically eliminated from the Bible many features of ancient religion; for example, theogony and theomachy. The Old Testament does not even have a word for " goddess," although particular pagan goddesses are mentioned by name.

arrows: " For against me are the Almighty's arrows whose poison my spirit drinks; the terrors of God are arrayed against me " (Job 6: 4). Cf. Iliad 1: 43-67 where Apollo's shafts are the cause of pestilence as well as death.

Wallowing in dirt was a widespread manifestation of grief for the dead. Priam " grovels in the filth " for the slain Hector (Iliad 22: 414). See the biblical contexts where the grief-stricken wallow (*hitpallēš*) in the dust (Jeremiah 6: 26; 25: 34; Ezekiel 27: 30; Micah 1: 10). Ugaritic uses the same root (*plṭ*) in describing the conventional ways of expressing grief.

Achilles fears the flies may enter the wounds of Patroclus so that worms may breed and shame the corpse, though Thetis promises to prevent it and preserve the flesh fair for a year if necessary (Iliad 19: 23-33). Cf. the Gilgamesh Epic in which the worm on Enkidu's corpse dismays Gilgamesh and reminds him of his own mortality.

Burial is essential for the welfare of the dead. Iliad 19: 228-9 has an almost Hebrew ring, for it advocates burial after one day's weeping. Hebrew insistence on burial within a day typifies the Hebraic abhorrence of corpses.

The disgrace of the unburied corpse left to be devoured by dogs and carrion-eating birds appears often in Homer and Bible; cf. also Antigone: 205-6, 697-8, 1017, 1081-2. Leaving a prince unburied for the dogs and birds was so offensive that the gods would not accept the prayers and offerings of those guilty thereof (Antigone: 1016-1020). This horror of shaming the royal dead (even when the latter deserved the worst), explained King Jehu's order regarding the corpse of Jezebel: " Tend to this cursed one and bury her, for she is the daughter of a king " (2 Kings 9: 34).

A soldier's ghost could find no rest unless his body received condign rites. Elpenor's spirit asks that his body be burned with his armour, then buried in a mound by the shore for remembrance, and not left behind unwept and unburied (Odyssey 11: 72-78).

In Chapter 1 we compared the Homeric and biblical burning of slain heroes before burial. Variant forms of this custom are attested throughout Indo-European epic: Indic, Greek, Anglo-Saxon and Icelandic. Hittite and Homeric burial have much in common: the burning of the body, quenching the pyre with some beverage; dipping the bones in oil or wrapping them in fat, then placing them in linen or some fine garment; the burial, and finally a feast.[1] The burnings of Saul and Hector were thus linked by Hittite custom overland, even as they were presumably linked by Philistine custom imported by sea.

The realm of nether darkness, where the dead dwell, is *Érebos* (Iliad 8: 368; 16: 327; Odyssey 10: 528; 20: 356) located in the west (Odyssey 12: 81). In Egypt the abode of the dead is also in the west, and there can be little doubt that the Mycenaean and Egyptian concepts are related. However, *Érebos* is borrowed from Semitic, not from Egyptian. In Hebrew, *'éreb* is " evening " referring to the sunset; and *ma*ᶜᵃ*rāb* (from the same root) is " west." In Ugaritic *'rb špš* means " setting of the sun "=*m'rb* " sunset." In Akkadian *erêb šamši* is " setting of the sun " or " west." Since Homeric *Érebos* is a Semitic word for " west," designating the Egyptian meaning of " the West " as the abode of the dead, the same idea must have permeated the Semitic world as well. We can, therefore, call the concept East Mediterranean because of its spread, even though Egypt (where it is first attested as far as our records go) may have been the centre from which the idea fanned out.

The epithet of the god Hades, "he of the famed steeds," appears in Iliad 5: 654. In Ugaritic, we meet with a related concept in the Rephaim, the divine inhabitants of the land of the dead, who ride in horse-drawn chariots.

[1] O. R. Gurney, *The Hittites*, pp. 164-169.

Unlike the older literatures of the Near East, the East Mediterranean texts of the Amarna/Mycenaean Age confront us with the
pervasive theme of romantic love and marriage. The older
attitude is preserved in the Bellerophon story, where the adulter-
ous wife would seduce an upright youth, but on failing to do so,
maligns him. This story with its portrait of woman in the role of
trouble-maker occurs in the Egyptian Tale of the Two Brothers
and in the Joseph Cycle of Genesis. The older traditions of the
Bible portray woman as a bad (albeit necessary) influence on man,
starting with mother Eve. In the Gilgamesh Epic, Ishtar (the
divine prototype of womankind) is depicted as a bane to her
husbands and lovers. With the Indo-European invasions, a new
attitude infiltrated the East Mediterranean. Hattusili III (Apology
9: 3: 1 ff.) regards his marriage as divinely decreed. The
Apology is full of expressions of tenderness for his destined bride,
glorifying the love of man and wife, and the blessings of progeny
within the framework of a happy marriage. Greek (like Indic)
Epic is full of this theme. The love of Achilles and Briseis, of
Odysseus and Penelope, of Hector and Andromache, etc.,
permeate Homer. Helen cannot be substituted by another
woman; she is prized above all women and none can take her
place. The same goes for Hurrai in the Ugaritic Legend of Kret;
and for Sarah or Rachel in Genesis. It is all too easy to assume
that a romantic approach to woman is universal. The Gilgamesh
Epic is far from devoid of sex, but completely lacks any trace of
romance, even though the subject of marriage is raised. A good
Middle Egyptian illustration is afforded by Sinuhe, who marries a
chieftain's daughter and has stalwart sons from her; yet when he
has a chance to return to Egypt, he abandons her and his children
for all time without any expression of regret.

The concept of *mênis* "wrath" permeates Homer. A *mênis* is
caused by an affront and touches off dire consequences far beyond
any reasonable objective. The wrath of Achilles, because Aga-

memnon took away Briseis, not only punished Agamemnon, but sent many brave Achaeans to Hades. When the tragic effects of Achilles' wrath had come to pass, Achilles had to admit that the sorry business made no sense and that all would have been better off had Artemis slain Briseis with a shaft on the day he (Achilles) got her (Iliad 19: 56-60). The theme of the *mênis* is not limited to the Wrath of Achilles. An older *mênis*, The Wrath of Meleager, is incorporated in the Iliad (9: 529-599). The wrath idea occurs in the Gilgamesh Epic, where Enkidu affronts Ishtar and her wrath is not assuaged until she accomplishes his death. At Ugarit, Anath, enraged by the insults of Aqhat, is not satisfied until she has him murdered. But the wrath that is most akin to the wrath of Achilles is the "Wrath of Samson," who because his wife has been given to another, goes on a destructive rampage and refuses to behave rationally until he has slain many a Philistine (Judges 15: 1-8). This has all the elements of a Homeric *mênis*: the affront, the dire consequences, and the dissipation of the rage only after mad acts of vengeance. Gods as well as heroes are subject to *mênis*. "The Wrath of God" in the Bible is a reflex thereof. The Old Testament examples are many. When Israel aroused God's jealousy with the Golden Calf: "Yahweh smote the people because they fashioned the calf that Aaron had made" (Exodus 32: 35). The psychology of divine wrath is stated in Ezekiel 5: 13 where God says: "And (when) My wrath will be spent (after total destruction in v. 12!), I shall allay Mine anger from them and be appeased; and they shall know that I Yahweh have spoken in My jealousy when I complete My wrath against them."

One of the lessons inculcated by the epic is that we should accept condign terms on time. Agamemnon refused the ransom offered by Chryses for his daughter, and instead persisted in harshness (Iliad 1: 22-32). Calchas accordingly tells Agamemnon that now he will have to restore the girl without the ransom he could have had (Iliad 1: 95-100). Meleager refused gifts and would not defend his city; eventually he had to defend his city, but it was too late to receive the gifts that would have brought him honour. In Genesis 38, Judah knew that he was wrong in assuming an attitude that could only deprive Tamar of bearing his heir. Finally, he was unwittingly instrumental in enabling her to produce the heir, but in a way that put him to shame.

The epic dwells on two kinds of dedication to comrades: the hero's devotion to a particular friend, and the commander's concern for his troops. Individual devotion is illustrated by Gilgamesh and Enkidu, by Achilles and Patroclus, or by David and Jonathan. The commander's concern for his men is illustrated by Odysseus who earnestly sought to secure not only his own life but also the return of his comrades (Odyssey 1: 5; etc.), or by Menelaus who would have settled for a third-part of his own fortune if only his companions could have been saved at Troy (Odyssey 4: 97).

The Gilgamesh Epic is our earliest text stating the heroic preference for fame rather than life without glory. Hector does not want to die before accomplishing something that will guarantee his lasting renown (Iliad 22: 304-5). And when Odysseus faces death alone at sea, he wishes he could have died while fighting at Troy for the body of Achilles, for then the Achaeans would have spread his fame (Odyssey 5: 311).

Honourable treatment required gifts, as we have had occasion to observe. Gifts cemented friendships and were vital in establishing good relations. Particularly after a long absence from home, returning home was honourable in proportion to the gifts one brought with him (Odyssey 11: 355-361); and it is shameful to tarry long and return emptyhanded (Iliad 2: 298). Note the gifts that Odysseus claims to have got from Egypt in Odyssey 14: 285-6. Particularly interesting is the fact that it was Arete, the wife of his host among the Phaeacians, that urged the giving of gifts for Odysseus (Odyssey 11: 335-341); even as it was

Utnapishtim's wife who urged the presentation of some valuable parting gift for Gilgamesh on the eve of his departure. The gifts that Odysseus brought home from the Phaeacians are to be compared with the gifts that the Shipwrecked Sailor brought home from the magic isle, and with the gifts that the Hebrews extracted from the Egyptians on the eve of the Exodus homeward-bound to the Promised Land. The emphasis on gifts is an important part of the epic repertoire.

The ability to lie, deceive and beat the other fellow through chicanery was admired by onlookers if not by the victims themselves. The maternal grandfather of Odysseus was Autolycus, who, together with his sons, excelled all men in thievery and oaths. The success of Autolycus is attributed to the sacrifice he gave to Hermes (himself quite a deceiver!), who befriended him (Odyssey 19: 394-8). Odyssey 19: 203 informs us that Odysseus, uttering many lies, made them seem like truth. This is mentioned as a compliment, not a condemnation. Athene, the guardian deity of Odysseus, was also expert at deception, like her mortal favourite. This standard of character—which equates successful skulduggery with intelligence—permeates the Patriarchal Narratives as well. Jacob's impersonation of Esau to secure the blessing of primogeniture to which Esau was entitled, is a case in point. Jacob's and Laban's relationship was characterised by mutual cheating. Laban palmed off the wrong bride (Leah) on Jacob, who had laboured for Rachel. Jacob later made off with more than his just share of Laban's flocks by a calculated combination of an agreement and some shrewd practices in animal breeding. Note that Jacob (like Odysseus) is a hero, admired by the ancient as well as modern readers of the text.

Men and gods share the same world and the same sun gives light " to the immortals and to mortal men " (Odyssey 3: 2-3). In fact, men and gods are kinsmen, for Zeus is " the father of men and gods." Hebrew poetry sometimes reflects the same view inherited from the pagan literary past (Proverbs 3: 4), exhorts us to "find favour and good wit in the eyes of god(s) and men." Also in Jotham's parable, the vine asks: "Shall I cease (producing) my wine that gladdens gods and men" (Judges 9: 13).

The view that the blood (*haîma*) is the soul (*thūmós*) (Odyssey 3: 455) appears also in the Bible: "for the soul (*néfeš*) of the flesh is (in)[1] the blood (*dām*)" (Leviticus 17: 11). This idea is basic in Hebrew sacrifice and diet. The blood must be poured into the ground and not eaten under any circumstances. The taboo against blood has to do with the sanctity of life; and the sparing of blood must be connected with the continuity of the soul after death.

Animals sometimes receive the treatment appropriate for men. When Odyssey 17: 326-7 tells of the "black fate" that seized Argos when he saw Odysseus in the twentieth year, his death is described in terms befitting a hero. Iliad 16: 466-469 tells of the slaying of the mortal horse Pegasus as though he were a hero, with a soul (*thūmós*) that leaves him. After cataloguing the heroes, the Iliad (2: 761-770) lists the best of the horses and human heroes; the best horses were the mares of the son of Pheres driven by Eumelus and the best man was Telamonian Ajax (except for Achilles and his horses who were out of the combat). The Bible (like much of the literature in ancient Western Asia and Egypt) treats animals almost on a par with people; especially domestic cattle (e.g., Jonah 3: 7-8; 4: 11). The most striking of many examples we might cite is perhaps the slaying of the firstborn in Egypt. The firstborn of Egyptian cattle and human beings were slain; the firstborn of Hebrew cattle and human beings were spared. Rabbinic law forbids the

[1] The Hebrew preposition for "in" should perhaps be omitted in the translation because it can be the equivalent of English "is, are." Hebraists may compare passages like Proverbs 3: 26 and Job 23: 13.

sale of cattle to Gentiles[1] which reflects the kinship felt between men and their livestock. Just as a Jew cannot sell a member of his own people into foreign bondage, he should not sell Jewish cattle to foreigners.

Homer speaks of immortal, as well as mortal, horses that fought at Troy. Iliad 10: 547 describes horses, wondrous like the sun's rays.

The decoration of real or idealised palaces in the ancient world appears in variant forms throughout the literatures of the East Mediterranean. For example, the use of metals and precious stones, especially for embellishing the surface, is reflected in several literatures. Alcinous' palace was of bronze, cyanus, gold and silver (Odyssey 7: 84-90). At Ugarit, Baal's palace is of gold, silver and lapis-lazuli.

The common vocabulary of Semites and Greeks cannot be attributed to any single factor. Some words are loans, that moved into Greek from Semitic or vice versa. Others are East Mediterranean words common to several languages in the area, attributable to either substratum or to diffusion from some (often unknown) language or other in the area. For example, it is hard to dissociate Greek *taur-* " bull " from Semitic *ṯawr-* " bull." Since the word occurs in East and West Semitic (both Northwest and Southwest) with normal inner-Semitic phonetic correspondences, it is presumably a native Semitic word. The " bull " had an importance transcending its value as a domestic animal. Its role in religion and ritual was considerable. Not only was it a sacrificial animal in Semitic and Greek cults, but its function as the beast in bull-grappling was significant enough to warrant its prominence in Sumero-Akkadian art and literature, prior to its documentation in the Minoan sphere. The word *ṯawr* probably moved with the phenomenon of bull-grappling into the Aegean;

[1] E. J. Bickermann, " The Altars of the Gentiles," *Revue International des Droits de l'Antiquité*, 3rd series, v, 1958, pp. 137-164; see p. 139.

in any case the Mesopotamian representations of the cultic sport are earlier than the Minoan. *Boûn agelaíēn* (Odyssey 20: 251) "a heifer of the herd" invites comparison with Hebrew *'égel* "calf," *'eglā* "heifer."

In our survey of Homer, we have been obliged to single out numerous details. Literary criticism of all kinds tends to fragmentise the compositions under investigation. This is inevitable and necessary. And yet we must not lose sight of the unity of our great classics. The ancient Greeks accepted both Homeric epics as the two halves of one tradition. Modern scholarship (in line with a theory of late antiquity), separates the author of the Iliad from the author of the Odyssey, and often goes on to fragmentise each composition. The reader has seen how pre-Greek materials were used in the Homeric epics, so there is no ground for any "classical fundamentalism" whereby Homer was inspired to utter both epics, whole, without historic antecedents. At the same time, there is a unity embracing both the Iliad and Odyssey inherent in the tradition itself, as well as in the past that preceded it. The Iliad and Odyssey are often supposed to represent two widely different stages of early Greek history. The Iliad is presumed to be the earlier and more heroic age; the Odyssey is supposed to be the later and more agricultural age. This, however, is wide of the mark.

In the pre-Greek Near East, the totality of earthly life was conceived as composed of two halves: war and peace. The most graphic illustration that comes to mind is the Standard of Ur from the mid-third millennium. It has two main panels: one of war, the other of peace. Together the panels form a single composition. This concept, which is built into the Homeric text, is clearly expressed in the description of the Shield of Achilles (Iliad 18: 478 ff.), depicting peace and war as the two aspects of human life. Peace does not mean any ideal tranquillity, but rather the absence of open major warfare. On the

Shield, two cities are portrayed, one during peacetime and one involved in war. The peaceful one (: 491 ff.) is the scene not only of a marriage, but also of strife and litigation because of manslaughter. The other city (: 509 ff.) is the scene of war with all the typical features of Homeric military tactics. Then follows (: 541 ff.) a description of agricultural and pastoral activities. The Shield of Achilles epitomises the Iliad and Odyssey. The Iliad is the " war panel " and the Odyssey the " peace panel." Two societies are not depicted in the two Homeric epics; one society is reflected in both epics but under the different conditions of war and peace.[1] The Iliad portrays the heroes as warriors because they are involved in the Trojan War. Let us not forget that it also represents those warriors as rich in land and cattle back home. The Odyssey does not have pitched battles, because the war is over. Instead it portrays the festive board, sullied with manslaughter and strife, as in Hephaistos's " peaceful city " on the Shield of Achilles. Ancient Greece correctly assumed the unity of the two Homeric epics; and we shall be able to do the same once we see that the tradition required the two halves to make up the whole canonical picture of the Heroic Age.

Homeric criticism and Pentateuchal criticism are reflexes of the same intellectual currents. Both must now be tempered by the new understanding of the traditions, forced on us by the same mass of archaeological discovery.

[1] The Books of Judges and Ruth both deal with the period of the Judges. The Book of Judges portrays the heroes at war, whereas Ruth portrays the same age during peace.

VIII

Further Observations on the Bible

The Bible is of complex composition, varying in scope according to the different ecclesiastical bodies. The Samaritans include only the Five Books of Moses in their Bible, and it is evident from the Dead Sea Scrolls that before the start of the Christian Era the Pentateuch was the most stabilised part of Hebrew Scripture. Normative Judaism embraces the conventional Pentateuch, Prophets and Hagiographa of the familiar Hebrew Old Testament. The Septuagint, however, is far more inclusive, containing, as it does, Apocrypha and Pseudepigrapha. Qumranite and other sectarian Jews possessed still other sacred writings. Protestant Bibles usually contain the normative Jewish Old Testament plus the New Testament; Catholic Bibles have, in addition, the Apocryphal Books. Various Eastern Orthodox Churches include different Pseudepigrapha. Accordingly, there is no one biblical corpus; and the component books of either Testament are in many cases extremely heterogeneous individually.

The older cultures did not develop the concept of canonical writings. There is no Bible in Egypt or Mesopotamia. Neither country had a collection of sacred writings that excluded other writings from comparable status. Unlike any canonical book of the Bible, there was never an official " Book of the Dead " in Egypt. Any Egyptian who ordered and could afford to purchase a " Book of the Dead " might have one made for him, and the various exemplars of the Book of the Dead diverge widely from each other. So much so that we should not speak of *The* Book of the Dead, because there is no one copy that an Egyptian would have recognised as *The* (one and only) Book.

Only two people in East Mediterranean antiquity developed " canonical "[1] Scripture: the Greeks and the Jews. The Greeks treated Homer as their Scripture *par excellence*, much as the Jews regarded the Bible. The establishment of the Textus Receptus of Hebraic Scripture and Homeric Epic were parallel manifestations of the same movement. Hebrew and pagan Greek scriptures were each considered the divinely inspired guide for life. Just as the Jew and Christian turn for guidance to the Bible, the ancient Greek turned to the Homeric text.

The analogy between the Greeks and Hebrews goes much further. Minos has rightly been compared with Moses. Both are greater-than-life-size figures who received the law from the supreme god on a sacred mountain (see Dionysius of Halicarnassus, *Roman Antiquities* 2 : 61 concerning Minos). The law is the constitution of the world and society. So far the same general notion can be traced back to Mesopotamia, for on the stela of Hammurapi's Code, the god Shamash, enthroned on a mountain, reveals to Hammurapi the immutable law that must forever govern society. However, in some respects, Moses and Minos have analogues not shared with Hammurapi. The most notable is that Moses and Minos is each seconded by a master craftsman; Moses has his Bezalel, and Minos his Daedalus. As far as we can tell, this is an East Mediterranean feature.

The East Mediterranean framework of the World of the Hebrews is a foregone conclusion for plain geographical reasons, but it is nonetheless interesting to see the Hebraic expression of

---

[1] Strictly speaking, " canonical " is not quite exact for the Greeks; and anachronistic even for the Jews, who did not establish their Canon until around A.D. 100. But in retrospect, we see that both peoples shared parallel tendencies towards canonisation of Scripture.

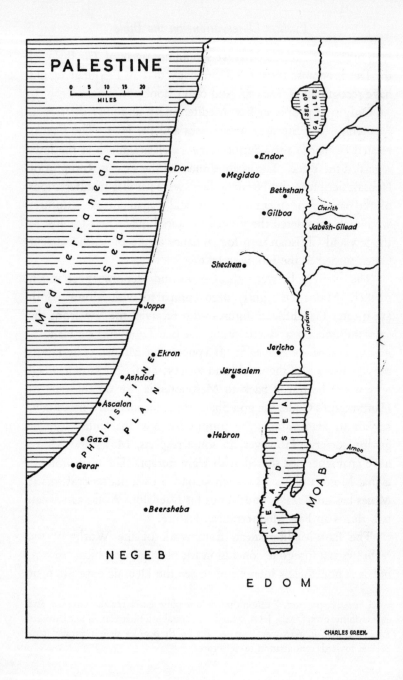

the fact. In Genesis 10, where the people of the known world are arranged according to ethnic affinities, the very first group is the Japhethite, including the Aegean peoples such as the Ionian Greeks and their offshoots, such as the Cypriotes (v. 4). The linguistic diversity of the area is reminiscent of the Homeric description of the Trojan allies: " From these (i.e., the Ionian offshoots) were separated the islands of the nations in their lands—each according to its own language—according to their clans among their nations "(v. 5).

Sea-mindedness is built into the idioms of early Hebrew as well as Greek literatures. A great host can be compared with sand in Greek epic (Iliad 2: 800), even as Israel's progeny will be innumerable as the " sand of the sea " (Genesis 32: 12; cf. Judges 7: 12). A landlocked people would not use this and many other expressions showing familiarity with the sea.

Books and groupings of books in the Bible—and ultimately the Bible as a whole—should be understood *in toto* as well as in their component parts.

The Pentateuch, with all its diversity, was considered an integral whole by Jews and Samaritans alike. If broken down into its component parts typologically, it appears to be a patchquilt of badly stitched sources. For the Pentateuch tells about the cosmos, social institutions, litigation, war, agriculture, grazing, royalty, sacrifice, etc., It is interesting to note that these topics are all worked into the composition of the Shield of Achilles. The description of the Shield opens with the portrayal of earth, sea and heaven (Iliad 18: 483-489) and closes with the portrayal of the cosmic river Oceanus (: 607-608). Note also the portrayal of social institutions, litigation, war, agriculture, grazing, royalty, etc. (: 490 ff.). Even sacrifice comes into the picture (: 558-560). The Torah, being the guide for life, had to cover the various aspects of life as the ancient Hebrew conceived it. The Shield shows us that such diverse themes as cosmology, law, sacrifice, etc., were "part of the same picture" according to ancient East Mediterranean *Weltanschauung*. We must, therefore, keep our eye on the totality of the Pentateuch, as well as on the sum of its parts.

If we examine the sequence of the Hebrew books from Genesis through Kings, we find that they cannot be a group of books simply thrown together in chronological order, for they are not merely in chronological order. They fit together tightly. Where the Pentateuch leaves off, Joshua begins; where Joshua ends, Judges continues; and so with the books of Samuel and Kings. If we then examine the separate books, we find that they have earlier sources imbedded in them. Some of these sources were definitely in written form when they were excerpted by the biblical authors. "The Book of the Story of Man" (Genesis 5: 1 ff.) can only be a pre-biblical written source because *séfer* "book" designates only an inscribed text; the same holds for the Book of the Wars of Yahweh (Numbers 21: 14). Some of the other *named* sources of the Pentateuch may also have been written even though they are not called *séfer* "a book"; e.g., "This is the Story of Heaven and Earth" (Genesis 2: 4), "This is the Story of Noah" (Genesis 6: 9), "This is the Story of the Sons of Noah" (Genesis 10: 1), etc.

The high literacy of Canaan during the Amarna/Mycenaean Age is attested by the Ugaritic tablets. The aristocratic, mercantile and official character of the Patriarchs goes hand in hand with the literacy of the Age. Ugarit has yielded documents regulating the activities of the merchants of Ur(a). Ugarit has also yielded the Epic of Kret dealing with the promised line of King Kret. It would, therefore, be in keeping with Canaanite culture if the Patriarchal Narratives (*qua* Epic of Kings) was written during Mycenean times, before the Judges came along. Indeed for the Period of the Judges (*ca.* 1100 B.C.) one passage suggests a degree of popular literacy: "And (Gideon) captured a lad of the men of

Succoth, and interrogated him; and he inscribed for him (the names of) the princes of Succoth and its elders: seventy-seven men" (Judges 8: 14). Unless the word *ná'ar* "lad" has some special meaning like "scribe" or "official," the passage conveys the impression that it was nothing unusual for a youth found at random in a Canaanite town to be literate.

That certain parts of our Bible circulated in oral form before they were committed to writing is not only possible but likely. However, the high literacy of the age points to a maximum of written sources lying behind Scripture.

The Book of Judges illustrates well what classical scholars called the work of the rhapsodes, "stitchers of songs." Judges is for the most part a number of different cycles about various Judges of different tribes "stitched together." Some cycles (like Samson's) are told in some detail. One (Deborah's) is given in two versions: prose (Chapter 4) and poetic (Chapter 5). Some are reduced to a tantalising minimum. Judges 5: 6 conveys the impression that Shamgar was so famous a figure that events in his day could be dated by being referred to him. And yet all we know of him is stated in one verse (Judges 3: 31): "And after him (Ehud), there was Shamgar son of Anath; he smote six hundred Philistines with an oxgoad; and also he saved Israel." It would be a gross mistake to conclude that the Book of Judges is only the sum of what an editor excerpted. The Book as a whole gives a coherent picture of an era and propounds the thesis that the institutions of pre-monarchic Israel were so chaotic (Judges 17: 6; 18: 1; 19: 1; 21: 25)—as the narratives in chapters 17-21 bring out—that centralised, hereditary kingship was necessary.

It is clear that some of the early sources were comprehensive writings excerpted more than once by the biblical author. For example, the Book of Jashar is excerpted twice: first, in Joshua 10: 13; then, in 2 Samuel 1: 18. But the incorporation of such earlier sources does not mean that the Pentateuch or Former

Prophets is the work of an editor who pasted together various documents. Once we view the work as a whole, we see that it is a fresh creation though not a *creatio ex nihilo*. The same holds for Homeric Epic that has been subjected to the same kinds of modern literary criticism.

We keep coming back to the principle of taking ancient writings on their own terms. Heroic epic and saga (Indic as well as Greek and Hebrew, etc.) combine action with genealogy. This is necessary because the action is performed by aristocrats who require genealogies. In biblical criticism, the old genealogies are usually detached and attributed to P of the 5th century, B.C. That they should not be detached from the narrative is indicated by Homeric epic, where the two are combined so artistically that no one should ever think of rending them asunder; especially since it would mean breaking the lines and destroying the meter.

The most important document found at Ugarit for both Biblical and Homeric studies is the Epic of Kret. It anticipates the Helen-of-Troy motif in the Iliad and Genesis, thus bridging the gap between the two literatures.

I Kings 17: 3 tells us that the Wady of Krit (which was probably named after the hero of the Kret text) was opposite the Jordan. We should note that in the Hebrew Bible "jordan" (Heb. *yardēn*, Septuagint *iordánēs*) is not a proper name but a common noun, because the River is called "The Jordan" or "This Jordan" or "the Jordan of Jericho" but never "Jordan"[1] by itself in the manner of true proper names. That "jordan" is a noun meaning "river" is indicated by Mandaic, in which any river is a "jordan." The term is familiar in the ancient Aegean area; note, for example, "Crete where the Kydonians

---

[1] In the two passages where the article is omitted (Psalm 42: 7; Job 40: 23), "Jordan" is not the specific river but harks back to the personified River God.

dwelt about the streams of Iardanus " (Odyssey 3: 291-2).[1] In fact *iardan* seems to be an East Mediterranean word for " river." Aegean influence in Palestine probably accounts for the names of the Wady of Krit and of the Jordan, where the Philistines exercised control down to David's reign, for Beth-Shan overlooking the Jordan was a Philistine stronghold until after Saul's death.

The prevalence of royal epic (the Kret and Aqhat texts) in Canaan has shown us that the Patriarchal Narratives are (among other things!) royal epic. Like Kret, the Patriarchs are plainly described as the founders of a line of kings in Genesis 17: 6 and 35: 11. The Septuagint translators of Genesis 23: 6 knew enough Homer to realise that Abraham could properly be called " king " in the Mycenaean sense of an aristocratic warrior in command of a contingent of troops. A coalition of such " kings " wages war against another coalition of kings in Genesis 14, even as the Achaean and Trojan coalitions of kings wage war in the Iliad albeit on a grander scale.

Once we recognise the factor of royal epic in Genesis, we see that the Helen-of-Troy motif permeates the Patriarchal Narratives. We do not refer only to the abductions that wrested Sarah and nearly wrested Rebecca from their aristocratic husbands. The abduction and seduction of Dinah is a related theme in the Narratives, involving also a *mênis* of her brothers Simeon and Levi that results in bloody vengeance. Neither Sarah nor Dinah is ever condemned. Like Helen and Hurrai, Sarah and Dinah are heroines according to the standards of royal epic. Like Helen, Sarah is wondrously fair and ageless. Twenty years after Helen left her husband and child, she still retained the charms of youth. Sarah outdid her; for even after Sarah had passed her ninetieth birthday (Genesis 17: 17), kings could not resist her beauty (Genesis 20: 2 ff.).

[1] For streams of Iardanus also in Elis, see Iliad 7: 135.

Sarah's name means "princess" in normal Hebrew, and "queen" in Akkadian. It is conceivable that (like David afterwards, whose name *dāwíd* means "leader, chief"[1]) her title came to be used as her name.[2]

The Mycenaean kingship depicted in Homer is the best possible collateral information for understanding early Hebrew kingship, which is not yet recognised as kingship even though Midrashic literature not only understood it but called it by its right name.

As in all comparative studies, we must beware of equating parallel and related structures. Greeks were not Hebrews, however close their interrelations were during the Mycenaean Age. One difference is the commercial interests of the Patriarchs *vis-à-vis* the total disregard for commerce among the Mycenaean heroes. Unlike the Homeric sackers of cities, who thrived on plunder, Abraham refuses any personal share of the plunder acquired by his coalition after its victory over the four invading kings in Genesis 14: 22-23. Abraham is repeatedly described as wealthy in gold and silver as well as in livestock and slaves. In Genesis 23: 16, his commercial interests are hinted at by the phrase "current for the merchant" describing the four hundred shekels of silver that he paid out. The commercial pursuits of the Patriarchs are explicitly mentioned in two different contexts confirming their commercial activities: once when the Shechemites invite Jacob's family to join the Shechem community (Genesis 34: 10); the other when Joseph provisionally welcomes his brothers to settle in Egypt (Genesis 42: 34). On both occasions, trading privileges are offered. Abraham could afford to turn down a personal share in the plunder because he had a peaceful and adequate source of income; viz., legitimate trade: an occupation that his descendants continued for at least three

[1] Some scholars, however, now interpret his name as meaning "victory."
[2] That she is the destined mother of kings is stated in Genesis 17: 16.

generations according to the text of Genesis. The traditions of Abraham now fit into a documented historic context thanks to the correspondence of Hattusili III found at Ugarit. That Hittite monarch (doubtless continuing an activity conducted by his predecessors for generations) sponsored merchants in Canaan from Ur(a). He regulated their activities, enforcing their collection of what was due them from their native debtors, but prohibiting them from buying real-estate or settling down in Canaan. Ur of the Chaldees, the birthplace of Abraham, was a northern commercial colony probably founded by the Sumerian Empire called the Third Dynasty of Ur during its heyday (*ca.* 20th century B.C.). All of the connections of the Patriarchal Narratives are northern, with no trace of direct contact with Sumer and Akkad. The southern identification of Ur of the Chaldees began during the second half of the nineteenth century when the decipherment of the Sumero-Akkadian inscriptions produced references to Sumerian Ur. That identification received an impetus during the 1920's as a result of C. Leonard Woolley's important and widely publicised excavations at Sumerian Ur. The Royal Tombs yielded such splendid finds that the success of the expedition gave the illusion of finality to a specious identification. Older books—including many a forgotten tome of the nineteenth century—correctly locate Ur of the Chaldees in the general Haran area. Possibly the name " Ur " (of the Chaldees) was perpetuated as Orrhai,[1] a powerful centre of Aramaism, down into Christian times where (under the name of Edessa) it was the stronghold of Syriac Christianity. The Patriarchs are depicted as Arameans as long as they remained in their native land.

Ur of the Chaldees, and Haran, were centres of the lunar Sin-and-Nikkal cult like the mother city of Sumerian Ur. Nikkal (the moon goddess) came to be worshipped throughout Canaan

[1] Now " Urfa."

287

and even penetrated Egypt. The movement that brought Abraham into Canaan explains why only Nikkal of the whole Mesopotamian pantheon, was widely worshipped in Canaan. (There was no need for the moon god " Sin," because the Canaanites were already worshipping the moon under his Canaanite name " Yarih "; since he had no consort before the Mesopotamian impact, Nikkal came in under her Mesopotamian name.)

The invitation of the Shechemites to Jacob (Genesis 34: 10) is remarkable in that it covers the same topics regulated by Hattusili for his merchants: (a) trading activities, (b) settling down, (c) owning real-estate. Hattusili's merchants were not permitted to settle down or buy real-estate; but the Shechemites, to induce Jacob to unite with them, conceded precisely the two rights normally wanted by, but withheld from, the merchants.

Abraham's purchase of the field of Machpelah from Ephron the Hittite, in the presence of the representatives of the whole Hittite enclave, is, as we have already observed, known to be according to Hittite law. The Hittites treat Abraham as an official of their own Hittite empire, for they address him thus: " You are an exalted prince (" king " in the Septuagint) in our midst." It is significant that Abraham of Ur is accorded this title only in the midst of a community belonging to the nation whose sovereign sponsored the merchants of Ur(a).

Recently published cuneiform texts from northern sites make the southern identification of Patriarchal Ur less and less tenable on other grounds. Alalakh confronts us with the following variants: *Ú-ra, Ú-ri-e^{ki}* and *Ú-ur-ri*.[1] Nuzu confronts us with *^{al}ú-ri* GAL " Great Ur " and *^{al}ú-ri* TUR " Little Ur "; var. *^{al}úr-ra* GAL.[2] There is little likelihood that any of these references

[1] D. J. Wiseman, *The Alalakh Tablets*, London, 1953, p. 157 (C 142, 13, 154: 10).

[2] E. R. Lacheman, *Harvard Semitic Series* 14, 1950, text 75: 3; 195: 2.

have to do with Ur in Sumer, though they doubtless refer to more than one northern Ur.

One of the chief themes in the Patriarchal Narratives is the preoccupation with leadership. A great issue is made over Abraham's heir. The text dramatises not only the birth of Isaac but also his triumph over Ishmael's rivalry. The same, *mutatis mutandis*, may be said of Jacob's triumph over Esau. This pervasive theme goes hand in hand with the fact that the text is royal epic, establishing the line founded by the first *basileús* of the Jews, Abraham. The royal prerogatives of the line are substantiated in the text not only by birth, but by blessings, birthright and possession of the household gods.

At first it seems strange to attribute to the Patriarchs the roles of aristocratic warriors and merchants, simultaneously. That this combination of roles is genuine, and not contrived, is borne out by the administrative texts from Ugarit, which list *bdl . mrynm* (400: III: 6) " merchants of the charioteer warriors " and similarly *bdl . mdrǵlm* (44: VI: 17) " merchants of the *m.*-warriors."[1] However we interpret the syntactic relationship of the two nouns in each case, it is clear that commerce and the military *élite* could and did mix. It stands to reason that if the king had commercial agents to represent his interests throughout his commercial empire, his merchants would on serious occasions turn to him for protection against the threat of attack. The King of Battle epic, as noted in Chapter II, tells how Sargon of Akkad's merchants in Anatolia summoned him to rescue them from the attack of a local king. Sargon heeded their call and re-established his suzerainty there. This epic naturally enjoyed wide currency not only in Mesopotamia but also throughout the far-flung

---

[1] That merchants often had troops attached to them, is also clear from another Ugaritic tablet (Virolleaud, *Palais royal d'Ugarit* II: 35: 4-5) which singles out merchants without troops of their own, in a way that indicates that merchants ordinarily did have troops.

commercial empire, for fragments of it have been found not only at Assur but even in Egypt. The Phoenicians probably had the same type of merchant-warrior princes, except that they fared by sea rather than overland.

One of the differences between the Homeric heroes and the Hebrew Patriarchs is their contrasting methods of getting land. The Greek heroes acquired land by conquest. The Patriarchal Narratives depict the Fathers as purchasing land in Canaan. Genesis 23 tells of Abraham buying land from the Hittites around Hebron; Genesis 33: 19 states that Jacob bought land around Shechem from the Sons of Hamor.

We must shun one-sided approaches to complex questions. The near-sacrifice of Isaac is a case in point. The principal function of the story in epic saga may well be to remind the public to obey the behests of God, no matter how exacting they be. If Abraham was ready to sacrifice his son and heir, we should certainly withhold nothing that God wants from us. But this application of the story does not explain all the factors inherent in the story itself. Just as God saved Isaac in the nick of time and provided a ram to substitute for him on the altar, Artemis saved Iphigeneia at Aulis by snatching her away and putting a stag in her place on the altar (*Cypria*, Loeb edition, pp. 494-5). This parallel shows that the essential elements of the story are East Mediterranean with reflexes in both Greece and Israel.

Students of Scripture have long observed that the Isaac saga is smaller in scope and in detail than the sagas of either his father Abraham or of his son Jacob. It is quite likely that his original saga has been trimmed down for good reasons. Scripture makes it clear that unlike the conceptions of Abraham and of Jacob, Isaac was conceived through divine agency. Like the Mycenaean Greek heroes, Isaac could claim paternity at two levels; the human and the divine. His human father, through whom he obtained his specific position in his people's history, was Abraham; but his superhuman quality was derived from the deity that visited Sarah. This is of a piece with the dual paternity of Homeric heroes, who hold the office of their human fathers, but are super-men because of their divine fathers. Normative Judaism has divested itself of this ancient approach to the paternity of heroes, in spite of the tell-tale text in Genesis. Midrash does not hesitate to call Moses half-god and half-man,[1] but it too fails to pick up the thread of the nativity of Isaac, probably because the puritanic trend set in early enough to nip the Isaac midrashim in the bud. It is in every way conceivable that some of the original Isaac Cycle survived to re-echo in Christianity. Jesus derives his human-office of Messianic King from Joseph, but his divine quality from his Divine Father. Moreover, the Church tradition that connects the sacrifice of Isaac with the sacrifice of Christ apparently rests on sound exegesis, for the sacrifice of Isaac would have meant not only the sacrifice of Abraham's son but of God's.

If we take the story of Israel as unfolded in Scripture, as a whole, there emerges the pattern of a national epic. The central event in the consciousness of Israel was the Exodus, rather than later developments such as the establishment of the Davidic Dynasty. The reason for this is evident and intelligible. The nationhood of Israel required the union of the various segments of the people, schematised as the Twelve Tribes. Accordingly, the Exodus Story is careful to make all of the tribes the equal recipients of God's salvation from Egypt to the Promised Land. David was Judean, and that by itself ruled out any chance of his Dynasty being the ideological rallying point of all the Tribes. To the contrary, when his successors Hezekiah and Josiah tried to reunite the nation, they built their programme around the Passover Pilgrimage commemorating the Exodus.

[1] See L. Ginzberg, *Legends of the Jews* III, 1911, p. 481. Actually the apotheosis of Moses is promised in Exodus 7: 1, where Yahweh says to him: " Behold I am making you a god (Elohim) *vis-à-vis* Pharaoh." Cf. Mark 9: 4.

It is noteworthy that the towering figure in Judaism is not David, but Moses, whose Levitical affiliation placed him outside the secular Twelve-Tribe structure. It would be going too far to write off his Levitical genealogy to tendentious invention. But it is clear that his being accepted as a Levite contributed to the success of his mission.

The Pentateuch cannot be compared with the Iliad as literature, because they are completely different types of compositions. However, they did serve a similar function for their readers. Not only were both accepted as the revelation par excellence, but they both served as the Epic of Nationhood for the scattered segments of the people.[1] All Israel could look to the Pentateuch for their national epic in which all the Tribes are treated with equal dignity. The reading of the Pentateuch during a national pilgrimage such as that celebrated under Josiah at Passover, would have the effect of cementing the Tribes together and instilling in them a feeling of unity. Indeed the oneness of the Hebrews is built into the Pentateuch at two levels: the Patriarchal and Exodus levels. The ancestors of the Tribes are brothers according to Genesis; it is to the Patriarchs that the Land is promised for their progeny; and it is the Patriarchs who also acquire the land by legal purchase and treaty. Accordingly, the Conquest under Joshua corresponds to the Return of the Heraclids in Greek tradition. The Conquest is ideologically a return to claim the land acquired by the Patriarchs, and temporarily abandoned by them through necessity.

---

[1] In both, all branches of the warrior people have a legitimate place and are treated with respect, in keeping with the epic mood. Trojans are just as brave and honourable as the Achaeans. Hector (as well as Achilles) remains an honoured name. Conflicts among the noble leaders do not mean that one side becomes debased. The Sons of Korah thus remain honoured in Israel (Psalms 42, 44, 45, 46, 47, 48, 49, 84, 85, 87, 88) even though they are descended from Korah who wrongly challenged the authority of Moses (Numbers 16).

It is often surmised (falsely, I think) that the Scroll of the Law found in Josiah's reign, and read at his Passover reunion, was only a part of Deuteronomy. It is apparent, that to be appropriate for Passover, it must have included the Exodus, and to cement the tribesmen into a nation in accordance with Josiah's programme, it should also have included the Patriarchal Narratives. It is much more likely that Josiah's scroll was pretty much like our modern Pentateuch,[1] which must have been fixed at a very early date because the Samaritans (whose beginnings are pre-Josianic) have a Pentateuch quite similar to the familiar Jewish Pentateuch. As we have already noted, our Pentateuchal text was fairly well established before the rift between the Samaritans and Judeans. That the whole Pentateuch could be read during the week of Passover is in keeping with the reading of the Homeric epics at a Greek panegyris; and the verses of the Iliad alone far outnumber the verses of the Pentateuch.

The function of reciting (actually chanting—for Scripture and national epic were sung, not read) Pentateuch and Homer at national reunions is the same in both cases. The narrative knits the segments of the nation together telling how they achieved their place in history in the course of a great event (the Exodus or Trojan War). All of the tribes and their leaders are heroic. The text brings in each tribe by name. The catalogue of the Tribes in Exodus (or in the Patriarchal Blessings) is functional, for at a reunion, like Hezekiah's or Josiah's Passover, there must be an honoured place for all. The same holds for a Greek panegyris; no matter where the participant comes from, his tribe and heroic predecessors will be mentioned by name in the course of the recitation of the Iliad.

---

[1] The so-called P stratum of the Pentateuch, generally attributed to the fifth century B.C., is replete with very ancient material: much of it pre-Israelite. It is not surprising that an outstanding Old Testament scholar like Ezekiel Kaufmann considers P early, antedating in any case D.

We have just mentioned themes that are major features of Hebraic and Aegean tradition. The methodology inherent in this book calls for singling out details within the fabric of the whole, as well as major parallels. We shall accordingly proceed by taking a number of points, more or less in the order of their sequence in the biblical text.

We have mentioned various types of kingship in the early East Mediterranean. The biblical text is clear enough if we pay attention to the context and wording; but midrashic literature often calls the phenomenon by its familiar name. For example, Midrash plainly states that Moses was the King of Israel.[1] Theoretically, anybody in the Hebraic genealogies was eligible for kingship by dint of his extraction from the Patriarchs who were kings.

The Conquest under Joshua could not have been a primitive assault, because a civilised land like Canaan with well-fortified cities could easily have repulsed an attack that was militarily naïve. The biblical account makes it clear that Joshua's attack was launched after the collection and evaluation of intelligence data. Spies were sent to search out the land and lay the groundwork. Moreover the invasion was timed with the Sabbatical year (Leviticus 25: 2) when the land was vulnerable agriculturally and economically. The inclusion of spying in the epic repertoire appears also in the Homeric epics.

The capture of Jericho (and Ai) in some evident respects is the Hebrew reflex of what evoked the saga of the sack of Troy. The Greeks and Hebrews sacked many a city, but certain special cities assumed importance in the tradition. It is quite possible that behind the Joshua accounts of the capture of Jericho and Ai, lay one or possibly two epics that occupied a position in Israel comparable with the Greek epic cycle about Troy.

[1] L. Ginzberg, *Legends of the Jews* III, p. 251. His kingship was not hereditary, for neither his father nor his son was king.

When Joshua needed more time for a victory, the heavenly bodies were immobilised to hold off the sunset until he might achieve victory. The incident is excerpted from the Book of Jashar—a pre-biblical national epic extending from at least the Conquest to the ascendancy of David. Battles ended with sunset or dusk; so heroes, on special occasions when they needed more time, were vouchsafed victory by the stoppage of the sun in Greek as well as Hebrew saga.[1] Midrash also has it that God granted the prayer of Moses to hold back the sun until Israel destroyed the Amalekite foe.

The Hebrew institution of the ban (*ḥērem*), for all its ruthlessness, served practical purposes. It gave the foe good reason to surrender their city without a struggle, and it took the profit out of chaotic looting. The genocide aspect of the *ḥērem* is unfortunately paralleled in Homeric tradition, too.

The Hebrew heroes of the Conquest received inalienable land grants, in perpetuity, for their heirs, in exchange for which they owed continued military service to the nation. Leviticus 25 makes the theory of real-estate quite clear. God owned the Land and the People. The Hebrews (as slaves of God because of His taking them out of Egypt) were entrusted with His Land as His tenants. They were at the same time to be the landed warrior and administrative ruling class. All this is basically paralleled in Greece where the aristocracy had inalienable land and where the subjected natives were reduced to servitude.

The warrior class, who became the landed aristocracy, were called the *gibbôrê ḥáyil*; from them came the leadership of the nation. Aristocrats (among Hebrews and Greeks) often had harems that included women of common or even servile origin, as well as well-born aristocratic ladies. Normally, the successors would be chosen from the sons born by ladies; but on occasion those born by servile or common wives achieved the ascendancy.

[1] Iliad 18: 239-242 (cf. 2: 412-8); Joshua 10: 13-14.

In the latter case, tradition could dwell on the phenomenon as " worthy of saga."[1]

Iliad 15: 333-6 tells of Medon, the bastard son of Oileus, who slew a kinsman of his stepmother Eriopis. Now this Medon, who stemmed from a lowly mother and slew a relative of his father's well-born wife, is nonetheless a hero. We are to compare his lowly maternity and his slaying the kin of his well-born stepmother, with the account of Abimelech. Abimelech, the son of Gideon (Jerubbaal) by a Shechemite concubine, slew the many well-born sons of his father (except Jotham, the youngest, who escaped by hiding) and was made king by the grandees of Shechem (Judges 9: 1-6) and ruled over Israel for three years (9: 22). What we have to bear in mind is that Abimelech (for all the inferiority of his mother and for all his own rascality) was nevertheless a member of the ruling class because he was the son of the ruler Gideon.

Another aristocrat born of a lowly mother was Jephthah.[2] Jephthah was the son of a harlot, and he was scorned and driven out by his half-brothers, but he was still a *gibbôr ḥáyil* as Judges 11: 1 plainly states.

This has the greatest bearing on the institution of the leaders called *šôfᵉṭîm* " Judges." The prevailing view is simply that the Judges were inspired, not hereditary, leaders. But this misses the point; the Judges were normally from the ruling aristocracy, quite like the kings in Homer. Succession from father to son was not the important thing. The Odyssey tells us that while there was no guarantee that Telemachus would succeed Odysseus as ruler of Ithaca, the ruler would be chosen from one

---

[1] Note also that Gideon is a *gibbôr ḥáyil*, although his becoming Judge is the more worthy of saga because he was the youngest in a family belonging to a poor clan in the tribe of Manasseh (Judges 6: 12, 15). This type of elevation is not from the dregs of society, but from the lower rungs on the ladder of aristocracy.

[2] For the nobility of his father, see Numbers 26: 29 and Judges 11: 1.

of the many " kings " (=members of the ruling class) in Ithaca.

The key to the institution of the Judges is Mycenaean kingship, whose heyday was precisely in the Period of the Judges (12th and 11th centuries) in the same East Mediterranean cultural continuum. The kings did not necessarily inherit rulership from their fathers but they sometimes did like Odysseus from Laertes, or Abimelech from Gideon. In any case, the kings came from the fighting and landed aristocracy whose Hebrew name is *gibbôrê ḥáyil*. The title for " ruler " varies in both Greek and Hebrew. The two commonest designations in Greek are *basileús* and *(w)ánax*. In Hebrew, *nāśî'* is familiar in the Patriarchal Narratives; and *šôfẹṭ* in the Book of Judges. But *mélek*, the normal Hebrew word for " king " also appears in both sets of documents.[1] It is useful to remember that in Ugaritic, the cognates of *mélek* and *šôfẹṭ* are parallel equivalents of each other.

As in Mycenaean society, so too in the Period of the Judges, petty groups would form coalitions in times of general emergency. The leader with the largest following would be the president of the confederacy.

The comparative study of the Judges and Mycenaean kingship shows that the prevailing theory of "charismatic leadership " in ancient Israel is based on one factor but misses the other factor. The Judges are not inspired leaders raised from the masses, but rulers who normally emerged from the aristocracy. They may come from smaller tribes, and even from smaller clans within the tribes; they may be younger sons, or even sons of socially inferior mothers; but such details only make their tale more worthy of saga. They regularly are sired by *gibbôrê ḥáyil*, from whom they derive their membership in the ruling class.[2]

[1] But there are still other terms for the leader; e.g., *śâr, nāgîd, rôzēn, gᵉvîr, rôš, qāṣîn*, etc.

[2] The text, as we have indicated above, often bears this out specifically, and when it does not, it nowhere gives any reason to suppose that the Judge was raised from the common people by inspiration alone.

Sometimes, a feature common to Homer and Bible will be common in the one and rare in the other. The Iliad expatiates on the gory wounds from which individual heroes perish. This is far less common in the Hebrew; however, compare Judges 3: 22 which tells that Ehud stabbed Eglon, plunging in " the hilt after the blade; and the fat enveloped the blade, for he did not draw the dagger from his belly." (Note also Judges 4: 21 for the details of how Jael wounded Sisera mortally.) The distinctive, though brief, manner in which the hero slew his foe, is familiar from Homer. It is the distinctiveness of each killing that we should note; hardly any two are the same. We are not dealing with a cliché such as " he ran him through with his sword and slew him " but with the inflicting of a mortal wound that is different from all other wounds in the particular tradition.

The most intimate tie-in between the Judges and the Aegean World is the Samson Cycle, which unfolds within a Philistine milieu. Historic period and social climate combine to produce the most Mycenaean atmosphere in all the Old Testament. Like the Wrath of Achilles, the Wrath of Samson over the woman who is taken away from him leads to the violent death of many a man ere his wrath is assuaged. There are still other elements in the Samson Cycle that we may term " Mediterranean." Samson's inflicting of damage on his enemies by turning loose foxes with firebrands is to be compared with Hannibal's strategy of creating havoc by turning loose cattle with torches ablaze upon them. Although Samson's trick has a folkloristic ring, it stemmed from an actual tactical usage, current around the shores of Mediterranean.

Judges 1: 6-7 tells of cutting off the thumbs and big toes of captured heroes so as to render them unfit for warfare. Plutarch, *Life of Lysander:* 9 tells that the Athenians cut off the right thumb of prisoners so that they could no longer wield the spear but only ply the oar.

Saul is the son of Kish the *gibbôr ḥáyil* (1 Samuel 9: 1), so that he was a member of the ruling class even though he was from a junior clan of a small tribe (v. 21).

The East Mediterranean setting of Scripture enables us to make sense of David's personality. That he was both warrior and king fits together easily. But when we ponder his other qualities: singer, poet and dancer (2 Samuel 6: 16), we run into an apparent contradiction that disappears only when we compare him with a figure such as Tyrtaeus. The music, poetry and dancing were all part of the complex for training the troops. Athenaeus tells of " the warlike character of the dance " for " in war, they recite poems of Tyrtaeus from memory and move in time to them " (" Doctors at Dinner "; cf. Loeb Classics, *Elegy and Iambus* I, p. 57). War dances are portrayed on Cappadocian seal cylinders and the dancing performed by warriors is mentioned in the Iliad (3: 393-4). David's (like Tyrtaeus') training of troops through his poetry is clearly stated in 2 Samuel 1: 18.

As in Greece, so in Israel, historiography and drama were rooted in the epic. The device of reconstructing history in the form of verbatim speeches is inspired by the epic.[1] It is characteristic of both Herodotus and Thucydides. A parade example of it appears in the speech of Rabshakeh in 2 Kings 18: 17-35, precisely in one of the finest expressions of Hebrew historiography.

Not only historical writing, but also classical drama is rooted in the epic. Greek drama tends to take its heroes and situations from the epic: Agamemnon, Ajax, Helen and many other characters (including Oedipus) are borrowed by the dramatists from the epic. Greek drama uses dialogue instead of action. And the central problem of the Greek tragedies is why we suffer so at the hands of God. The movement that evoked Greek tragedy in the fifth century B.C. was spread over the East Mediterranean, evoking a parallel response in Israel. The Book of Job has as its

---

[1] Gilgamesh, Ugaritic and Homeric epic are full of this device.

central figure a hero of the pre-Hebraic epic past.[1] The story in the prose Prologue and Epilogue are of Canaanite epic antiquity comparable with the Homeric epic antiquity of the stories in Aeschylus, Euripides and Sophocles. The creative contribution of the Greek and Hebrew dramatists is enshrined in the dialogues. Action is reduced to the same minimum in Job as in the Greek drama. And as in Greek tragedy, Job deals with the problem of why man suffers so at the hands of God.

Almost every facet of biblical study will be enriched by re-examination in its East Mediterranean framework. We are in for many surprises, but it is safe to predict that the surprises will be in keeping with the plain meaning of the ancient texts.

If archaeology had yielded only the Epic of Kret, we would have had enough to bridge the gap between the Iliad and Genesis. But the reader has seen how our new sources are so rich that we have only begun to apply them to the many-sided problem before us. The years ahead bid fair to be the most fruitful in the annals of Classical and Biblical scholarship. Our debt to the Bible and Classics is so great that this type of research will deepen our understanding of our culture and of ourselves.

EPILOGUE (9 MARCH 1962)

The evolution of this book has been dramatic from start to finish. While it was in galley proof, I first discovered that the Minoan language was specifically Northwest Semitic, of a type that the ancient Greeks would have called "Phoenician" (see the Post-script to Chapter VI). The correctness of this discovery might not have convinced Semitists, because the unfamiliarity of the Minoan syllabary would almost surely have failed to dispel their mis-givings. But fortunately, while this book was going into page

[1] For Ezekiel 14: 14 classifies Job with Ugaritic Daniel.

proof, the unexpected happened. I re-examined the four "Eteocretan" texts from two Cretan sites. They are written in plain Greek letters and date from between 600 and 300 B.C. Scholars have agreed, since their first discovery in the 1880's, that they must be written in the pre-Greek speech of Crete. But the identity of that language remained a dark mystery until February 1962. Knowing at last the specific Semitic character of Linear A, I looked for Northwest Semitic words on the four Eteocretan stone inscriptions. All four turned out to be funerary, which is convenient because there are many Phoenician and other Northwest Semitic funerary texts for providing background material.

Scholars will find my first scientific reports on the Northwest Semitic decipherments of Linear A and Eteocretan in the July 1962 issue of the *Journal of Near Eastern Studies* ably edited by Professor Keith C. Seele. As a sample, and as a demonstration that the decipherment of Eteocretan is sound, I herewith offer the complete translation of a nine word phrase: *meumarkrkoklesues* to be divided into *me u mar krk o kl es u es*, in which any competent Semitist should be able to see "whoever he be, lord of a city or any man at all," referring to the passerby, be he lord or commoner.

No competent Semitist is likely to oppose the Northwest Semitic character of the Minoan language. The evidence, especially of Eteocretan, is too clear for that. There will probably be some difference of opinion as to whether "Phoenician" is the right label. I am using "Phoenician" in the broad sense that the Greeks used it. For reasons that I shall explain in a more technical study, I mean by "Phoenician" in this context all the Northwest Semitic dialects used along the Palestinian, Lebanese and Syrian coastline, including biblical Hebrew.

As of now it appears that the common background of Greek and Hebrew civilisations is due mainly to the Northwest Semitic factor that covered the entire East Mediterranean (Palestine,

Syria, the coast of Asia Minor, Cyprus, Crete and the Aegean) down to 1500 B.C. For a clear statement of the essential unity and Phoenician character of the area, see Raymond Weill's important book, *Phoenicia and Western Asia*, Harrap, London, 1940, pp. 16, 18.

Before the Bible was sent to press as a bold thesis (but whose truth I never doubted). It ends with the specific proof that establishes beyond cavil that *Greek and Hebrew civilisations are parallel structures built upon the same East Mediterranean foundation.*

BIBLIOGRAPHY

ALBRIGHT, W. F., " Abraham the Hebrew," *Bulletin of the American Schools of Oriental Research* No. 163, Oct. 1961, pp. 36-54.

ALEXIOU, S., *Hē Minōikē Thea meth' Hupsōmenōn Kheirōn* Heraclion, Crete, 1958.

ANDRAE, W., and SCHAFER, H., *Die Kunst des alten Orients*, 3rd ed., Propyläen-Verlag, Berlin, 1925.

BAUMGARTNER, W., " Israelitisch-griechishche Sagenbeziehungen," in the collection of his articles entitled *Zum Alten Testament und seiner Umwelt*, Brill, Leiden, 1959.

BOMAN, T., *Das hebräische Denken im Vergleich mit dem Griechischen*, 3rd ed., Göttingen, 1959.

BRICE, W. C., *Inscriptions in the Minoan Script of Class A*, Society of Antiquaries, London, 1961.

BRUNDAGE, B. C., " Herakles the Levantine: A Comprehensive View," *Journal of Near Eastern Studies* 17, 1958, pp. 225-236.

CAMPBELL THOMSON, R., *The Epic of Gilgamesh: Text, Transliteration and Notes*, Oxford, 1930.

CHADWICK, J., " Minoan Linear A: A Provisional Balance Sheet," *Antiquity* 33, 1959, pp. 269-278.

COOKE, G. A., *A Text-book of North-Semitic Inscriptions*, Clarenden Press, Oxford, 1903.

DAVIS, S., " New Light on Linear A," *Greece & Rome* 6, 1959, pp. 20-30.

DEUEL, L., *The Treasures of Time*, World Publishing Co., Cleveland and New York, 1961.

DIRLMEIER, F., " Homerisches Epos und Orient," *Rheinisches Museum für Philologie* 98, 1955, pp. 18-37.

EISSFELDT, O., " Recht und Grenze archäologischer Betrachtung des Alten Testament," *Orientalistische Literaturzeitung* 49, 1954, pp. 101-108.

FRANKFORT, H., *Cylinder Seals*, Macmillan, London, 1939.

The Birth of Civilisation in the Near East, Doubleday (Anchor), Garden City, N.Y., 1956.

FRIEDRICH, J., *Die hetitischen Gesetze*, Bill, Leiden, 1959.

" Göttersprache und Menschensprache im hetitischen Schrifttum," in *Festschrift Albert Debrunner*, 1954.

FURUMARK, A., *Linear A und die altkretische Sprache* (mimeographed in 2 fascicles for private circulation), Berlin, 1956.

Bibliography

GARDINER, A., *Egyptian Grammar*, 3rd ed., Oxford, 1959.

Egypt of the Pharaohs, Clarendon Press, Oxford, 1961.

GARELLI, P. (ed.), *Gilgames et sa legende*, Klincksieck, Imprimerie Nationale, Paris, 1960.

GERMAIN, G., *Genèse de l'Odyssée*, Paris, 1954.

GINZBERG, L., *Legends of the Jews* I-VII, Jewish Publication Society, Philadelphia, 1909-38.

GORDON, C. H., *Ugaritic Literature*, Pontifical Biblical Institute, Rome, 1949.

Ugaritic Manual, Pontifical Biblical Institute, Rome, 1955.

Adventures in the Nearest East, Phoenix House, London, 1957.

Hammurapi's Code, Rinehart, New York, 1957.

World of the Old Testament, Doubleday, Garden City, N.Y., 1958.

"Western Asiatic Seals in the Walters Art Gallery," *Iraq* 6, 1939, pp. 3-34, pls. II-XV.

"The Daughters of Baal and Allah," *Moslem World* 33, 1943, pp. 50-51.

"The New Amarna Tablets," *Orientalia* 16, 1947, pp. 1-21, pls. I-II.

"Stratification of Society in Hammurabi's Code," in *The Joshua Starr Memorial Volume*, New York, 1953, pp. 17-28.

"The Origin of the Jews in Elephantine," *Journal of Near Eastern Studies* 14, 1955, pp. 56-58.

"Homer and Bible," *Hebrew Union College Annual* 26, 1955, pp. 43-108.

"Ugaritic Guilds and Homeric *Demioergoi*," in *The Ægean and the Near East: Studies Presented to Hetty Goldman*, Augustin, Locust Valley, 1956, pp. 136-143.

"Colonies and Enclaves," in *Studi Orientalistici in onore di Giorgio Levi della Vida*, Istituto per l'Oriente, Rome, 1956, vol. I, pp. 409-419.

"Abraham and the Merchants of Ura," *Journal of Near Eastern Studies* 17, 1958, pp. 28-31.

GURNEY, O. R., *The Hittites*, Pelican, London, 1952.

GRIFFITHS, J. GWYN, *The Conflict of Horus and Seth: from Egyptian and Classical Sources*, Liverpool University Press, Liverpool, 1960.

HAYES, W. C., *The Scepter of Egypt* I-II, Harper, New York, 1953-59.

KALLEN, H. M., *The Book of Job as a Greek Tragedy*, Hill and Wang, New York, 1959.

KAUFMANN, Y., *The Religion of Israel*, University of Chicago Press, Chicago, 1960.

KNUDTZON, J. A., *Die El-Amarna-Tafeln*, Vorderasiatische Bibliothek, Leipzig, 1907-15.

KRAMER, S. N., *History Begins at Sumer*, Doubleday (Anchor), Garden City, N.Y., 1959.

Sumerian Mythology, Harper (Torchbook), New York, 1961.

Bibliography

(ed.), *Mythologies of the Ancient World*, Doubleday (Anchor), Garden City, N.Y., 1961.

LACHEMAN, E. R., *Miscellaneous [Nuzu] Texts, Publications of the Baghdad School* VI, American Schools of Oriental Research, New Haven, 1939.

Miscellaneous Texts from Nuzi, Harvard *Semitic Series* 14, Harvard University Press, Cambridge, Mass., 1950.

LEHMANN, M. R., "Abraham's Purchase of Machpelah and Hittite Law," *Bulletin of the American Schools of Oriental Research* No. 129, Feb. 1953, pp. 15-18.

LESKY, A., review of "Homer and Bible," *Gnomon* 29, 1957. pp. 321-325.

LLOYD, S., *The Art of the Ancient Near East*, Thames and Hudson, London, 1961.

MARINATOS, S. and HIRMER, M., *Crete and Mycenae*, Harry N. Abrams Inc., New York (no date).

MARINATOS, S., "Diogeneis Basilêes," in *Studies Presented to David Moore Robinson*, pp. 126-134.

"*Grammátōn Didaskália*," in *Minoica* (the Sundwall Festschrift edited by E. Grumach), Akademie-Verlag, Berlin, 1958, pp. 226-231, pl. I.

MERCER, S. A. B., *The Tell el-Amarna Tablets*, I-II, Macmillan, Toronto, 1939.

MEYER, E., *Geschichte des Altertums* I-III, 2nd ed., Cotta'sche Buchhandlung, Stuttgart, 1907-37.

MURRAY, G., *The Rise of the Greek Epic*, 4th ed., Oxford University Press, Oxford, 1934.

NOTH, M., *The History of Israel*, 2nd English ed., A. & C. Black, London, 1960.

NOUGAYROL, J., *Le Palais royal d' Ugarit* III, Klincksieck, Imprimerie Nationale, Paris, 1955.

PAGE, DENYS L., *History and the Homeric Iliad*, University of California Press, Berkeley and Los Angles, 1959.

PARROT, A., *Sumer*, Thames and Hudson, London, 1960.

PENDLEBURY, J. D. S., *The Archaeology of Crete*, Methuen, London, 1939.

PERUZZI, E., "Recent Interpretations of Minoan (Linear A)," *Word* 15, 1959, pp. 313-324.

PORADA, *The Collection of the Pierpont Morgan Library* I (plates of seals), Bollingen Foundation, Washington, 1948.

PRITCHARD, J. B. (ed.), *Ancient Near Eastern Texts*, 2nd ed., Princeton University Press, Princton, 1955.

RACHEWILTZ, B. DE, *Egyptian Art*, Hutchinson, London, 1960.

SCHACHERMEYR, F., *Die ältesten Kulturen Griechenlands*, Kohlhammer, Stuttgart, 1955.

SCHMÖKEL, H., *Geschichte des Alten Vorderasien* (*Handbuch der Orientalistik* II, 3), Brill, Leiden, 1957.

SMITH, S., *The Statue of Idri-mi*, British Institute of Archaeology in Ankara, London, 1949.

STEUER, R. O., and SAUNDERS, J. B. DE C. M., *Ancient Egyptian and Cnidian Medicine: The Relationship of their Aetiological Concepts of Disease*, University of Calfornia Press, Berkeley and Los Angeles, 1959.

UNGNAD, A., *Babylonische Briefe*, Leipzig, 1914.

VANDIER, J., *Manuel d'archéologie égyptienne* I-III, Picard, Paris, 1952-58.

VELIKOVSKY, I., *Oedipus and Ikhnaton: Myth and History*, Doubleday, Garden City, N.Y., 1960.

VENTRIS, M., and CHADWICK, J., *Documents in Mycenean Greek*, Cambridge University Press, Cambridge, 1956.

VIROLLEAUD, C., *Palais royal d'Ugarit* II, Klincksieck, Imprimerie Nationale, Paris, 1957.

WADE-GERY, H. T., *The Poet of the Iliad*, Cambridge, 1952.

WAINWRIGHT, G. A., " Early Tin in the Ægean," *Antiquity* 18, 1944, pp. 57-64. " Some Sea-Peoples," *Journal of Egyptian Archaeology* 47, 1961, pp. 71-90.

WEBSTER, T. B. L., *From Myceuae to Homer*, London, 1958.

WEILL, R., *Phoenicia and Western Asia*, Harrap, London, 1940.

WILSON, J. A., *The Culture of Ancient Egypt*, Phoenix Books, University of Chicago Press, Chicago, 1956.

WHITMAN, C. H., *Homer and the Heroic Tradition*, Harvard University Press, Cambridge, Mass., 1958.

WISEMAN, D. J., *The Alalakh Tablets*, London, 1953.

WOLF, W., *Die Kunst Ægyptens: Gestalt und Geschichte*, Kohlhammer, Stuttgart, 1957.

WOLFSON, H. A., " The Philonic God of Revelation and his Latter-Day Deniers," *Harvard Theological Review* 53, 1960, pp. 101-124.

WOOLLEY, C. L., *Ur Excavations* II (British Museum and University of Pa. Museum), Oxford University Press, London, 1934.

YEIVIN, S., " Did the Kingdoms of Israel have a Maritime Policy? " *Jewish Quarterly Review* 50, 1960, pp. 193-228.

INDEX

Abimelech, 228 n., 251, 296

'*ābîr*, Yahweh as, 157

Abraham, his status, 25, 34-5, 56, 143, 239, 285, 286-8, 289; and "Helen of Troy" theme, 26, 133, 135, 228 n.; his purchase of land, 29, 94, 288, 290; other references, 104, 132-3, 147, 156, 244, 245 n., 248 n., 257.

Achaeans, 15, 18, 63, 292 n.

Achaemenian Empire, 27, 31, 32, 40, 191

Achilles, Homeric hero, 55, 65, 147, 160, 180, 181, 239, 243, 245-6, 254, 257, 266, 292 n.; and Thetis, 61, 67, 160, 194, 245-6; and Patroclus, 64, 71, 268, 272; in Hades, 85, 223; his armour, 160, 194, 276-7, 281-2; Wrath of, 222, 225, 227-8, 258, 270-1, 298

Adapa, legend of, 86-7

Aegean, the, 28, 36, 49, 51, 57, 59-60, 93, 117

Aegean culture, 19, 23, 40 n., 46, 55, 130, 162, 183, 214, 298; peoples, 30, 40, 120, 281; scripts, 206 ff.

aegis, the, 13

Aeneas, 243, 246

Aeschylus, plays of, 237, 267, 300

Agamemnon, 180, 181, 227, 229, 239, 258, 259, 260, 264, 271

agelaíos, 276

agriculture, 242, 276, 277

Ahab, 27, 42, 100, 260

Ai, 265, 294

Akhetaton (*see also* Tell el-Amarna), 116

Akkad, 24-5, 52, 54-5, 139, 190, 287, 289

Akkadian culture, 49-50, 60, 93; language, 28, 48-9, 52-3, 59, 118 n., 131, 211, 212, 224, 269, 286

"Akkadograms", 59

Alalakh, 27, 88 n., 213, 216, 288

Alalu, 92

Alcinous, 231, 239-40, 249, 275

Alishar, 58

Aliyan (Baal), 169, 188, 194, 196, 197, 199, 200, 201, 202, 203, 204

alphabet, 129-30, 216

Amalek, 12-13, 295

Amarna Age, 19, 23, 24, 28, 30, 32, 60-61, 86, 115, 116-17, 131, 143, 155, 175 n., 210, 214, 219, 227, 270, 282

Amarna Tablets, 28 n., 128, 239; *see also* Tell el-Amarna

Amenophis III, 117

Amenophis IV (Ikhnaton), 117, 118

Amon, 118, 120, 121, 122, 123, 124, 237

Amon-Re, 118, 122

Amorites, 78, 239

Amos, 260

Anath, Ugaritic goddess: and Aqhat, 69, 161, 163, 262, 267, 271; in Baal and Anath cycle, 126, 178, 181, 184-95 *passim*, 201, 202, 203, 227; her character, 62, 74, 141, 144, 161-2, 169, 171, 173, 174, 185, 186, 187,

307

Index

189, 193, 194, 202; as "younger" goddess, 92, 163, 172; in Egyptian texts, 127; mother of Shamgar, 61-2, 246, 283

Anatolia (*see also* Asia Minor), 38, 48, 55, 58, 60, 86, 95, 97, 116, 221, 224, 289

Anatolian culture, 19, 53, 55, 60, 93, 95, 97

Anchises, 96, 243, 246

Anu, 64, 69, 78, 92, 163, 193 n.

Aphrodite, 43, 96, 101, 246, 261

Apiru, 35, 36, 118

Apodulu, 214, 215

Apollo, 13, 267, 268

Aqhat, legend of, 69, 74 n., 134, 138, 155-70, 262, 263, 267, 271

Aramaeans, 27, 287

Aramaic language, 42, 49; texts, 190

archaeology, 12, 20, 40, 300

aristocracy, 238, 241, 243, 245, 253, 255, 282, 284, 295-7

arrows of God, 267

Arsai, 184-5, 193, 197

Artemis, 267, 290

Asherah, 92, 142, 144, 147, 172-3, 174, 184, 193, 194, 198, 201, 202

Asia Minor (*see also* Anatolia), 27, 28, 54, 93, 117 n., 248

Assyrian Empire, 32, 40; culture, 50, 58; settlements abroad, 27-8, 30, 58, 130; military achievements, 115; laws, 249-50

Astarte, 127, 141, 155, 181

Athena, 13, 77, 96, 115 n., 181, 234, 256, 257, 259, 265, 273

Az-mawet, 191

Baal, Ugaritic god, 54, 92, 136, 144, 151, 170, 171, 188, 254, 265; in legend of Aqhat, 155, 157, 161, 164, 165-6, 167, 169; Baal and Anath Cycle, 126, 178-85, 188-204 *passim*, 227; "daughters" of, 184-5; death of, 201; house (palace) of, 151, 193, 195-7, 199, 237, 275; resurrection of, 203-4; worship of, 42, 116, 233

Baal-zebub, 191 and n., 246-7

Babylonia, 22, 24, 73; of Sassanian Era, 247

Babylonian Empire, Old, 28, 54, 60, 91; influence abroad, 28-29, 36, 44, 57-8, 210, 214; language, 60, 86, 116; texts (*see also* Akkadian), 125, 126, 224, 264. See also Neo-Babylonian Empire.

Balaam, 41, 256

Balak, 41, 256

ban, *see ḥérem*

basileús, 239, 289, 297

Beelzebub, 191 n., 246-7

Bellerophon, 120, 226, 235, 263, 270

Beth-shan, 285

Bible, the, 131, 218, 226 n., 233, 278-300 *passim*; greatness of, 10, 26; traditional views of, 11, 19; relations with other literatures, 103, 135, 137, 155, 190, 192, 227, 254. *See also under Biblical proper names* (Abraham *to* Zedekiah) *and many themes.*

birthright, 289

bît-ḫillâni, 196

blood, 274; rain or plague of, 229-30.

blood-revenge, 15

book, 226 n., 282

Book of the Dead, 278-9; of the Story of Man, 282; of the Wars of Yahweh, 282; *see also* Jasher, Book of.

bow, 159, 160, 161-2, 263

Briseis, 228, 270, 271

brlt (Ugaritic), 153

brutality of war, 265-6

bull, as title for grandees, 148-9
Bull, Mighty, Pharaoh as, 100, 148
Bull of El (in Ugaritic epic), 135, 136-7, 157, 180, 183, 193, 204
Bull of Heaven, 51, 52, 69, 70, 74, cf. 201 (tauromorphic being)
bull-grappling, 51-2, 70, 275-6
burial, 18, 104, 268-9
burning of dead, 18, 269
Byblos, 100, 104, 120-1

Cain, 15-16, 255
calf as cult-image, 157
Calypso, 68, 162, 223
Canaan, 131, 170, 190, 192, 205, 282-3, 294; links with other areas, 28, 34, 38, 56, 60, 103, 104, 116, 130, 216; Patriarchs in, 35, 290; gods of, 127
Canaanites, 20, 49, 105, 184, 241
Canon (Scriptural and Homeric), 278-9
Caphtor, 30, 40 and n., 117 and n., 139, 194, 236
capital (financial), 36-7
Cappadocia, 58, 60, 299
captives, killing of, 265-6; marriage with, 251
Carchemish, 138
carpenters, 40, 78, 151
cattle, 274-5
champions, individual, 262-3
chariotry, 25-6, 38, 39, 114, 115, 118, 238, 269, 289
Cherethites, 40, 139
Cherith, Brook, 138
Christianity, 10, 246-7, 291
Cilicia, 26, 216
Circe, 87-8
colonies (*see also* enclaves), 26-7, 33, 56, 58, 248
comradeship, 64, 272

Contendings of Horus and Seth, 125-6
cosmology, 281-2
covenant relationship, 96, 137, 157, 256
craftsmen, 78, 253, 279
creation poem, 90-1
creation from clay, 62
creative word, 166
Cretans, 39 n., 132, 247
Crete, 28, 54, 57-8, 115, 117 n., 128-9, 139, 224, 236, 284; texts from, 206-17, 301; paintings in, 231. *See also under* Minoan
Cronos, 92, 171, 178
crown prince, rebellion of, 154
cuneiform script, 48, 209; texts, 12, 51, 59, 60, 131
Cypriote texts, 207, 216-17
Cypro-Minoan texts, 30, 131, 207
Cyprus, 24, 33, 124, 131, 221, 281
Cythera, 43-5, 101, 117 n.

Daedalus, 279
Dagon, 53, 92, 136, 179, 180, 213
Damascus, 27
damokor(os), 53 n.
dan, meaning of, 155
Dan (personal name), 216
Dan (place), 157, 267
Danaans, 224
Danatai, 156, 159
Daniel (Biblical), 155
Daniel (Ugaritic), 138, 155, 156-60, 164-70, 300 n.
Danites, 42, 256, 266-7
David, king of Israel, 17, 26, 39, 93, 105, 240, 241, 243, 291; as epic hero, 55, 65-6, 126, 135, 148, 151, 154, 164-5, 231, 242, 255, 262, 299; and Absalom, 154; and Jonathan, 64, 71, 148, 272; and Philistines,

Index

Index

Index

Index

Index

317

Index